P9-DZN-218

q796.357 Smit

Smith, Ron, 1949 Apr.
The Sporting news
selects baseball's 100
greatest players.

APR 13 1999	JUN 2 0 2005
APR 29 1999	JUN 2 0 2006
MAY 19 1999	JUL 2006
SEP 07 1999	AUG 1 0 2006
SEP 2 2 1999	JUN 6 2010
OCT 2 3 1999	AUG 15 2014
NOV 13 1999	
FEB 19 2000	
JUL 2 2001	
SEP 6 2004	
OCT 2 6 2004	

DISCARD

1-607-754-4243   MAR 17 1999

VESTAL PUBLIC LIBRARY
0 00 10 0205439 1

Vestal Public Library
Vestal, New York 13850

SELECTS

BASEBALL'S 100 GREATEST PLAYERS

A Celebration of the 20th Century's Best

written by
Ron Smith

FOREWORD BY WILLIE MAYS

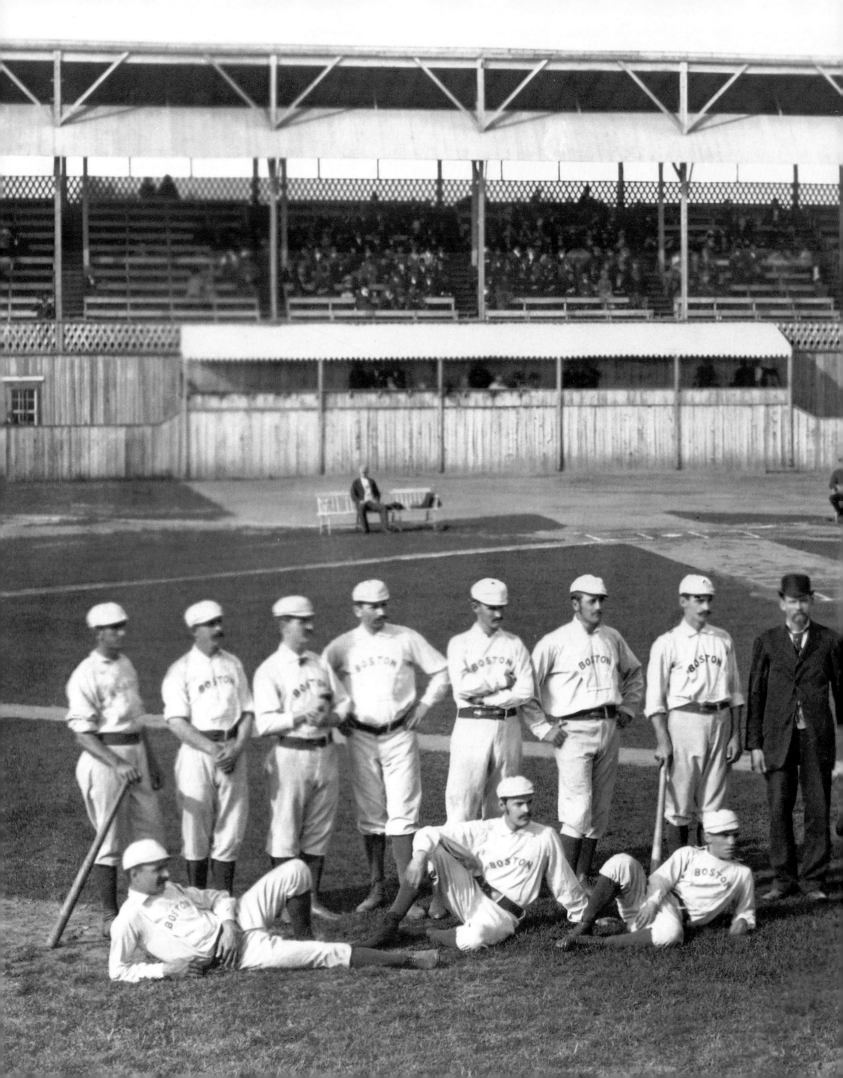

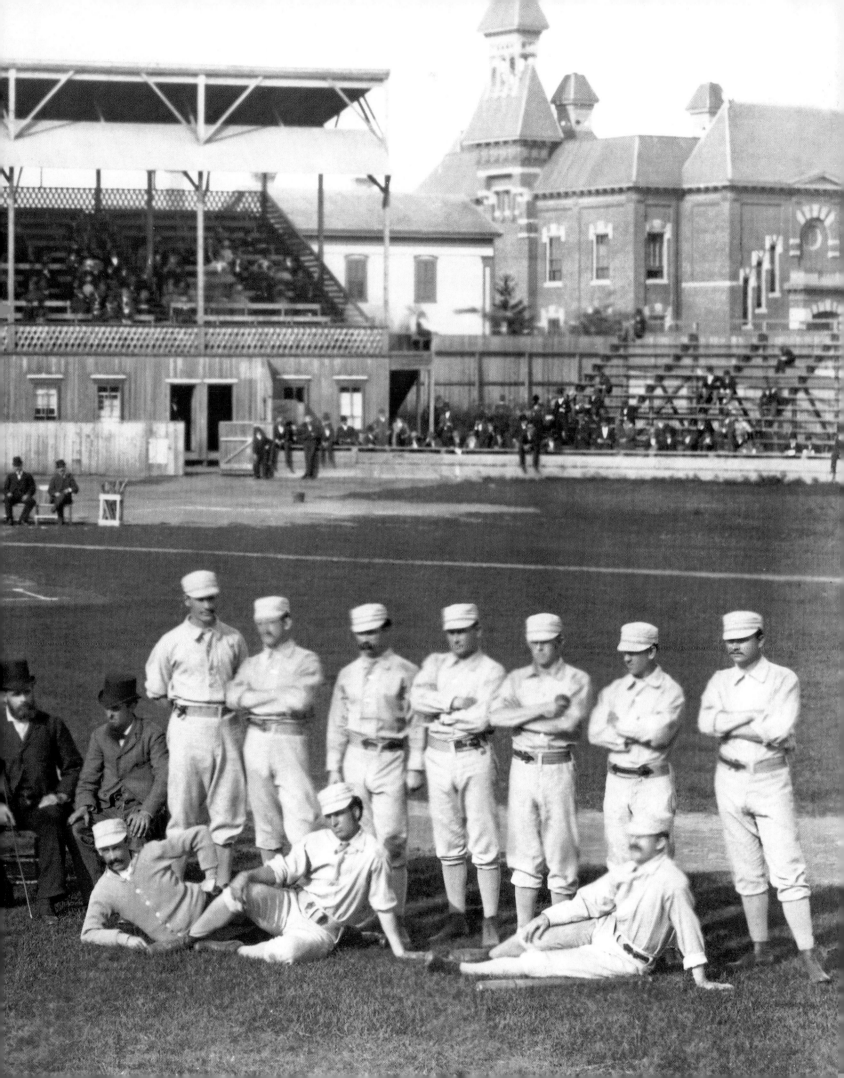

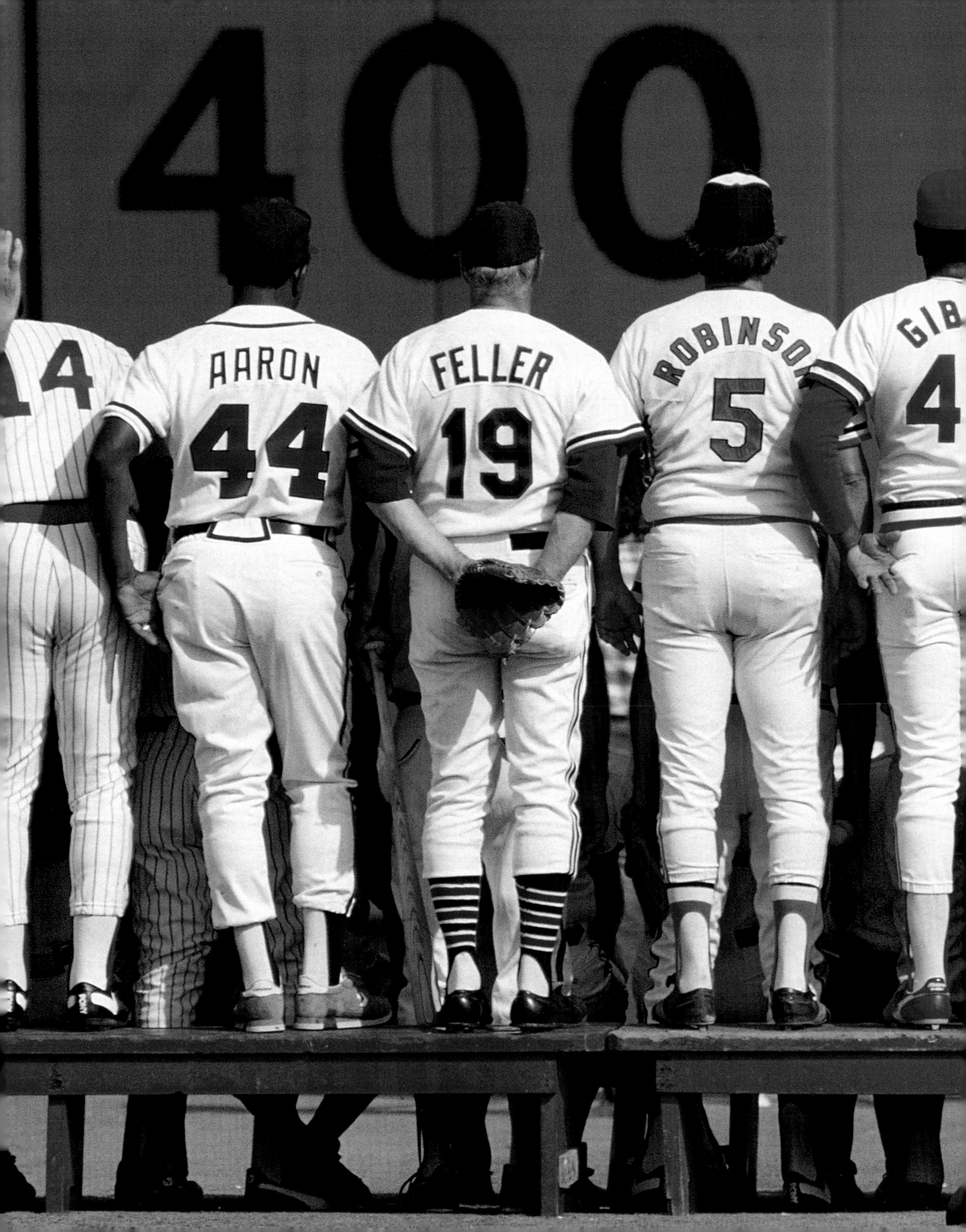
400
14
AARON
44
FELLER
19
ROBINSON
5
GIB
4

CONTENTS

Copyright ©1998 by The Sporting News Publishing Co., 10176 Corporate Square Drive, St. Louis, MO 63132. All rights reserved. Printed in the U.S.A.

No part of The Sporting News Selects Baseball's 100 Greatest Players may be reproduced or transmitted in any form or by any means, electronic or mechanical, including photocopy, recording or any information storage and retrieval system now known or to be invented, without permission in writing from the publisher, except by a reviewer who wishes to quote brief passages in connection with a review written for inclusion in a magazine, newspaper or broadcast.

The Sporting News is a registered trademark of The Sporting News Publishing Co., a Times Mirror Company.

ISBN: 0-89204-608-2

Special thanks to Craig Carter, who pulled together the 100 trivia quiz and Timeline, and to Dave Sloan, who compiled the breakdowns and handled proofreading duties. Also to Mike Bruner, Michael Behrens and Christen Webster for their design work. And especially to Dave Brickey, Vern Kasal, Jack Kruyne, Steve Romer and Ian Wilkinson for countless hours making the photographs in this book as good as they are.

The numbers in this book conform to the official Major League Baseball statistics, which are supplied by Total Baseball.

On the covers:

Front *(left to right)* Babe Ruth (The Sporting News Archives); Ken Griffey Jr. (Albert Dickson/The Sporting News); Willie Mays (The Sporting News Archives).

Back Cal Ripken celebrating his record-setting 2,131st consecutive game in 1995 (Albert Dickson/The Sporting News).

Contributing Photographers

Albert Dickson/The Sporting News—79T, 88, 108T, 108-109, 200T, 201, 211B.

Robert Seale/The Sporting News—118, 119B, 197B.

Ed Nessen/The Sporting News—79B, 109, 196, 197T.

Michael Conroy for The Sporting News—78.

Louis DeLuca—4-5.

Malcolm W. Emmons—Pages 12, 13T, 13B, 18, 40, 41T, 42B, 43, 49B, 58, 59B, 62, 73, 74T, 75, 106, 122T, 124, 129T, 132, 134, 150, 154, 156, 167, 174, 175T, 175B, 207, 208.

Rich Pilling/MLB Photos—41B, 107B, 135B, 141B, 157B, 177.

Tony Tomsic/MLB Photos—140.

Photo File/MLB Photos—42T, 48, 72T, 86, 87T, 129B.

Photo File—19T, 19B, 24, 25T, 25B, 28T, 28B, 29, 50B, 51, 53, 63T, 63B, 87B, 90T, 90B, 91, 116T, 116B, 125T, 128, 133B, 138B, 139, 155T, 155B, 166T, 166B, 203B, 206T, 209T, 209B.

Al Tielemans/Duomo—66, 123.

Bryan Yablonsky/Duomo—59T, 67B.

David Madison/Duomo—115.

Mitchell Layton/Duomo—169T.

UPI/Corbis-Bettmann—50T, 52B, 125B, 133T, 151B.

Lewis Portnoy/Spectra-Action, Inc.—70B, 71, 72B, 176B.

Otto Greule/Allsport—222-223.

Diane Johnson/Allsport—67T.

T.G. Higgins/Allsport—203T.

Focus West—135T.

National Baseball Hall of Fame Library, Cooperstown—36B, 37, 144T, 144B, 145.

Negro Leagues Baseball Museum, Inc.—45B, 105B, 146T, 146B, 147.

Courtesy of Boston Red Sox—157T.

Brewers Archive Photo—206B.

© The Phillies—70T.

Courtesy of Atlanta National League Baseball Club, Inc. © 1998, All rights reserved—138T.

Courtesy of Pittsburgh Pirates—49T, 176T.

Courtesy of Minnesota Twins—151T.

Courtesy of Baltimore Orioles—52T, 141T.

Courtesy of Cincinnati Reds—74B.

The Sporting News Archives—2-3, 9, 10, 11T, 11B, 14T, 14B, 15, 16T, 16B, 17, 20, 21T, 21B, 22T, 22B, 23, 26T, 26B, 27, 30T, 30-31, 31, 32T, 32B, 33, 34T, 34B, 35, 36T, 38, 39T, 39B, 44, 45T, 46, 47T, 47B, 54, 55T, 55B, 56T, 56B, 57, 60A, 60B, 60C, 64, 65T, 65B, 68, 69T, 69B, 76, 77T, 77B, 80T, 80B, 81, 82T, 82B, 83, 84, 85T, 85B, 89T, 89B, 92, 93T, 93B, 94T, 94B, 95, 96, 97T, 97B, 98T, 98B, 99, 100T, 100B, 101, 102, 103T, 103B, 104, 105T, 107T, 110T, 110-111, 111, 112, 113T, 113B, 114T, 114-115, 117, 119T, 120, 121T, 121B, 122-123, 126, 127T, 127B, 130, 131T, 131B, 136, 137T, 137B, 142T, 142B, 143, 148, 149T, 149B, 152T, 152B, 153, 158T, 158B, 159, 160T, 160B, 161, 162, 163T, 163B, 164, 168, 169B, 170, 171T, 171B, 172T, 172B, 173, 178T, 178B, 179, 180, 181T, 181B, 182, 183T, 183B, 184T, 184B, 185, 186, 187T, 187B, 188, 189T, 189B, 190, 191T, 191B, 192, 193T, 193B, 194, 195T, 195B, 198, 199T, 199B, 200B, 202, 204T, 204-205, 205, 210, 211T, 212T, 212B, 213, 214, 215T, 215B, 217T, 218B.

INTRODUCTION

It seems only fitting that *The Sporting News* should punctuate baseball's first full-calendar centennial by ranking the 100 best players of the century—players its writers and editors have been watching, analyzing, criticizing and describing for hungry readers since 1886. As the only pre-1900 sports weekly still in existence, TSN has been inexorably entwined with the national pastime through most of its existence.

So the task of whittling an all-time roster of about 15,000 players to a select few was not taken lightly. A selection committee, made up of 12 TSN editors, started the six-week voting process by culling a list that included every Hall of Fame member and numerous other fringe and active players to the 100 that would appear in the book.

Every editor was then asked to pick a Top 10, without rankings. After those votes were tabulated and the Top 10 was locked in place, each voter was asked to rank those players and select the next 15 to fill out a Top 25. This select/rank process was continued for 26-50, 51-75 and 76-100, always locking the players into a group before rankings were determined. The group breakdowns prevented one voter with a low opinion of an otherwise popular player from skewing that player's place in the rankings.

The voters were armed with clip files, statistical books, historical knowledge, personal observations and, of course, strong opinions that helped in their selections. The final rankings, obviously subjective and open to debate, represent the collective feelings of a TSN staff that has logged many hours tracking the sometimes-bumpy course of baseball history.

The decision to include and rank Negro League greats among the Top 100 also was difficult, primarily because the black stars of the first half century never were allowed to pit their skills against major league contemporaries. Glimpses of how they might fit into the big baseball picture are provided by quotes from major league greats who competed against them in barnstorming tours and word-of-mouth testimonials from other Negro Leaguers, writers and fans who watched them perform.

The profiles that appear in the book attempt to provide a quick glimpse into the player or pitcher's personality and playing style. The charts and lists that accompany each player attempt to provide a perspective you don't get from other sources.

A special thanks to the former managers and members of our Top 100 who took the time to provide special insights in the Top 10 lists that appear throughout the book.

FOREWORD

BY WILLIE MAYS

It's a great honor to be named the No. 2 player in baseball history. To tell you the truth, it's something I would never have dreamed possible back in high school, where my best sport was football. I played quarterback in those days and that helped me in baseball because it taught me to analyze the game. On defense, I was a safety and had to go all over the field. Later, as a center fielder, I did the same thing.

When I was growing up, Joe DiMaggio was my hero because he was the kind of all-round player I wanted to be—hitting, running, fielding. The only time I actually played against Joe was in the '51 World Series. When he hit a home run, I clapped in my glove and then thought, "Hey, I'm playing for the Giants!" Lucky for me, nobody got that shot.

But I never could play like Joe because he was bigger and had that wide stance. I had to develop my own style. Fortunately, I was very creative in the outfield, I had the ability to hit for both power and average and my baserunning was something that I just had an instinct for. That combination of skills is probably why I'm ranked No. 2.

My defensive secret was that I always played according to the park. The Polo Grounds had a lot of room for me to roam, and I loved it. When the Giants moved to San Francisco, we played the first two years in Seals Stadium, which wasn't a big park, so I played shallow. It was important that I catch balls that were hit just over the infield. A lot of players didn't know how to play center field in Candlestick Park because they'd break for the ball and then the wind would blow it back to where they'd been.

New York was a fast city when I came up in 1951, so the Giants gave me a chaperone named Frank Forbes. He was a boxing commissioner and a friend of (Giants owner) Horace Stoneham. And they placed me with a family.

I was very lucky. (Giants manager) Leo Durocher was like my godfather, taking me around and keeping a close eye on me. Leo was into the movies and he introduced me to Frank Sinatra, who also would take me all over. Frank would just pick me up in his plane, so wherever I went I didn't have any (race) problems. I had already been to New York and played at the Polo Grounds with the Birmingham Black Barons of the Negro League. So I was not in awe of the big city.

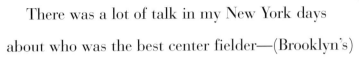

There was a lot of talk in my New York days about who was the best center fielder—(Brooklyn's) Duke Snider, (the Yankees') Mickey Mantle or myself. There's never going to be another city that could boast three great center fielders at the same time like that. But we were all good friends and there wasn't any jealousy at all.

It was great playing for the Giants because we competed against great players like Henry Aaron. Henry and I were good friends. We would talk about hitting, about pitchers. I'd even borrow his bats when I got tired late in the season because he used a lighter bat.

You had some really good players at that time. The Braves had Ed Mathews, Joe Adcock, Billy Bruton, who was the fastest guy around. The Dodgers had Jackie Robinson, Duke Snider, Gil Hodges. Cincinnati had Gus Bell, Ted Kluszewski. The '50s and '60s in the National League were really good baseball, which I think is reflected by the number of players from that period that appear on this list.

This is just a great honor. I know Babe Ruth has to be No. 1 of all time. The Babe revived baseball when he came along; he put the home run on the map. He was baseball, so being second to Babe is not bad. I have the satisfaction of knowing that when they call my name, everybody knows me. If you'd have asked me when I was 15 in Birmingham if all this could happen, there's no way I would have said yes.

" BABE WAS NO ORDINARY MAN ...
RUTH POSSESSED A MAGNETISM THAT WAS
POSITIVELY INFECTIOUS. WHEN HE ENTERED A
CLUBHOUSE OR A ROOM, WHEN HE APPEARED
ON THE FIELD, IT WAS AS IF HE WAS THE
WHOLE PARADE. THERE SEEMED TO BE FLAGS
WAVING, BANDS PLAYING CONSTANTLY."

WAITE HOYT

BABE RUTH 1

abe Ruth played baseball like he lived his life: with loud, gaudy, entertaining gusto. There was nothing subtle about the happy-go-lucky Sultan of Swat, who paraded through his career, forged an enduring relationship with adoring fans and then withstood the test of time as the greatest power hitter in baseball history.

Ruth's legendary home run totals—714 in his career, 60 in 1927—are no longer records, but they still stand as the milestone power numbers by which all other players are judged. His legendary carousing still enhances the irascible image that colors his aura. More than anything, the magnetic Ruth is hailed as the savior of the game, the man who ushered in baseball's long-ball era and revitalized the game when it was mired in the bog of the 1919 Black Sox scandal.

The Babe, a former Baltimore orphan who started his career as a successful Boston Red Sox pitcher, set a major-league record with 29 homers in 1919, his final Boston season, and soared to the mind-boggling total of 54 in 1920, his first season with the New York Yankees. He quickly became a New York icon as he powered his way through the Roaring '20s and the Great Depression, leading the Yankees to four World Series championships and anchoring one of the most devastating lineups in baseball history.

Lost in the fog of Ruth's 12 American League home run titles, four 50-homer seasons and six RBI titles was a career .342 average that ties for eighth all-time in baseball's modern era. Not lost is the enduring image of a paunchy Babe signing autographs, hob-nobbing with celebrities or circling the bases with his distinctive trot.

A trot that carried Ruth to immortality as the greatest player of the 20th century.

THE ROARING '20s

The immortal Ruth dominated the 1920s (1920-29) like no power hitter since has dominated a decade. The totals are through the 1997 season:

HRs	Player	Decade
467	Babe Ruth	1920s
415	Jimmie Foxx	1930s
393	Harmon Killebrew	1960s
375	Hank Aaron	1960s
350	Willie Mays	1960s
347	Lou Gehrig	1930s
326	Duke Snider	1950s
316	Frank Robinson	1960s
313	Mike Schmidt	1980s
310	Gil Hodges	1950s
308	Dale Murphy	1980s
308	Mel Ott	1930s
300	Willie McCovey	1960s

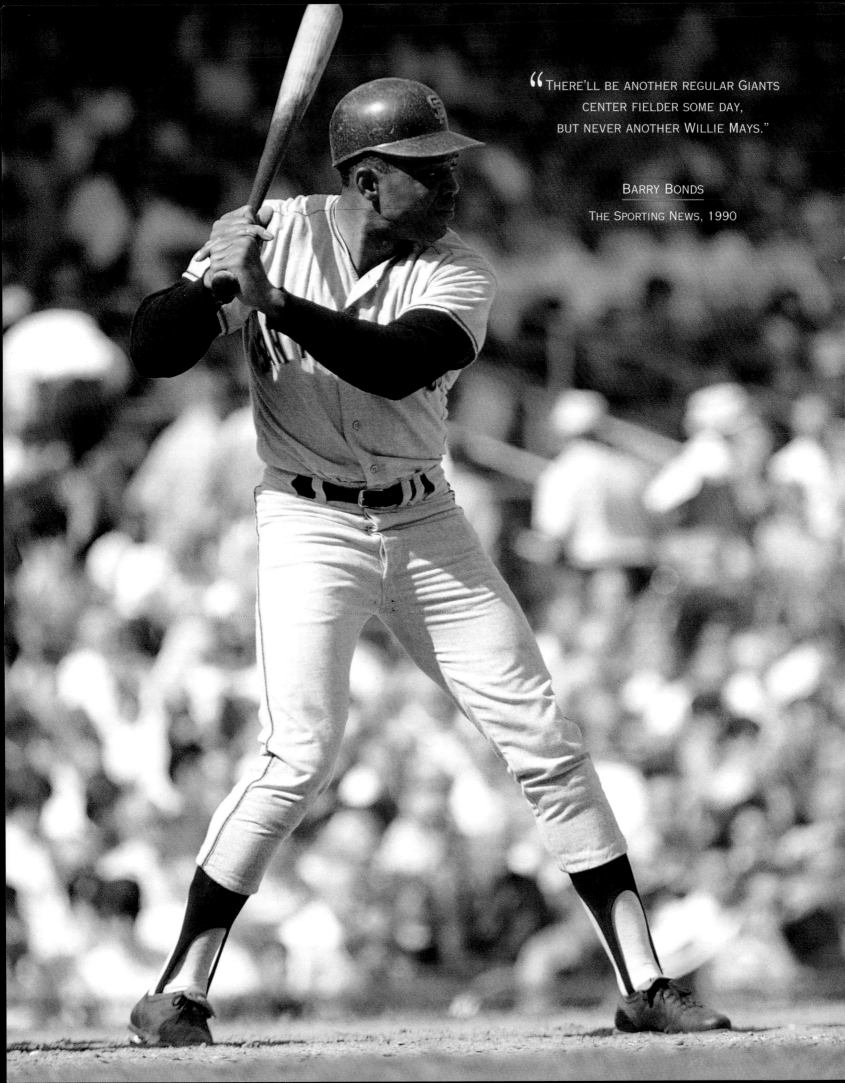

"There'll be another regular Giants center fielder some day, but never another Willie Mays."

Barry Bonds
The Sporting News, 1990

WILLIE MAYS 2

He might have been as close to baseball perfection as we'll ever get. And from the moment you walked into the stadium and took your seat, through the final out of every game, your eyes, by sheer magnetic force, were drawn to the youthful smile, the boundless enthusiasm and the graceful athleticism of Willie Mays.

The Say Hey Kid, the former New York and San Francisco Giants star who set the lofty standard by which center fielders will forever be judged, could dominate a game in ways beyond comprehension. Baseball lore is filled with accounts of incredible Mays catches and throws. He seemed to enjoy showcasing his daring baserunning ability for national audiences in a record-tying 24 All-Star Games. He was a career .302 hitter who could break up a pitching duel with an opposite-field bloop single. Or his powerful arms and sculpted 5-11 body could drive the ball out of any National League park.

Mays made an indelible stamp on the record

books with 3,283 hits (ninth on the all-time list) and 660 home runs (third). But memories somehow gravitate toward the graceful ease with which he made difficult defensive plays look easy and the head-to-the-outfield acceleration around second base on a ball into the gap. Mays appeared to be in perpetual motion—even when standing still. And that energy level and enthusiasm might have been his greatest weapon.

Mays used it to mesmerize fans for 22 major league seasons, from his 1951 rookie campaign with the New York Giants to his 1973 finale with the New York Mets. His love for baseball never wavered, and neither did the impact he had on the game.

BEST CLUTCH HITTERS
S E L E C T E D   B Y
AL KALINE

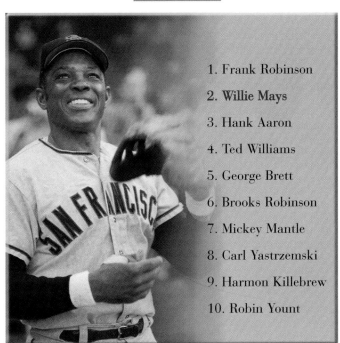

1. Frank Robinson
2. Willie Mays
3. Hank Aaron
4. Ted Williams
5. George Brett
6. Brooks Robinson
7. Mickey Mantle
8. Carl Yastrzemski
9. Harmon Killebrew
10. Robin Yount

3 TY COBB

N o player in history generated more emotion, created more havoc, bruised more egos and left more battlescars than Tyrus Raymond Cobb, a snarling wildcat who cut a bloody path to baseball immortality with a take-no-prisoners style, razor-sharp spikes, iron fists and acid tongue that spared nobody, friend or foe.

Exactly what motivated the 6-1, 175-pound Georgia Peach will forever remain a dark mystery. But his incredible baseball talents were fueled by equal parts anger, intensity, cunning, intimidation and a mean-spirited, win-at-all-costs drive that never wavered over an incredible 22 seasons with the Detroit Tigers and two more with the Philadelphia Athletics.

Cobb, the dominant player of the dead-ball era, was to bat control what Babe Ruth was later to the home run. A lefthanded hitter, he choked up on the bat with a split grip and drove the ball anywhere he wanted. If a little muscle was required, Cobb could supply it, and he was a master bunter. But he was at his best on the bases, where he used his speed to dominate and his spikes to deliver bloody messages.

Love him or hate him, this was no ordinary demon. When Cobb retired in 1928 at age 42, he owned an incredible 90 all-time records. His 12 American League batting titles (nine in succession), .366 career average and 2,246 runs scored still top the charts. His 892 stolen bases and 4,191 hits remain legends. Cobb also was an accomplished right fielder with an above-average arm.

While Cobb never won anybody's popularity poll, nobody could deny the impact he made on the early-century game and the respect he generated in the process.

When the first class of Hall of Fame players was elected in 1936, Cobb received 98.2 percent of the vote—topping contemporaries Ruth (95.1), Honus Wagner (95.1), Christy Mathewson (90.7) and Walter Johnson (83.6).

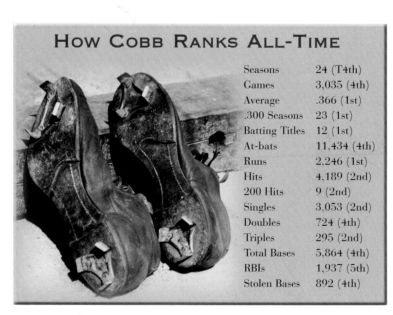

HOW COBB RANKS ALL-TIME

Seasons	24 (T4th)
Games	3,035 (4th)
Average	.366 (1st)
.300 Seasons	23 (1st)
Batting Titles	12 (1st)
At-bats	11,434 (4th)
Runs	2,246 (1st)
Hits	4,189 (2nd)
200 Hits	9 (2nd)
Singles	3,053 (2nd)
Doubles	724 (4th)
Triples	295 (2nd)
Total Bases	5,864 (4th)
RBIs	1,937 (5th)
Stolen Bases	892 (4th)

" HE COULD DO EVERYTHING BETTER THAN
ANY PLAYER I EVER SAW.
HE WAS ALWAYS THE FIRST ONE TO
DETECT WEAKNESSES OR MISTAKES
BY THE OPPOSITION AND BENEFIT BY THE
SAME."

WALTER JOHNSON

THE SPORTING NEWS, 1940

4 WALTER JOHNSON

He was the hardest-throwing pitcher of his era, the most successful fireballer in major-league history. Walter Johnson was to power pitching what Ty Cobb was to bat control. And every time Johnson delivered his fastball to overmatched hitters, he delivered a dose of much-needed pride to the fans of an overmatched franchise.

The 6-1, 200-pound Johnson used that fastball and pinpoint control to carve out 417 victories for the Washington Senators, a career total that ranks second all-time to Cy Young. He sling-shotted his heat homeward with a long right arm that whipped the ball from an exaggerated sidearm motion, mesmerizing overmatched hitters. For the first 15 years of his 21 major-league seasons, that fastball was his only pitch—an incredible testimony to the outstanding 2.17 ERA Johnson compiled over 5,914 ⅔ innings.

Johnson's success can be measured against two additional barriers that would have been the demise of many pitchers:

First, he piled up his wins for the lowly Senators, a team that did not enjoy success until 1924 and 1925—when Johnson was approaching age 40. Second, the Big Train never deviated from a gentlemanly demeanor that kept him from brushing back aggressive hitters, allowing them a sense of security they did not enjoy against the more mean-spirited pitchers of the era.

Johnson, baseball's first 3,000-strikeout pitcher and the all-time leader with 110 career shutouts, was one of the five charter members of the Hall of Fame, earning election with fellow greats Ty Cobb, Babe Ruth, Honus Wagner and Christy Mathewson in the class of 1936.

WALTER VS. THE WORLD

From 1910 through 1919, Johnson never failed to win 20 games for generally weak Senators teams:

Year	Johnson		Senators	
	W	L	W	L
1910	25	17	66	85
1911	25	13	64	90
1912	33	12	91	61
1913	36	7	90	64
1914	28	18	81	73
1915	27	13	85	68
1916	25	20	76	77
1917	23	16	74	79
1918	23	13	72	56
1919	20	14	56	84

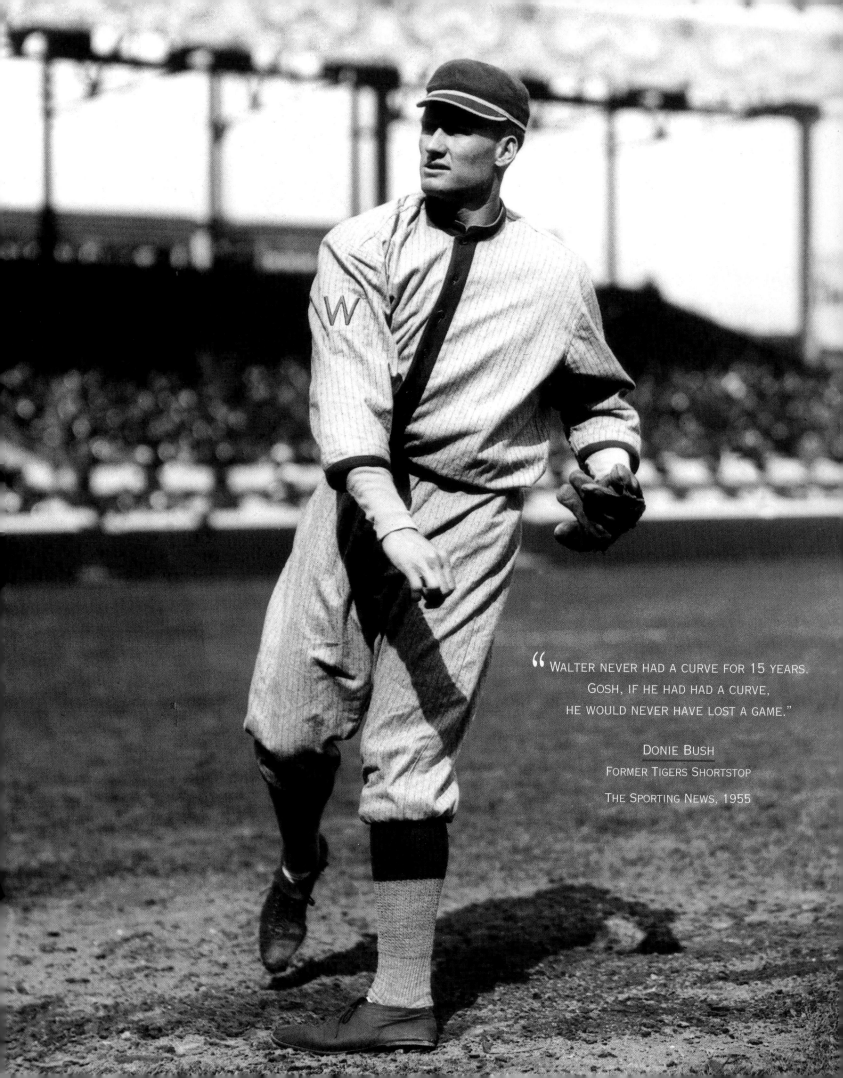

"WALTER NEVER HAD A CURVE FOR 15 YEARS.
GOSH, IF HE HAD HAD A CURVE,
HE WOULD NEVER HAVE LOST A GAME."

DONIE BUSH
FORMER TIGERS SHORTSTOP

THE SPORTING NEWS, 1955

"I REMEMBER HENRY AS A GREAT PLAYER.
HE COULD DO EVERYTHING. HE WAS ALWAYS A
QUIET GUY. HE LET HIS BAT DO THE TALKING."

WILLIE MAYS, 1982

HANK AARON 5

He was quiet, unassuming and shy, but no one in the second half century exerted more influence on the record books than Henry Aaron. He mesmerized teammates and fans with a soft-spoken dignity that defined his off-field personality for almost a quarter of a century while delivering a less-subtle message with the booming bat that helped him find baseball immortality.

That the home run would become Aaron's legacy seemed preposterous when he stepped onto the field as a skinny 6-foot rookie. But no one could have envisioned the unflinching work ethic and competitive fire that would allow Hammerin' Hank to pile up a record 755 home runs over a career that started in 1954 with the Milwaukee Braves and ended 23 seasons later in the same city with the American League's Brewers.

Aaron was a righthanded hitter with a fluid swing and lightning reflexes, but his secret to success was in the wrists—powerful wrists that allowed him to keep the hands back and drive the ball to all fields with tremendous force. The numbers never were spectacular—eight 40-homer seasons, never more than 47; 11 100- RBI seasons, never more than 132—but the bottom lines were: 3,771 hits (third all-time), 2,174 runs scored (tied for second), 2,297 RBIs (first), a career .305 average and, of course, the homers—41 more than Babe Ruth's previous record total.

Lost in the glare of the home run record and such contemporaries as Willie Mays and Mickey Mantle was Aaron's all-around consistency. He had outstanding speed, good instincts and one of the better right field arms in the game. The power combination of Aaron and Eddie Mathews drove the Milwaukee Braves to two pennants and a World Series victory (1957), but the Braves' Atlanta teams generally were weak. Still, Aaron was selected to a record 25 All-Star Games.

BEST HOME RUN HITTERS
SELECTED BY
HARMON KILLEBREW

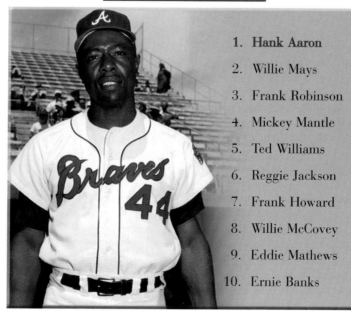

1. Hank Aaron
2. Willie Mays
3. Frank Robinson
4. Mickey Mantle
5. Ted Williams
6. Reggie Jackson
7. Frank Howard
8. Willie McCovey
9. Eddie Mathews
10. Ernie Banks

"I'M NOT A HEADLINE GUY AND WE MAY AS WELL
FACE IT. I'M JUST THE GUY WHO'S IN THERE
EVERY DAY, THE FELLOW WHO FOLLOWS BABE
IN THE BATTING ORDER."

LOU GEHRIG

THE SPORTING NEWS

LOU GEHRIG 6

Lou Gehrig will forever be lost in the glare of former New York Yankees teammate Babe Ruth's vast spotlight. But nothing about Gehrig's accomplishments should be minimized, from the 2,130 consecutive games he once played as the Iron Horse to his longtime link with Ruth as the enforcer of baseball's original Bash Brothers.

Gehrig was a rock-solid 6-foot, 210-pound left-handed slasher who rocketed line drives to all sections of the park, unlike the towering, majestic home runs that endeared Ruth to adoring fans. And unlike the gregarious Ruth, Gehrig was withdrawn, modest and unassuming, happy to let his teammate drink the fruits of their tandem celebrity.

But those who played with and against Gehrig understood the power he could exert over a game. As the Yankees' first baseman, cleanup hitter and lineup protection for Ruth, Gehrig was an RBI machine. He won four American League titles and tied for another and his 184-RBI explosion in 1931 is a still-standing A.L. record. His 13 consecutive 100-RBI seasons (1926-1938) were a byproduct of 493 career home runs and a not-so-modest .340 career average.

The Ruth-Gehrig relationship powered the Yankees to three World Series championships, and when Ruth left New York after the 1934 season, Gehrig and young Joe DiMaggio powered the team to three more. Ironically, Gehrig finally received his well-deserved recognition, but only because of a fatal disease that ended his career prematurely in 1939, tugging at the nation's heart strings, and took his life two years later.

GEHRIG'S RBI YEARS

Year	Total	A.L. Rank	Leader/2nd
1926	107	7th	Ruth (146)
1927	175	1st	Ruth (164)
1928	142	T1st	Ruth (142)
1929	126	4th	Simmons (157)
1930	174	1st	Simmons (165)
1931	184	1st	Ruth (163)
1932	151	T2nd	Foxx (169)
1933	139	2nd	Foxx (163)
1934	165	1st	Trosky (142)
1935	119	2nd	Greenberg (170)
1936	152	2nd	Trosky (162)
1937	159	3rd	Greenberg (183)
1938	114	T7th	Foxx (175)

7 CHRISTY MATHEWSON

He was an unusual combination of finesse, guile and controlled intensity, a baseball artist who turned out pitching masterpieces over the first 17 years of the 20th century. Christy Mathewson was the Greg Maddux of yesteryear and his National League-record-tying 373 career victories still stand as a testimony to artistic efficiency.

When Mathewson threw his first pitch for John McGraw's New York Giants in the summer of 1900, he provided a breath of fresh air for the rough-and-tumble game that scared away the more genteel, educated class of would-be fan. Matty, a product of Bucknell University, helped change baseball's image and he did it without the power style that characterized most pitchers of the era.

"You could sit in a rocking chair and catch Matty," said former Giants catcher Chief Meyers. Mathewson, a righthander, threw his vast assortment of pitches with an overhand delivery and pinpoint control. He pitched with savvy, seldom walked a batter and spotted pitches, letting his fielders do their job. His typical game required 80 to 90 pitches and he seldom topped 100. When in trouble, he often turned to his special fadeaway curve—a modern-day screwball that mesmerized both left-handed and righthanded batters.

Mathewson, a first-ballot Hall of Fame selection in the charter class of 1936, also mesmerized record keepers with his numbers. The Big Six topped 20 victories in 13 of his 17 seasons, 30 wins four times. His 37 wins in 1908 still stand as a modern N.L. record and his three straight 30-win streak from 1903-05 has been matched only once. His three-shutout 1905 World Series performance against Connie Mack's Philadelphia A's has never been duplicated.

THE OVER-35 GANG

When Mathewson won a modern National League-record 37 games in 1908, he joined the short list of 35-game winners in the 20th century:

W-L	Pitcher/Team	Year
41-12	Jack Chesbro, Yankees	1904
40-15	Ed Walsh, White Sox	1908
37-11	Christy Mathewson, Giants	1908
36-7	Walter Johnson, Senators	1913
35-8	Joe McGinnity, Giants	1904

"WITH JOHNSON, IT WAS BRUTE FORCE.
WITH MATHEWSON, IT WAS KNOWLEDGE AND
JUDGMENT, PERFECT CONTROL AND FORM. IT
WAS A PLEASURE TO WATCH HIM PITCH."

CONNIE MACK, 1943

"(WILLIAMS) IS THE MOST REMARKABLE HITTER
I EVER SAW. ... I NEVER SAW A HITTER WHO
COULD SWING AS LATE AS HE DOES AND HIT
THE BALL AS GOOD."

BILL DICKEY

THE SPORTING NEWS, 1946

TED WILLIAMS 8

Love him or hate him, you had to appreciate the work ethic Ted Williams applied to putting bat on ball. The incredible eyesight, the lightning reflexes, the perfect timing, the powerful forearms and the unwavering patience were scientifically defined components of a Boston Red Sox hitting machine that terrorized American League pitchers from 1939 to 1960.

If Williams wasn't the greatest pure hitter of all-time, he certainly was of his era. A lefthanded swinger, he stood erect, hands holding bat in a vice-like grip, straight up and close to his left shoulder. As the pitch arrived, Williams would throw his gangly body forward, keeping his hands back, back, back ... until a blurry, split-second swing would whip out another line drive. Always a perfectionist, Williams refused to swing at a bad pitch, a discipline that made him the most-walked hitter in history behind Babe Ruth.

But the self-discipline that so defined Williams the hitter often was lost on Williams the man. Quick-tempered, arrogant, opinionated and independent, the sensitive Williams, a sometimes-erratic defender in left field, fought career-long battles against critical sportswriters and fickle Boston fans. His feud with the media might have cost him three Most Valuable Player awards—in 1941 when he batted .406 but lost out to Joe DiMaggio; in 1942 when he won a Triple Crown but lost out to Joe Gordon; and in 1947 when he won a second Triple Crown and lost again to DiMaggio.

The Williams bottom line includes two MVPs, six A.L. batting titles, 2,654 career hits, a .344 average, 19 All-Star Game selections and 521 home runs—numbers that could have been higher if he had not lost four prime seasons to military duty during World War II and the Korean War.

BEST CLUTCH HITTERS
SELECTED BY BILL RIGNEY

1. Ted Williams
2. Stan Musial
3. Willie Mays
4. Al Kaline
5. Hank Aaron
6. Joe DiMaggio
7. Johnny Mize
8. Frank Robinson
9. Tony Gwynn
10. Tommy Henrich

9 ROGERS HORNSBY

As a man, Rogers Hornsby was truculent, aloof and a self-absorbed loner who always spoke his mind and seldom worried about the consequences. As a ballplayer, Rajah lived up to his nickname—proud, brash and majestic, especially when he stepped up to the plate and let his never-silent bat do the talking.

Hornsby possessed cat-like reflexes and sprinter speed, qualities that doubled his impact as a devastating hitter with power and one of the best-fielding second basemen of the first half-century. He stood deep in the box and rocketed line drives to all fields, a hitting style that helped him string together the best six-season offensive stretch in baseball history.

Playing for the St. Louis Cardinals, Hornsby posted averages of .370, .397, .401, .384, .424 (the second highest single-season average in history) and .403 from 1920-'25, winning six straight National League batting titles, two Triple Crowns and adulation as the greatest right-handed hitter of the modern era. He doubled as player/manager of the 1926 Cardinals, but it was during that World Series-championship season that his confrontational style wore thin with management.

Over the rest of Hornsby's 23-year playing career, he changed uniforms five times—always posting big numbers, always defying the authority figures he seemed to resent. He never wavered on either count, finishing his career with the second-highest batting average in history (.358) and a Ty Cobb-like aura that haunted him throughout a lengthy managerial stint.

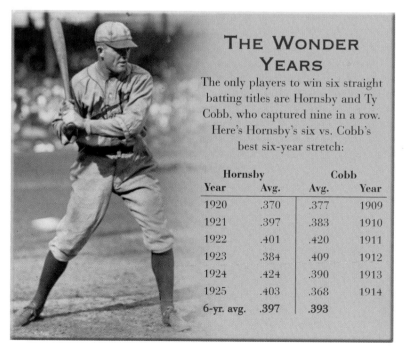

THE WONDER YEARS

The only players to win six straight batting titles are Hornsby and Ty Cobb, who captured nine in a row. Here's Hornsby's six vs. Cobb's best six-year stretch:

Hornsby		Cobb	
Year	Avg.	Avg.	Year
1920	.370	.377	1909
1921	.397	.383	1910
1922	.401	.420	1911
1923	.384	.409	1912
1924	.424	.390	1913
1925	.403	.368	1914
6-yr. avg.	.397	.393	

"I DON'T LIKE TO SOUND EGOTISTICAL, BUT EVERY TIME
I STEPPED UP TO THE PLATE WITH A BAT IN MY HANDS,
I COULDN'T HELP BUT FEEL SORRY FOR THE PITCHER."

ROGERS HORNSBY, 1953

10 STAN MUSIAL

He had the menacing look of a cobra—crouched at the hips, legs close together in the back of the box with right heel elevated, bat cocked straight up, eyes peering over the right shoulder in a hypnotic search for a moving target. When the ball arrived, Stan (The Man) Musial uncoiled, driving another hit into his impressive record book.

Musial mesmerized adoring St. Louis Cardinals fans with 3,630 such hits over a 22-year career that covered all or parts of three decades and produced a .331 career average. Always affable, friendly and quick with a smile, the 20-year-old right fielder/first baseman began his St. Louis love affair in 1941 and powered the Cardinals to three World Series championships over the next five years while winning two of the seven National League batting titles he would claim before his retirement in 1963.

Musial was not a Ruthian-type power hitter, but careless pitchers usually paid for their mistakes. Musial muscled up for 475 career home runs,

including five in a memorable 1954 doubleheader against the New York Giants, and finished with 1,377 extra-base hits, second only to Hank Aaron on the all-time list. Musial ranks in the top five of numerous all-time categories, he's one of four players to win three MVP awards and he appeared in a record-tying 24 All-Star Games, hitting a record six All-Star home runs.

But Musial's greatest legacy might have been the goodwill he brought to a city and the game in general. His love for baseball was genuine, his rapport with the fans was enduring. Musial was living proof that an unyielding, take-no-prisoners intensity is not necessarily a prerequisite for success.

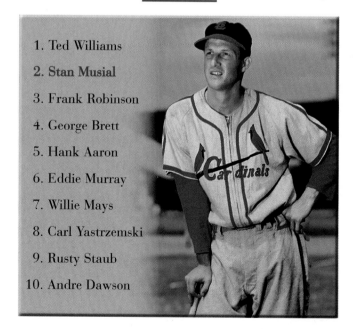

BEST CLUTCH HITTERS
SELECTED BY
JIM FREY

1. Ted Williams
2. Stan Musial
3. Frank Robinson
4. George Brett
5. Hank Aaron
6. Eddie Murray
7. Willie Mays
8. Carl Yastrzemski
9. Rusty Staub
10. Andre Dawson

"No man has ever been a perfect ballplayer. Stan Musial, however, is the closest thing to perfection in the game today. ... He's certainly one of the great hitters of all time."

Ty Cobb, 1953

11 JOE DiMAGGIO

Aloof and mysterious, graceful and dignified, the very essence of Joe DiMaggio defied his status as an American icon. But years after he retired from a Hall of Fame baseball career, years after his marriage to movie star Marilyn Monroe had ended, years after his name had been immortalized in song by Simon and Garfunkel and in television lore by Mr. Coffee commercials, DiMaggio maintained his status as a genuine hero.

That unwanted superstardom was thrust upon a 21-year-old do-everything center fielder when he made a spectacular 1936 debut with the New York Yankees, the team he would lead to 10 American League pennants and nine World Series championships in an incredible 13-season career interrupted by three years of military service. DiMaggio, who roamed the expansive center field pasture at Yankee Stadium like a gazelle, was a fearless righthanded hitter with extra-base and home run power. It was love at first sight for fickle New York fans, who immediately accorded him the hero status passed down from Babe Ruth and Lou Gehrig.

On the field, DiMaggio handled his burden with respect and quiet dignity. He fought through numerous injuries to compile a .325 career average, win two A.L. batting titles and top 100 RBIs nine times. His 1941 record 56-game hitting streak is a legendary feat and he shares the major league record for

MVP awards, with three. Off the field, the Yankee Clipper unsuccessfully fought against a hero status that just wouldn't go away.

The DiMaggio aura, which was passed on to fellow center fielder Mickey Mantle after his 1951 retirement, lives on today, like the Yankee World Series dynasty he helped create.

56 AND COUNTING

Some quick facts and figures from DiMaggio's record 56-game hitting streak in 1941:

Average	.408
At-Bats	223
Runs	56
Hits	91
Doubles	16
Triples	4
Home Runs	15
RBIs	55
1st Hit	May 15
Last Hit	July 16

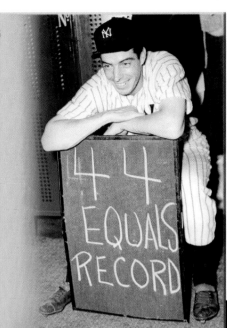

" WHERE HAVE YOU GONE, JOE DIMAGGIO? A NATION TURNS ITS LONELY EYES TO YOU."

SIMON AND GARFUNKEL, 1967

12 GROVER ALEXANDER

G rover Cleveland Alexander spent 20 major-league seasons creating two legends: an on-field master who posted a National League-record-tying 373 career victories and an off-field drifter who battled alcoholism and other problems to an inglorious end. The control that so defined his pitching success was notably absent in a demonic vice that defined and overpowered his personal life.

The slim 6-1 Alexander, the product of a Nebraska farm life, burst upon the big-league scene in 1911 with the greatest rookie performance in history: 28-13, 2.57 ERA for the Philadelphia Phillies. His smooth, effortless, three-quarters and sidearm motions mesmerized opposing hitters and his laser-like fastball and sweeping curves were delivered with pinpoint precision. "Alex had the most perfect control of any pitcher I ever saw," Hall of Fame third baseman Max Carey once said, and he was a fast worker who operated with an instinct and confidence that belied his off-field demons.

Alexander's 1915, '16 and '17 seasons were masterpieces. He was 31-10, 33-12 and 30-13; his ERAs were 1.22, 1.55 and 1.83; he led the N.L.

in innings and strikeouts all three years; and he posted 36 shutouts, including a still-standing record of 16 in 1916. His seven-season, 190-victory Philadelphia tenure was followed by 12 less-spectacular, but still-productive, seasons with the Chicago Cubs and St. Louis Cardinals.

Alexander is best remembered for one dramatic 1926 performance when, at age 39 and reportedly hung over after a night of revelry, he entered the seventh inning of World Series Game 7 with two out and the bases loaded to face New York Yankees slugger Tony Lazzeri. He struck Lazzeri out on four pitches, preserving the Cardinals' 3-2 lead, and pitched the final two innings preserving St. Louis' first World Series championship.

OLD PETE VS. BIG SIX

Alexander and Christy Mathewson, who share the N.L. record with 373 career wins, are the only pitchers to win 30 games in three straight seasons:

ALEXANDER

Year	W	L	IP	ShO	ERA
1915	31	10	376.1	12	1.22
1916	33	12	389.0	16	1.55
1917	30	13	388.0	8	1.83

MATHEWSON

Year	W	L	IP	ShO	ERA
1903	30	13	366.1	3	2.26
1904	33	12	367.2	4	2.03
1905	31	9	338.2	8	1.28

"HE MADE ME WANT TO THROW MY BAT AWAY WHEN I WENT TO THE PLATE. HE FED ME PITCHES I COULDN'T HIT."

JOHNNY EVERS
FORMER CUBS SECOND BASEMAN

13 HONUS WAGNER

His 5-11, 200-pound gorilla-like frame featured a thick, massive chest, long arms and legs so bowed you could roll a barrel between them. Hall of Fame pitcher Lefty Gomez, who enjoyed the good fortune of never having to face Honus Wagner, once quipped, "He was the only ballplayer who could tie his shoelaces without bending down."

Wagner, a.k.a. the Flying Dutchman, was nobody's prototypical athlete. But when he stepped onto a baseball field, he magically transformed into one of the most versatile players in the history of the game. Wagner could pitch or play any infield or outfield position, but he is most fondly remembered as the first great shortstop of the 20th century and the National League's most proficient batsman of his era.

Wagner was to Pittsburgh what Ty Cobb was to Detroit and Babe Ruth to New York. From 1900 to 1917, he mesmerized Pirates fans with his deceptive range, over-sized, shovel-like hands that sucked every

ground ball into his undersized mitt and a rifle arm that allowed him to make plays from deep in the hole—and beyond.

Offensively, Wagner overmatched the usually dominant pitchers of the dead-ball era. His career total of 3,415 hits (seventh on the all-time list) produced an average of .327, 16 .300 seasons and a National League-record-tying eight batting titles, second only to Cobb's career mark of 12. When the first Hall of Fame class was selected in 1936, Wagner and Ruth tied for second in the voting, behind only Cobb and ahead of Christy Mathewson and Walter Johnson.

THE 10-YEAR ITCH

Wagner was the greatest hitter of the century's first decade, winning seven of his eight batting championships before 1910. Ten other players captured four or more titles in a decade, with Tony Gwynn (through 1997) doing it twice:

No.	Player	Decade
9	Ty Cobb	1910s
7	**Honus Wagner**	**1900s**
7	Rogers Hornsby	1920s
6	Rod Carew	1970s
5	Wade Boggs	1980s
4	Napoleon Lajoie	1900s
4	Harry Heilmann	1920s
4	Ted Williams	1940s
4	Stan Musial	1950s
4	Roberto Clemente	1960s
4	Tony Gwynn	1980s
4	Tony Gwynn	1990s

" I HOLD OUT FOR HANS WAGNER AS THE GREATEST OF THEM ALL. WAGNER WAS A GREAT BALLPLAYER AT 20. HE WAS STILL A GREAT BALLPLAYER AT 43. IN ALL MY CAREER, I NEVER SAW SUCH A VERSATILE PLAYER"

JOHN MCGRAW

THE SPORTING NEWS, 1931

14 CY YOUNG

His name is synonomous with masterful pitching and career success often is measured by an award bearing his name. If Cy Young wasn't the greatest pitcher in baseball history, he certainly was the game's first great hurler and the one destined for an immortality that transcends what he accomplished on the field.

Denton True Young, a Civil War baby boomer who delivered his first pitches with oranges on his father's Ohio farm, burst upon the major-league scene with the Cleveland Spiders in 1890 and began a string of fifteen 20- and 30-win seasons a year later. For turn-of-the-century hitters, the 6-2, 210-pound righthander was a magician who could pitch every other day and seemed to sense their every weakness.

Young's secret was a photographic memory that allowed him to mentally chart every batter and an assortment of pitches that kept them guessing and flailing weakly at his pinpoint deliveries. He used four motions, all of which started with his back to the plate, and his fastball was among the fastest of the period. He threw two curves, a big breaker from an overhand motion and a "swerve" that was delivered sidearm. A superb changeup was part of an act that baffled hitters until 1911, when Young retired after 22 seasons—12 in the N.L. with Cleveland, St. Louis and Boston; 10 in the A.L. with Boston and Cleveland.

Young is most celebrated for his career-record 511 victories, but just as amazing are his career records for innings pitched (7,356), 300-inning seasons (16) and complete games (749). He also started for the Red Sox in baseball's first World Series game in 1903.

A CY OF RELIEF

Young was 33 years old when he opened the 1900 season. He went on to compile 230 victories over the first 10 years of the century, the third highest single-decade total in history:

Wins	Pitcher	Decade
265	Walter Johnson	1910s
236	Christy Mathewson	1900s
230	Cy Young	1900s
218	Joe McGinnity	1900s
208	Grover Alexander	1910s
202	Warren Spahn	1950s
199	Lefty Grove	1930s
199	Robin Roberts	1950s
192	Jack Chesbro	1900s
191	Juan Marichal	1960s

"I don't expect to see a second Cy Young.
Men who combine his coordinated talents
of mind and arm are not born often."

John McGraw

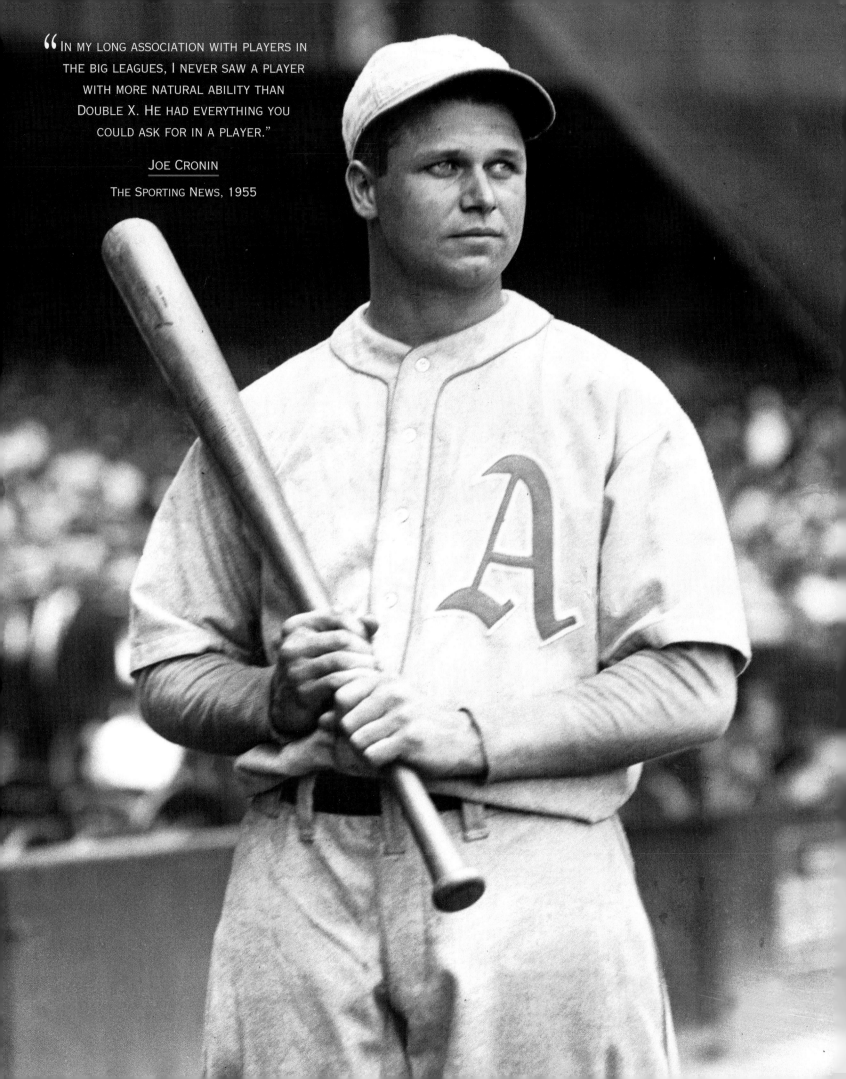

"IN MY LONG ASSOCIATION WITH PLAYERS IN THE BIG LEAGUES, I NEVER SAW A PLAYER WITH MORE NATURAL ABILITY THAN DOUBLE X. HE HAD EVERYTHING YOU COULD ASK FOR IN A PLAYER."

JOE CRONIN

THE SPORTING NEWS, 1955

JIMMIE FOXX 15

There was nothing quite like a Jimmie Foxx home run: powerful, muscular arms whipping a 37-ounce bat into a pitch with incredible speed; ball rocketing from home plate to places beyond even faster. Blink and you might miss the split-second experience. Watch closely and you might even see the vapor trail.

Unlike a Babe Ruth homer that was majestic and almost serene, a Foxx homer was brute force. Such power generated from a 5-11, 195-pound former Maryland farmboy, who emerged in 1925 as the strongman of Connie Mack's Philadelphia Athletics lineup and the first serious challenger to Ruth's power-hitting dominance. Foxx was a menacing figure when he stood at the plate, with a fixed glare, waving the bat with biceps that bulged from sleeves cut deliberately short.

From his breakthrough 1929 season with the A's through his 1940 fifth season with the Boston Red Sox, Foxx never failed to hit 30 homers or drive in 100 runs, a remarkable 12-year stretch that included a 1932 season in which he almost reached baseball immortality. His 58 home runs fell just two short of Ruth's 1927 single-season record and his 20-year total of 534 ranked second all-time to Ruth for many years. Foxx punctuated his Hall of Fame career with a .325 average, two American League batting titles and record-tying totals of 13 100-RBI seasons and three A.L. MVP awards.

Perhaps the real measure of Double X was the contributions he made in other areas of the game. His defensive versatility allowed managers to use him at catcher, first and third base, and in the outfield with full confidence; and his friendly, amiable personality belied his powerful personna and made him a popular clubhouse figure.

5-YEAR PLAN

If you combine the best five one-season home run totals of baseball's top sluggers, only Babe Ruth ranks ahead of Foxx. The totals are through the 1997 season:

Tot.	Name/Seasons
276	Babe Ruth (60, 59, 54, 54, 49)
241	Jimmie Foxx (58, 50, 48, 44, 41)
240	Mark McGwire (58, 52, 49, 42, 39)
240	Willie Mays (52, 51, 49, 47, 41)
237	Harmon Killebrew (49, 49, 48, 46, 45)
234	Ralph Kiner (54, 51, 47, 42, 40)
232	Lou Gehrig (49, 49, 47, 46, 41)
225	Mickey Mantle (54, 52, 42, 40, 37)
224	Hank Aaron (47, 45, 44, 44, 44)
220	Ernie Banks (47, 45, 44, 43, 41)

" BENCH IS THE GREATEST ATHLETE WHO EVER
HAS PLAYED THE GAME. IT'S ALMOST PITIFUL THAT
ONE MAN SHOULD HAVE SO MUCH TALENT."

SPARKY ANDERSON

THE SPORTING NEWS, 1970

JOHNNY BENCH 16

I t might not seem fair, but Johnny Bench is the standard by which catchers will be judged forever. From the rock-solid 210-pound frame that guarded home plate like a stone wall to the cannon-sized arm that bewildered baserunners with laser-like throws to second base, Bench gave future generations of catchers a floor plan for Hall of Fame success.

From the first moment of his 1967 debut with the Cincinnati Reds, there was little doubt about the impact he would have on the game. Bench's incredible tools—the arm, the huge hands that could hold seven baseballs at one time, the cat-like quickness—allowed him to play the way no other catcher had dared. Not only did he do everything better than his predecessors, he redefined the position with his one-handed style, the one-handed sweep tag that shocked veteran baseball people and the helmet and oversized glove that became a part of every catcher's equipment.

Bench could dominate games from behind the plate, where he earned 10 Gold Gloves and set National League records with 9,260 putouts and 10,110 total chances while compiling a .990 fielding percentage. Or he could dominate with a bat that produced six 100-RBI seasons, three N.L. RBI titles and 389 home runs— 327 as a catcher, second only to Carlton Fisk on the all-time list.

Bench, a 12-time All-Star who played through 10 broken bones in his feet and numerous knee problems throughout a 17-year career, also earned a pair of N.L. MVP awards and was a driving force for the Big Red Machine that won consecutive World Series championships in the mid-1970s.

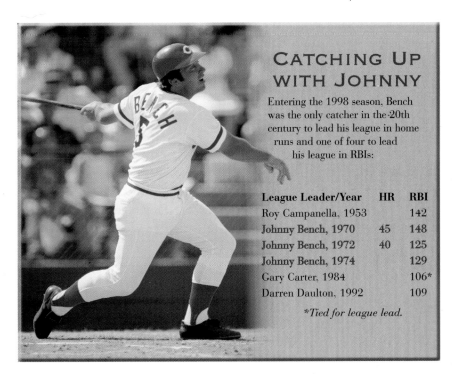

CATCHING UP WITH JOHNNY

Entering the 1998 season, Bench was the only catcher in the 20th century to lead his league in home runs and one of four to lead his league in RBIs:

League Leader/Year	HR	RBI
Roy Campanella, 1953		142
Johnny Bench, 1970	45	148
Johnny Bench, 1972	40	125
Johnny Bench, 1974		129
Gary Carter, 1984		106*
Darren Daulton, 1992		109

*Tied for league lead.

17 MICKEY MANTLE

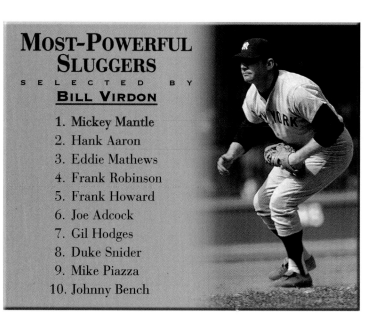

When he cut his Oklahoma ties in 1949 he was called the Commerce Comet, and when he retired from baseball 20 seasons later he was known affectionately, simply, as The Mick. In between, a naive country boy named Mickey Mantle rose to prominence as a national icon and the centerpiece of a New York Yankees dynasty that captured 12 American League pennants and seven World Series championships over a glorious 14-year span.

The husky, blond, switch-hitting 19-year-old with blacksmith arms, sprinter speed and an unassuming, home-spun charm arrived in 1951 as the heir apparent to center fielder Joe DiMaggio, a New York idol who was playing his final season. In the Babe Ruth-Lou Gehrig-DiMaggio tradition that had helped the Yankees achieve baseball superiority for three decades, Mantle, 5-11, 200 pounds of unprecedented power from both sides of the plate, quickly won over fans with his tape-measure home runs and an almost-mystical aura that would transcend his 18-year big-league career.

Mantle, a 16-time All-Star, was plagued by a series of early knee problems that would compromise his all-around skills and prematurely trigger a late-career decline, but his power-hitting feats were legendary. Not only were his home runs long, they were frequent. Twice he topped 50—in 1956 when he won an A.L. Triple Crown and in 1961 when he joined teammate Roger Maris in the chase of Ruth's single-season record—en route to a career total of 536. And 10 times he complemented that power with .300-plus averages that helped him win three A.L. MVP awards.

But Mantle's greatest legacy was written in the 12 World Series in which he set numerous fall classic records, including home runs (18) and RBIs (40).

MOST-POWERFUL SLUGGERS

SELECTED BY **BILL VIRDON**

1. Mickey Mantle
2. Hank Aaron
3. Eddie Mathews
4. Frank Robinson
5. Frank Howard
6. Joe Adcock
7. Gil Hodges
8. Duke Snider
9. Mike Piazza
10. Johnny Bench

"(MANTLE) HITS THE LONGEST BALL IN THE GAME.
HE CAN BELT IT AS FAR AS BABE RUTH OR TED WILLIAMS,
MAYBE FARTHER. HE IS FAST, HE CAN FIELD, HE CAN THROW
AND HE CAN HIT."

CHARLEY GEHRINGER, 1952
HALL OF FAME SECOND BASEMAN

"He can do everything. He hits the ball a mile, he catches so easily he might as well be in a rocking chair, throws like a bullet. Bill Dickey isn't as good a catcher."

Walter Johnson

JOSH GIBSON 18

He was to Negro League baseball what Babe Ruth was to the all-white game of his era. The Josh Gibson legend is filled with stories of long, longer and longest home runs, other incredible batting feats and testimonials from longtime teammates and supporters that he was at least equal to the Sultan of Swat, maybe even better.

The baseball world will never know for sure because Gibson, a barrel-chested 220-pound catcher, never had the chance to test his skills in the major leagues. But those who watched him play from 1930 to 1946 for the Homestead Grays and Pittsburgh Crawfords described an intimidating hitter who seldom struck out and powered mammoth home runs from a flat-footed stance with a simple flick of his wrists. His upper-body strength was incredible; his batting averages and home run totals (a reported 75 in one season) were hard to believe.

Gibson, a wide-smiling quiet man with broad shoulders and thick arms, also was an outstanding catcher, once described by pitching great Walter Johnson as better than New York Yankees contemporary Bill Dickey. Other major league players who competed against Gibson and various other Negro League stars during offseason barnstorming games were equally impressed.

Sadly, Gibson was just 35 years old and still active when he suffered a cerebral hemorrhage and died suddenly in January 1947, a few months before Jackie Robinson would gain national attention by breaking baseball's color barrier with the Brooklyn Dodgers.

THE BEST OF THE BEST

Negro League pitching great Satchel Paige named the five toughest hitters he had ever faced in a 1953 story that was printed in Collier's magazine:

1. Josh Gibson
2. Charley Gehringer
3. Larry Doby
4. Joe DiMaggio
5. Ted Williams

"SATCH'S FASTBALL NOW IS JUST A CHANGE
OF PACE TO THE BALL HE USED TO THROW.
BUT HIS CONTROL IS STILL PHENOMENAL."

DIZZY DEAN, 1952

SATCHEL PAIGE 19

I f Satchel Paige wasn't the best pitcher in baseball history, he might have been the most colorful. Enthusiastic, outlandish and endearing, he was a relentless showman who always made baseball fun for the multitudes who flocked to parks to see him pitch over the better part of four decades, most of which was spent dominating the 1920s, '30s and '40s Negro Leagues.

Paige was a physical anomaly who tested his rubber arm to the limit in working an estimated 2,600 games, as many as 200 in several year-round seasons. His fastball was dominant through most of his Negro League days, but he later tantalized major-league hitters with his off-speed deliveries as a 42-year-old Cleveland Indians rookie (1948) and a successful St. Louis Browns reliever (1951-53). Paige even made a major-league curtain call in 1965 for Charlie Finley's Kansas City Athletics, working three scoreless innings against Boston—at age 59.

The tall, lanky righthander delivered his blazing fastball with a windmill delivery and perfect control, often juicing up expectant fans by following through on crazy predictions and stunts (like pulling teammates off the field and then striking out the side). Ever the baseball ambassador, Paige filled ballparks for the struggling Negro Leagues while drifting from team to team, but his reputation really spread during seasons with the Pittsburgh Crawfords and Kansas City Monarchs.

Paige did not get to test his skills at the major-league level until well after his prime, when he was forced to rely on cunning and guile rather than his once-dominant fastball. But still he became an American folk hero who charmed teammates and audiences with self-effacing humor and home-spun stories. And, of course, that room-lighting smile.

STAYING YOUNG

This was Paige's advice for a long, active life:

1. Avoid fried meats, which angry up the blood.
2. If your stomach disputes you, lie down and pacify it with cool thoughts.
3. Keep the juices flowing by jangling around gently as you move.
4. Go very light on the vices, such as carrying on in society. The social ramble ain't restful.
5. Avoid running at all times.
6. Don't look back. Something might be gaining on you.

"THE BIG THING ABOUT CLEMENTE IS THAT HE CAN HIT
ANY PITCH. I DON'T MEAN ONLY STRIKES. HE CAN HIT A BALL
OFF HIS ANKLES OR OFF HIS EAR."

JUAN MARICHAL

THE SPORTING NEWS, 1972

ROBERTO CLEMENTE 20

He strutted through 18 major league seasons like a high-strung thoroughbred and gained baseball immortality in a tragic career-ending death while acting as a life-sustaining humanitarian. Proud, honest, intense, sensitive and incredibly talented: Adjectives simply oozed from the sometimes-complicated persona of Roberto Clemente.

Clemente, who learned the game on the sandlots of his native Puerto Rico, was baseball's prototypical right fielder from 1955 to 1972, complete with speed, razor-sharp instincts and an arm that was feared by base-runners throughout the National League. He patrolled the vast right field pasture at Pittsburgh's Forbes Field for most of his career, defiantly staking his claim to greatness with 12 Gold Gloves and defensive comparisons to outfield contemporary Willie Mays.

Clemente's hitting style was unorthodox, but effective enough to produce four N.L. batting titles, a 1966 MVP citation and 15 All-Star invitations. Clemente, 5-11 and 180 pounds with chiseled features and quick wrists, stood away from the plate and kept hands and bat cocked until the last possible second, seemingly pulling line drives right out of the catcher's mitt with an inside-out swing. Clemente, who went through his career complaining of aches and pains that never seemed to affect his play, was a notorious bad-ball hitter who posted a .317 career average and led the Pirates to two World Series championships.

Clemente never forgot his roots and was revered in Puerto Rico as a national hero. He was part of a team flying relief supplies to earthquake-ravaged Nicaragua on December 31, 1972, when the small aircraft exploded and crashed into the ocean. His untimely death occurred only a few months after he had recorded his 3,000th career hit and prompted a special election that gave him immediate distinction as baseball's first Hispanic Hall of Famer.

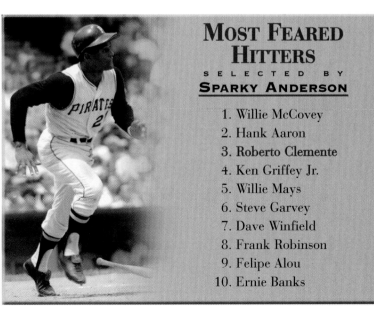

MOST FEARED HITTERS
SELECTED BY SPARKY ANDERSON

1. Willie McCovey
2. Hank Aaron
3. Roberto Clemente
4. Ken Griffey Jr.
5. Willie Mays
6. Steve Garvey
7. Dave Winfield
8. Frank Robinson
9. Felipe Alou
10. Ernie Banks

21 WARREN SPAHN

tan Musial called him "an artist with imagination." The Brooklyn Dodgers once named their new pitching machine "The Warren Spahn." Other National League hitters simply flailed helplessly at his wide assortment of strategically placed pitches for 21 major-league seasons and then retired quietly to their seat on the bench.

That's the effect Spahn had on hitters from 1942-65 as he carved out 363 victories, more than any lefthander in baseball history. An artist, indeed, but more accurately a pitching scientist who could paint corners with his pinpoint control, confound batters with different-speed fastballs, curves, sinkers and screwballs and get them to chase tantalizing pitches barely out of the strike zone.

Spahn, a thin 6-footer who posted all but seven of his victories for the Boston and Milwaukee Braves, delivered those pitches from a slow, rock-back motion that fueled a high, fluid leg kick and a machine-like overhand delivery. The hitter looked for the ball amid the illusion of flailing arms and legs. No two pitches looked alike or arrived in the same spot. When Spahnie was sharp, games were fast and the results predictable.

An affable, fun-loving prankster off the field, Spahn was all-business on the mound. He also was the model of consistency, posting a lefthander-record 13 20-win seasons over a 17-year stretch beginning in 1947. He claimed one Cy Young Award and pitched the Braves to three N.L. pennants and one World Series victory in a career that was interrupted by three years of military service in World War II.

BEST BIG-GAME PITCHERS
SELECTED BY
CHUCK TANNER

1. Sandy Koufax
2. Warren Spahn
3. Goose Gossage
4. Rollie Fingers
5. Wilbur Wood
6. Steve Carlton
7. Catfish Hunter
8. John Candelaria
9. Juan Marichal
10. Greg Maddux

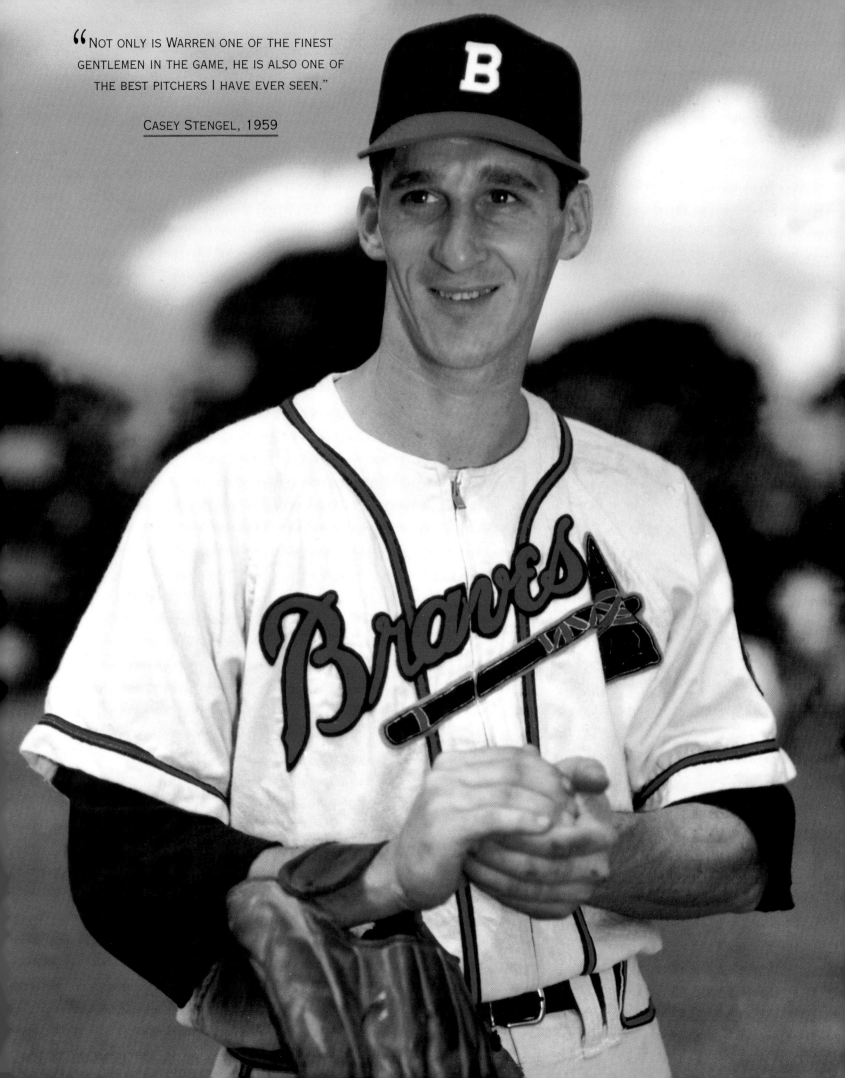

"NOT ONLY IS WARREN ONE OF THE FINEST
GENTLEMEN IN THE GAME, HE IS ALSO ONE OF
THE BEST PITCHERS I HAVE EVER SEEN."

CASEY STENGEL, 1959

22 FRANK ROBINSON

When you cut through all the superlatives, two capture the essence and intensity of the man. Frank Robinson, the self-made star with skinny legs and a big stick, was fearless and inspirational—qualities that earned him the contempt of opponents and the respect and admiration of teammates and fans.

There was nothing flashy about the right fielder who made his first memorable impressions in 1956 as a 20-year-old rookie for Cincinnati. Competing for prestige in a baseball era that would be dominated by such names as Mays, Mantle, Aaron and Clemente, Robinson played with a recklessness, intimidating self-confidence and scowling demeanor that infuriated opponents. He always slid hard, he never fraternized with the enemy and he wielded a booming bat that would produce 586 career home runs.

Even his batting style was confrontational. Robinson crowded the plate like a boxer trying to work inside, defiantly daring the pitcher to throw a strike. He crouched and leaned forward, bat pointed upward, and glared toward the mound over an upraised shoulder. Pitchers who greeted his insolence with fastballs to the ribs usually paid a stiff price in subsequent at-bats.

When Cincinnati sent Robby to Baltimore in an unpopular 1965 trade, the young-and-talented Orioles got the outspoken clubhouse leader who would help them win four American League pennants and two World Series in a six-year span. Robinson punctuated that team success with a 1966 Triple Crown and distinction as the only player to win MVP awards in both leagues.

The aging Robinson punctuated his career in 1975 with another distinction—he became Cleveland's player/manager and the first black manager in major league baseball history.

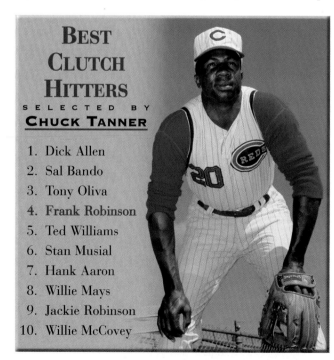

BEST CLUTCH HITTERS

SELECTED BY
CHUCK TANNER

1. Dick Allen
2. Sal Bando
3. Tony Oliva
4. Frank Robinson
5. Ted Williams
6. Stan Musial
7. Hank Aaron
8. Willie Mays
9. Jackie Robinson
10. Willie McCovey

" He took terrific talent and made it even better with his intensity. It has never been any secret that anyone who played against Frank hated him while the guys who played with him loved him."

Davey Johnson, 1982

Former Orioles Teammate

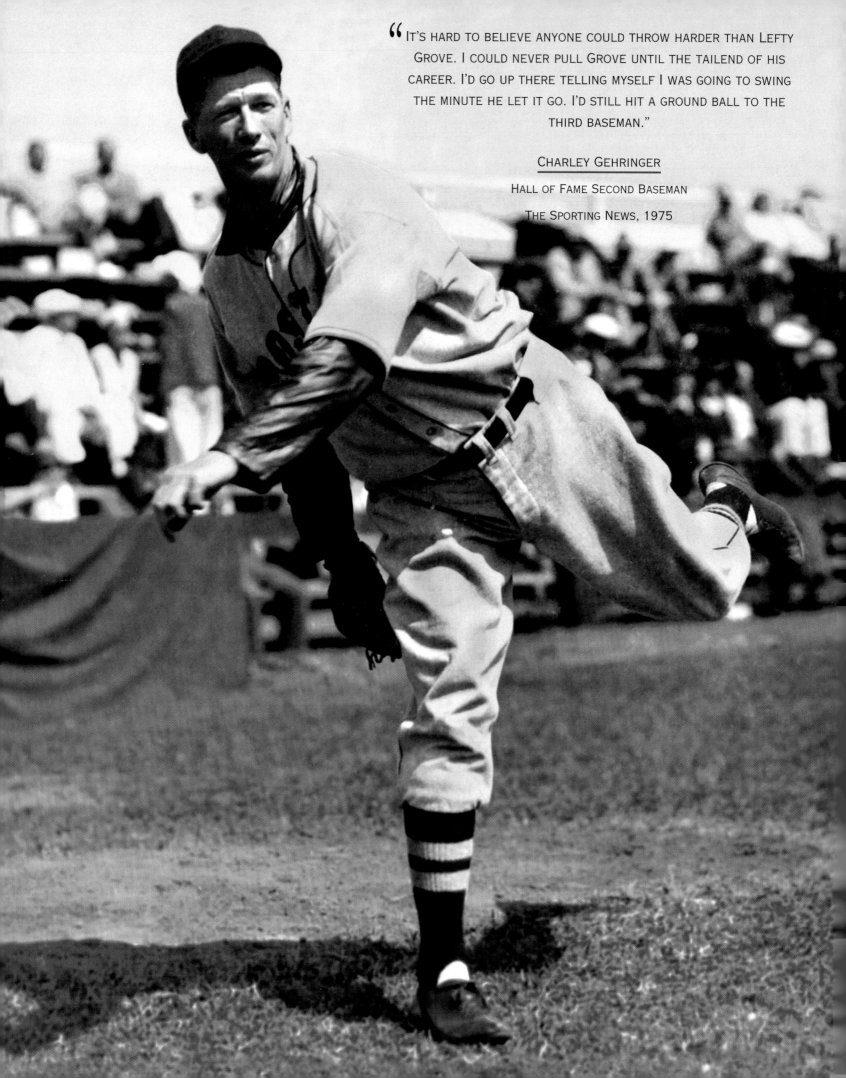

"IT'S HARD TO BELIEVE ANYONE COULD THROW HARDER THAN LEFTY GROVE. I COULD NEVER PULL GROVE UNTIL THE TAILEND OF HIS CAREER. I'D GO UP THERE TELLING MYSELF I WAS GOING TO SWING THE MINUTE HE LET IT GO. I'D STILL HIT A GROUND BALL TO THE THIRD BASEMAN."

CHARLEY GEHRINGER

HALL OF FAME SECOND BASEMAN

THE SPORTING NEWS, 1975

LEFTY GROVE 23

Opposing hitters never had a chance against a Lefty Grove fastball, which sailed past them like a meteor unleashed by some other-worldly force. Neither did teammates against the Lefty Grove temper, which erupted into sometimes-violent tantrums when things did not go just right over the virulent lefthander's 17-year major league career.

Suffice to say the lean 6-3, 200-pounder was both fast and furious. And incredibly successful, thanks to that uncontrollable intensity he brought to the clubhouse and the mound. When he made his big-league debut for Connie Mack's Philadelphia Athletics in 1925, his fastball was as wild as it was fast, and batters stepped into the box with trepidation.

The high-kicking Grove, who would go days without speaking to a teammate because of a defensive lapse, tamed his fastball but never lost the edge his early wildness provided. He enjoyed the first of eight 20-win seasons in 1927 and compiled a 152-41 record from 1928 to 1933, a six-year stretch in which the A's won three American League pennants and two World Series. His marquee season was 1931, when he fashioned a 31-4 record that would stand as the A.L.'s last 30-win effort until 1968.

When cost-cutting Mack traded Grove to the Red Sox after the 1933 season, he suffered an arm injury that forced him to transform from a thrower into a pitcher. Relying on a suddenly-improved curveball and sinker, Grove posted 105 Boston victories that gave him a final career mark of 300-141, remarkable when you consider he did not make his big-league debut until the age of 25.

THE WINNING EDGE

Grove compiled the best winning percentage among modern-era pitchers with 300 or more victories:

Pct.	Player	W-L
.680	Lefty Grove	300-141
.665	Christy Mathewson	373-188
.642	Grover Alexander	373-208
.634	Kid Nichols	361-208
.627	Eddie Plank	326-194
.618	Cy Young	511-316
.603	Tom Seaver	311-205
.599	Walter Johnson	417-279
.597	Warren Spahn	363-245
.574	Steve Carlton	329-244
.559	Don Sutton	324-256
.551	Early Wynn	300-244
.542	Gaylord Perry	314-265
.537	Phil Niekro	318-274
.526	Nolan Ryan	324-292

24 EDDIE COLLINS

Pound for pound, Eddie Collins might have been the best player in baseball history. Ty Cobb thought he was; so did Collins' former Philadelphia Athletics manager, the esteemed Connie Mack. The 5-9, 175-pound Collins, a graduate of Columbia University, certainly was one of the most cerebral players during his quarter-of-a-century reign as the game's premier all-around second baseman.

Collins, who began his career in 1906 with Mack's Athletics, covered more ground than early-century contemporary Nap Lajoie, made the double-play pivot more gracefully than late-career rival Rogers Hornsby and was especially adept at retreating into the outfield to pick off potential bloop hits. The slashing left-handed hitter was a perfect fit for the dead-ball era in which he spent most of his career and learned to play the game.

The speedy Collins, an outstanding bunter and consummate team player, might have been at his most dangerous best on the basepaths. He stole 67 bases in 1909 and 81 a year later en route to a career total of 744, but he always will be remembered for his daring dash to the plate in Game 6 of the 1917 World Series with the run that secured a Chicago White Sox championship.

Collins also will be remembered for other things: He was an innocent member of the 1919 Black Sox team that conspired to throw the World Series; he was a member of Philadelphia's famed $100,000 infield (Stuffy McInnis at first, Collins at second, Jack Barry at shortstop and Home Run Baker at third) in 1913-14; he was a .333 career hitter who pounded out 3,315 hits. Ironically, Collins never won an A.L. batting title because his career spanned the same period as Cobb.

ROGERS HORNSBY'S ALL-TIME TEAM

Hornsby selected his all-time team, with Collins at his second base position, for Look magazine in 1952:

1B: George Sisler
2B: Eddie Collins
3B: Pie Traynor
SS: Honus Wagner
LF: Joe Jackson
CF: Tris Speaker
RF: Babe Ruth
C: Mickey Cochrane
   Bill Dickey
RHP: Grover Alexander
   Walter Johnson
LHP: Lefty Grove
   Carl Hubbell

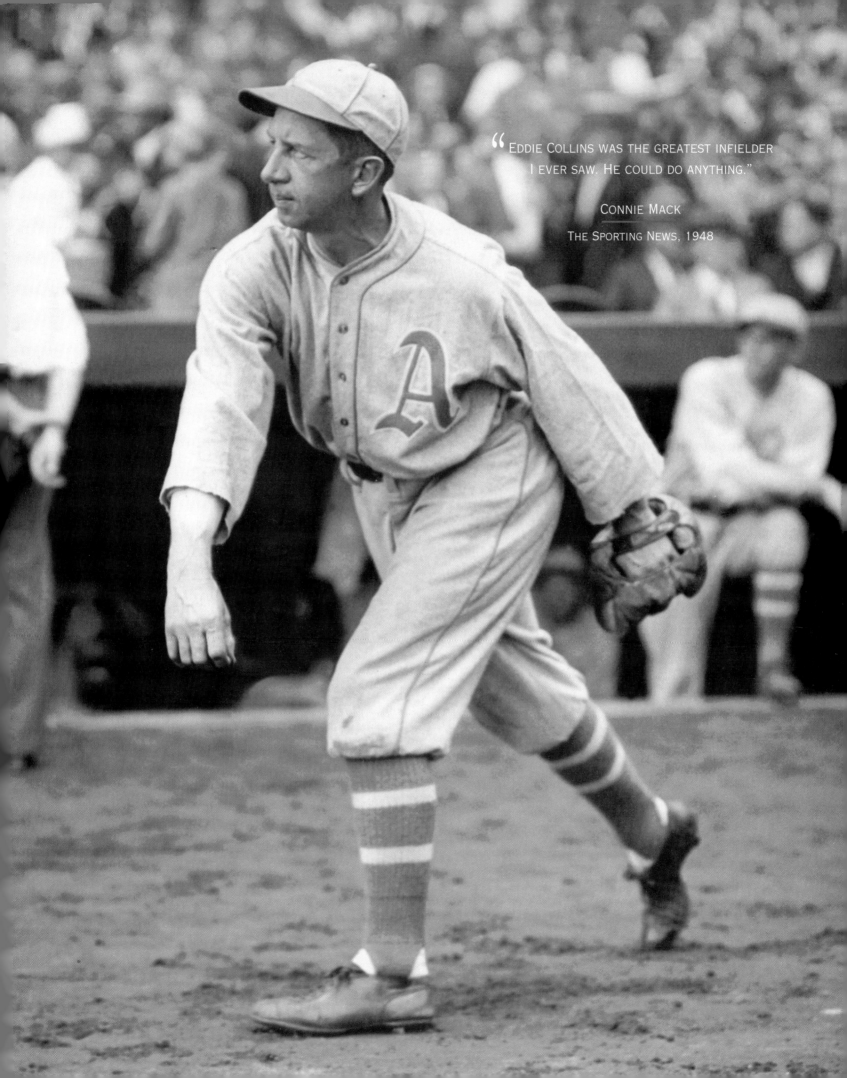

"EDDIE COLLINS WAS THE GREATEST INFIELDER
I EVER SAW. HE COULD DO ANYTHING."

CONNIE MACK
THE SPORTING NEWS, 1948

"Pete Rose is an original. He plays the game like nobody else, and his attitude, his enthusiasm, is contagious."

Ruly Carpenter, 1979
Longtime Owner of the Phillies

PETE ROSE 25

Arrogant. Cocky. Aggressive. Smart. Intense. Enthusiastic. There aren't enough words to describe the boundless energy Pete Rose brought to baseball for 24 seasons, first as the sparkplug that jump-started Cincinnati's Big Red Machine to World Series titles in 1975 and 1976 and then as the father figure for a 1980 Phillies team that gave Philadelphia its long-awaited first championship.

Rose joined the Reds in 1963 and his perpetual-motion style, whether running to first base after a walk or charging to and from the dugout between innings, quickly earned him the nickname Charlie Hustle. He obviously relished the love/hate relationship his take-no-prisoners attitude created with the fans. From a crouching, uncoiling stance he slashed line drives all over the field from both sides of the plate, he ran the bases instinctively with aggressive abandon and he prodded opponents into untimely mistakes while inspiring laid-back teammates.

The versatile Rose, who played five infield and outfield positions, seldom missed a game, a durability that allowed him to break one of baseball's most cherished records—Ty Cobb's hit total of 4,191. Rose, a .303 career batter,

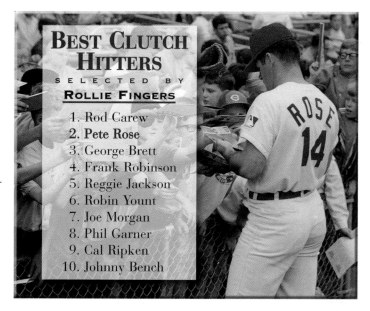

BEST CLUTCH HITTERS
SELECTED BY
ROLLIE FINGERS

1. Rod Carew
2. **Pete Rose**
3. George Brett
4. Frank Robinson
5. Reggie Jackson
6. Robin Yount
7. Joe Morgan
8. Phil Garner
9. Cal Ripken
10. Johnny Bench

collected hit No. 3,000 in 1978 for Cincinnati, became the game's second 4,000-hit man in 1984, his only season with Montreal, and stroked No. 4,192, the record-breaker, in 1985 while serving as player/manager of the Reds, his hometown team. Rose's record of 3,562 games may never be approached.

But the immortality those records should have ensured was cheated by the human side of Rose, who, after months of legal maneuvering, was handed a lifetime ban in 1989 by then-commissioner A. Bartlett Giamatti for betting on baseball games. The ban, which was followed by a five-month prison sentence for income tax evasion, has denied Rose the honor he probably relishes more than any other—inclusion in baseball's Hall of Fame.

Player	Rank	From	To		1890-99	1900-09	1910-19	1920-29	1930-39	1940-49

Player	Rank	From	To
Cy Young	(14)	1890	1911
Willie Keeler	(75)	1892	1910
Nap Lajoie	(29)	1896	1916
Honus Wagner	(13)	1897	1917
Sam Crawford	(84)	1899	1917
Christy Mathewson	(7)	1900	1916
Eddie Plank	(68)	1901	1917
Ed Walsh	(82)	1904	1917
Ty Cobb	(3)	1905	1928
Eddie Collins	(24)	1906	1930
Walter Johnson	(4)	1907	1927
Tris Speaker	(27)	1907	1928
Joe Jackson	(35)	1908	1920
Grover Alexander	(12)	1911	1930
Harry Heilmann	(54)	1914	1932
Babe Ruth	(1)	1914	1935
Rogers Hornsby	(9)	1915	1937
George Sisler	(33)	1915	1930
Frank Frisch	(88)	1919	1937
Pie Traynor	(70)	1920	1937
Goose Goslin	(89)	1921	1938
Lou Gehrig	(6)	1923	1939
Bill Terry	(59)	1923	1936
Charley Gehringer	(46)	1924	1942
Al Simmons	(43)	1924	1944
Mickey Cochrane	(65)	1925	1937
Jimmie Foxx	(15)	1925	1945
Lefty Grove	(23)	1925	1941
Mel Ott	(42)	1926	1947
Paul Waner	(62)	1926	1945
Bill Dickey	(57)	1928	1946
Carl Hubbell	(45)	1928	1943
Chuck Klein	(92)	1928	1944
Dizzy Dean	(85)	1930	1947
Lefty Gomez	(73)	1930	1943
Hank Greenberg	(37)	1930	1947
Joe Medwick	(79)	1932	1948
Joe DiMaggio	(11)	1936	1951
Bob Feller	(36)	1936	1956
Ted Williams	(8)	1939	1960
Early Wynn	(100)	1939	1963
Stan Musial	(10)	1941	1963
Warren Spahn	(21)	1942	1965
Yogi Berra	(40)	1946	1965
Ralph Kiner	(90)	1946	1955
Jackie Robinson	(44)	1947	1956
Duke Snider	(83)	1947	1964
Roy Campanella	(50)	1948	1957
Satchel Paige	(19)	1948	1965
Robin Roberts	(74)	1948	1966
Whitey Ford	(52)	1950	1967
Mickey Mantle	(17)	1951	1968
Willie Mays	(2)	1951	1973
Eddie Mathews	(63)	1952	1968
Ernie Banks	(38)	1953	1971
Al Kaline	(76)	1953	1974
Hank Aaron	(5)	1954	1976
Harmon Killebrew	(69)	1954	1975
Roberto Clemente	(20)	1955	1972
Sandy Koufax	(26)	1955	1966
Brooks Robinson	(80)	1955	1977
Frank Robinson	(22)	1956	1976
Bob Gibson	(31)	1959	1975
Willie McCovey	(56)	1959	1980
Juan Marichal	(71)	1960	1975
Lou Brock	(58)	1961	1979
Carl Yastrzemski	(72)	1961	1983
Gaylord Perry	(96)	1962	1983
Willie Stargell	(81)	1962	1982
Joe Morgan	(60)	1963	1984
Pete Rose	(25)	1963	1986
Steve Carlton	(30)	1965	1988
Jim Palmer	(64)	1965	1984
Nolan Ryan	(41)	1966	1993
Johnny Bench	(16)	1967	1983
Rod Carew	(61)	1967	1985
Reggie Jackson	(48)	1967	1987
Tom Seaver	(32)	1967	1986
Rollie Fingers	(97)	1968	1985
Mike Schmidt	(28)	1972	1989
George Brett	(55)	1973	1993
Dave Winfield	(94)	1973	1995
Dennis Eckersley	(98)	1975	1998
Eddie Murray	(77)	1977	1997
Paul Molitor	(99)	1978	1998
Ozzie Smith	(87)	1978	1996
Rickey Henderson	(51)	1979	1998
Cal Ripken	(78)	1981	1998
Wade Boggs	(95)	1982	1998
Tony Gwynn	(49)	1982	1998
Roger Clemens	(53)	1984	1998
Kirby Puckett	(86)	1984	1995
Barry Bonds	(34)	1986	1998
Greg Maddux	(39)	1986	1998
Mark McGwire	(91)	1986	1998
Ken Griffey Jr.	(93)	1989	1998

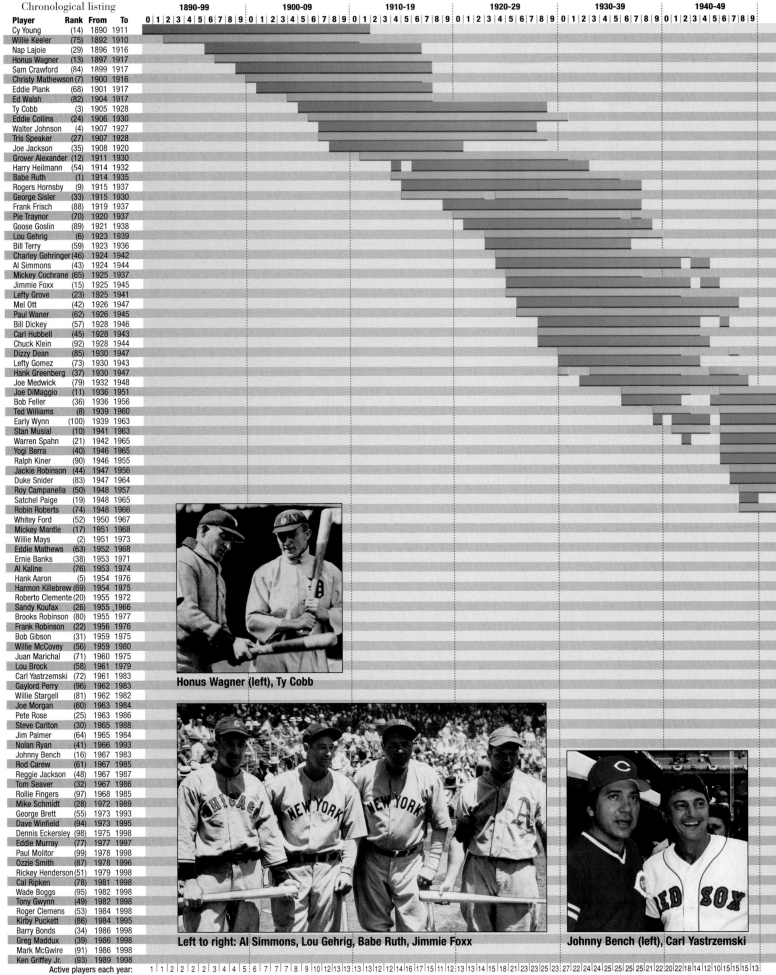

Honus Wagner (left), Ty Cobb

Left to right: Al Simmons, Lou Gehrig, Babe Ruth, Jimmie Foxx

Johnny Bench (left), Carl Yastrzemski

Active players each year: 1 1 2 2 2 3 4 5 6 7 7 8 9 10 13 13 13 13 12 12 14 16 17 15 11 12 13 14 15 18 21 23 23 25 23 27 24 24 24 25 25 25 21 22 20 18 14 12 10 15 15 13

TOP 100 TIMELINE

A chronological breakdown of the Top 100, accompanied by an alphabetical listing and a yearly total of active players. Negro League stars Josh Gibson, Buck Leonard, Cool Papa Bell and Oscar Charleston do not appear because they never played in the major leagues.

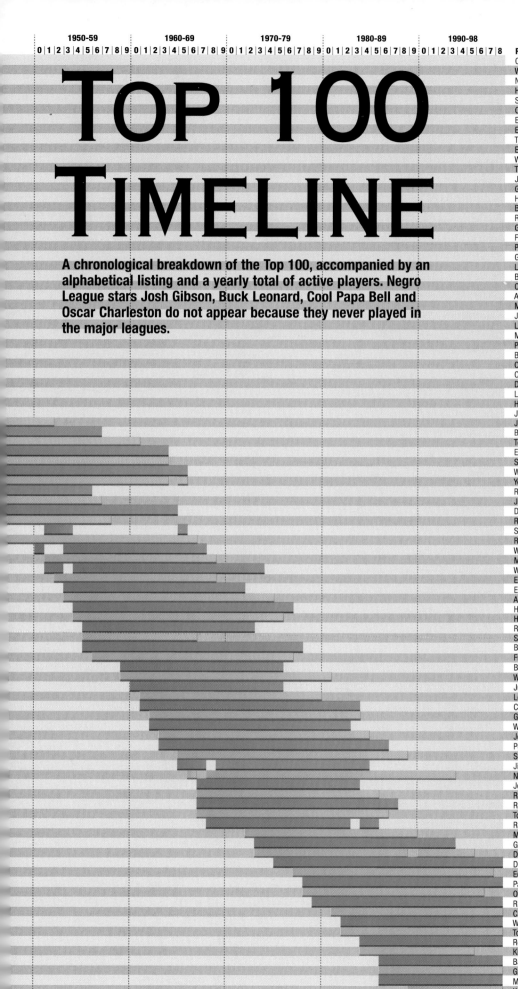

Chronological listing

Player	Rank	From	To
Cy Young	(14)	1890	1911
Willie Keeler	(75)	1892	1910
Nap Lajoie	(29)	1896	1916
Honus Wagner	(13)	1897	1917
Sam Crawford	(84)	1899	1917
Christy Mathewson	(7)	1900	1916
Eddie Plank	(68)	1901	1917
Ed Walsh	(82)	1904	1917
Ty Cobb	(3)	1905	1928
Eddie Collins	(24)	1906	1930
Walter Johnson	(4)	1907	1927
Tris Speaker	(27)	1907	1928
Joe Jackson	(35)	1908	1920
Grover Alexander	(12)	1911	1930
Harry Heilmann	(54)	1914	1932
Babe Ruth	(1)	1914	1935
Rogers Hornsby	(9)	1915	1937
George Sisler	(33)	1915	1930
Frank Frisch	(88)	1919	1937
Pie Traynor	(70)	1920	1937
Goose Goslin	(89)	1921	1938
Lou Gehrig	(6)	1923	1939
Bill Terry	(59)	1923	1936
Charley Gehringer	(46)	1924	1942
Al Simmons	(43)	1924	1944
Mickey Cochrane	(65)	1925	1937
Jimmie Foxx	(15)	1925	1945
Lefty Grove	(23)	1925	1941
Mel Ott	(42)	1926	1947
Paul Waner	(62)	1926	1945
Bill Dickey	(57)	1928	1946
Carl Hubbell	(45)	1928	1943
Chuck Klein	(92)	1928	1944
Dizzy Dean	(85)	1930	1947
Lefty Gomez	(73)	1930	1943
Hank Greenberg	(37)	1930	1947
Joe Medwick	(79)	1932	1948
Joe DiMaggio	(11)	1936	1951
Bob Feller	(36)	1936	1956
Ted Williams	(8)	1939	1960
Early Wynn	(100)	1939	1963
Stan Musial	(10)	1941	1963
Warren Spahn	(21)	1942	1965
Yogi Berra	(40)	1946	1965
Ralph Kiner	(90)	1946	1955
Jackie Robinson	(44)	1947	1956
Duke Snider	(83)	1947	1964
Roy Campanella	(50)	1948	1957
Satchel Paige	(19)	1948	1965
Robin Roberts	(74)	1948	1966
Whitey Ford	(52)	1950	1967
Mickey Mantle	(17)	1951	1968
Willie Mays	(2)	1951	1973
Eddie Mathews	(63)	1952	1968
Ernie Banks	(38)	1953	1971
Al Kaline	(76)	1953	1974
Hank Aaron	(5)	1954	1976
Harmon Killebrew	(69)	1954	1975
Roberto Clemente	(20)	1955	1972
Sandy Koufax	(26)	1955	1966
Brooks Robinson	(80)	1955	1977
Frank Robinson	(22)	1956	1976
Bob Gibson	(31)	1959	1975
Willie McCovey	(56)	1959	1980
Juan Marichal	(71)	1960	1975
Lou Brock	(58)	1961	1979
Carl Yastrzemski	(72)	1961	1983
Gaylord Perry	(96)	1962	1983
Willie Stargell	(81)	1962	1982
Joe Morgan	(60)	1963	1984
Pete Rose	(25)	1963	1986
Steve Carlton	(30)	1965	1988
Jim Palmer	(64)	1965	1984
Nolan Ryan	(41)	1966	1993
Johnny Bench	(16)	1967	1983
Rod Carew	(61)	1967	1985
Reggie Jackson	(48)	1967	1987
Tom Seaver	(32)	1967	1986
Rollie Fingers	(97)	1968	1985
Mike Schmidt	(28)	1972	1989
George Brett	(55)	1973	1993
Dave Winfield	(94)	1973	1995
Dennis Eckersley	(98)	1975	1998
Eddie Murray	(77)	1977	1997
Paul Molitor	(99)	1978	1998
Ozzie Smith	(87)	1978	1996
Rickey Henderson	(51)	1979	1998
Cal Ripken	(78)	1981	1998
Wade Boggs	(95)	1982	1998
Tony Gwynn	(49)	1982	1998
Roger Clemens	(53)	1984	1998
Kirby Puckett	(86)	1984	1995
Barry Bonds	(34)	1986	1998
Greg Maddux	(39)	1986	1998
Mark McGwire	(91)	1986	1998
Ken Griffey Jr.	(93)	1989	1998

Alphabetical listing

Player	Rank	From	To
Aaron, Hank	(5)	1954	1976
Alexander, Grover	(12)	1911	1930
Banks, Ernie	(38)	1953	1971
Bench, Johnny	(16)	1967	1983
Berra, Yogi	(40)	1946	1965
Boggs, Wade	(95)	1982	1998
Bonds, Barry	(34)	1986	1998
Brett, George	(55)	1973	1993
Brock, Lou	(58)	1961	1979
Campanella, Roy	(50)	1948	1957
Carew, Rod	(61)	1967	1985
Carlton, Steve	(30)	1965	1988
Clemens, Roger	(53)	1984	1998
Clemente, Roberto	(20)	1955	1972
Cobb, Ty	(3)	1905	1928
Cochrane, Mickey	(65)	1925	1937
Collins, Eddie	(24)	1906	1930
Crawford, Sam	(84)	1899	1917
Dean, Dizzy	(85)	1930	1947
Dickey, Bill	(57)	1928	1946
DiMaggio, Joe	(11)	1936	1951
Eckersley, Dennis	(98)	1975	1998
Feller, Bob	(36)	1936	1956
Fingers, Rollie	(97)	1968	1985
Ford, Whitey	(52)	1950	1967
Foxx, Jimmie	(15)	1925	1945
Frisch, Frank	(88)	1919	1937
Gehrig, Lou	(6)	1923	1939
Gehringer, Charley	(46)	1924	1942
Gibson, Bob	(31)	1959	1975
Gomez, Lefty	(73)	1930	1943
Goslin, Goose	(89)	1921	1938
Greenberg, Hank	(37)	1930	1947
Griffey Jr., Ken	(93)	1989	1998
Grove, Lefty	(23)	1925	1941
Gwynn, Tony	(49)	1982	1998
Heilmann, Harry	(54)	1914	1932
Henderson, Rickey	(51)	1979	1998
Hornsby, Rogers	(9)	1915	1937
Hubbell, Carl	(45)	1928	1943
Jackson, Joe	(35)	1908	1920
Jackson, Reggie	(48)	1967	1987
Johnson, Walter	(4)	1907	1927
Kaline, Al	(76)	1953	1974
Keeler, Willie	(75)	1892	1910
Killebrew, Harmon	(69)	1954	1975
Kiner, Ralph	(90)	1946	1955
Klein, Chuck	(92)	1928	1944
Koufax, Sandy	(26)	1955	1966
Lajoie, Nap	(29)	1896	1916
Maddux, Greg	(39)	1986	1998
Mantle, Mickey	(17)	1951	1968
Marichal, Juan	(71)	1960	1975
Mathews, Eddie	(63)	1952	1968
Mathewson, Christy	(7)	1900	1916
Mays, Willie	(2)	1951	1973
McCovey, Willie	(56)	1959	1980
McGwire, Mark	(91)	1986	1998
Medwick, Joe	(79)	1932	1948
Molitor, Paul	(99)	1978	1998
Morgan, Joe	(60)	1963	1984
Murray, Eddie	(77)	1977	1997
Musial, Stan	(10)	1941	1963
Ott, Mel	(42)	1926	1947
Paige, Satchel	(19)	1948	1965
Palmer, Jim	(64)	1965	1984
Perry, Gaylord	(96)	1962	1983
Plank, Eddie	(68)	1901	1917
Puckett, Kirby	(86)	1984	1995
Ripken, Cal	(78)	1981	1998
Roberts, Robin	(74)	1948	1966
Robinson, Brooks	(80)	1955	1977
Robinson, Frank	(22)	1956	1976
Robinson, Jackie	(44)	1947	1956
Rose, Pete	(25)	1963	1986
Ruth, Babe	(1)	1914	1935
Ryan, Nolan	(41)	1966	1993
Schmidt, Mike	(28)	1972	1989
Seaver, Tom	(32)	1967	1986
Simmons, Al	(43)	1924	1944
Sisler, George	(33)	1915	1930
Smith, Ozzie	(87)	1978	1996
Snider, Duke	(83)	1947	1964
Spahn, Warren	(21)	1942	1965
Speaker, Tris	(27)	1907	1928
Stargell, Willie	(81)	1962	1982
Terry, Bill	(59)	1923	1936
Traynor, Pie	(70)	1920	1937
Wagner, Honus	(13)	1897	1917
Walsh, Ed	(82)	1904	1917
Waner, Paul	(62)	1926	1945
Williams, Ted	(8)	1939	1960
Winfield, Dave	(94)	1973	1995
Wynn, Early	(100)	1939	1963
Yastrzemski, Carl	(72)	1961	1983
Young, Cy	(14)	1890	1911

13 15 15 17 19 22 22 20 19 21 22 23 25 27 24 27 25 26 26 25 25 26 25 26 25 22 21 21 22 23 22 22 24 22 22 20 21 19 18 17 17 17 17 15 15 13 12 11

" Koufax is the greatest.
He's the best pitcher I've ever seen."

Juan Marichal, 1966

SANDY KOUFAX

26

The ball shot out of his left hand and hurtled plateward in a white blur. The contorted grimace on Sandy Koufax's thin face was easier to see than the missile he had just launched. Such was the plight of overmatched National League hitters who had to face the Los Angeles Dodgers' ace during the most dominant six-year pitching exhibition of the second half-century.

Simply stated, the kid from Brooklyn was not your normal, everyday lefthander, from the day in 1955 when he joined his hometown Dodgers (skipping the minor leagues) until a day in 1966 when he told Dodgers management and fans he was retiring after 12 seasons because of an arthritic elbow he didn't want to damage beyond repair. The decision was shocking because Koufax, at age 30, had just completed a 27-9 season and a 129-47 six-year run that had vaulted him to the top of the pitching charts.

But that was vintage Koufax, an intelligent, straight-shooting pragmatist who didn't mince words off the field or pitches on it. His 6-2 frame held 210 pounds of muscle that delivered a blazing fastball and sharp curve to intimidated batters. Koufax, who was signed out of the University of Cincinnati, struggled with control and self-confidence through his six mediocre big-league seasons before transforming into one of the most proficient pitching machines ever constructed.

From 1961 to 1966, he was close to perfection. His .733 winning percentage was complemented by a record five consecutive N.L. ERA titles, one league MVP, three Cy Young Awards, four strikeout titles and key roles in three pennants and two World Series championships. Koufax also fired a then-career record four no-hitters, including a 1965 perfect game against the Chicago Cubs.

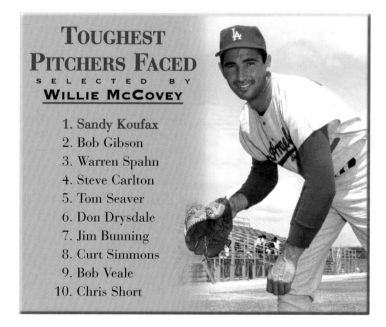

TOUGHEST PITCHERS FACED

SELECTED BY
WILLIE MCCOVEY

1. Sandy Koufax
2. Bob Gibson
3. Warren Spahn
4. Steve Carlton
5. Tom Seaver
6. Don Drysdale
7. Jim Bunning
8. Curt Simmons
9. Bob Veale
10. Chris Short

"(Speaker) used to drive the opposition crazy (by playing so shallow). He had an unbelievable instinct. He could sense a ball that was going deep if he was in short center. You'd drive the ball deep and he was waiting for it."

Chuck Dressen, 1956

Former Player and Manager

TRIS SPEAKER 27

He was easy to spot. The 6-foot, prematurely-gray, lefthanded-throwing center fielder positioned himself about 30 or 40 feet behind second base, always ready to dart forward and cut off another potential base hit or sprint back for anything hit over his head. Tris Speaker brazenly dared American League hitters to test his sure hands, speed and powerful arm for 22 glorious seasons, 20 of which were spent with the Boston Red Sox and Cleveland Indians from 1907-26.

The Gray Eagle also was easy to spot at the plate. From deep in the box with a closed stance, the crouching Speaker, bat held hip high and waggling nervously, would shoot line drives into both gaps and down both lines, a proficiency that helped him record a major league-record 792 doubles. Nine times he batted higher than .350, five times higher than .380 en route to a .345 career mark. But despite that lofty record and 3,514 career hits, Speaker's ledger shows only one A.L. batting title, thanks to an unfortunate career parallel with 12-time batting champion Ty Cobb.

Cobb, however, couldn't match Speaker's outfield cunning and nobody before or since has patrolled center field with such daring and aplomb. Believing that the singles he could cut off would far outnumber the triples that would sail over his head, Speaker played the shallowest center field in history, in effect serving as a fifth infielder. His signature play was darting toward second base behind an unsuspecting runner for a pickoff play and his proudest accomplishment might have been the A.L. record-tying 35 assists he recorded for Boston in 1909.

Speaker also was an accomplished baserunner who stole 432 bases and he played for three World Series champions—the Red Sox in 1912 and 1915 and the Indians in 1920.

TWO TIMING

Speaker holds the career record for doubles and shares the record for most times leading the league in that category. The numbers are through the 1997 season:

No.	Player	Led Lg.
792	Tris Speaker	8
746	Pete Rose	5
725	Stan Musial	8
724	Ty Cobb	3
665	George Brett	2
657	Nap Lajoie	5
646	Carl Yastrzemski	3
640	Honus Wagner	7
624	Hank Aaron	4
605	Paul Waner	2

"(SCHMIDT) GAVE US 110 PERCENT EVERY SINGLE NIGHT IN EVERY SINGLE AT-BAT. HE SET THE STANDARD FOR PROFESSIONALISM AROUND HERE."

BILL GILES
PHILLIES CHAIRMAN

THE SPORTING NEWS, 1990

MIKE SCHMIDT 28

Brooks Robinson and Pie Traynor had the golden gloves. Eddie Mathews and Harmon Killebrew had the game-breaking power. But no third baseman in the game's long history could match the near-perfect blend of defense, run production and speed that Mike Schmidt showcased during a Hall of Fame career in Philadelphia.

Over an 18-year run that opened in 1972, the even-tempered, always-cool Schmidt used those tools to help the Phillies carve out the most successful period in franchise history. He was the clubhouse leader and driving force for a team that won five National League East Division titles, two pennants and the 1980 World Series. In the process, he also carved out a personal legacy that put him in the select company of some of the game's greatest all-around players.

Every time he walked to the plate, there was an air of expectancy. From his righthanded upright stance with bat held high and feet spread well apart he was a home run waiting to happen—a big swing with plenty of bat speed and power to all fields. Thirteen times he hit 30 or more home runs in a season and a record eight times he led or shared N.L. home run honors en route to a career total of 548. From 1974 through 1987, which includes the strike-shortened 1981 campaign, he averaged 36.5 home runs and topped 100 RBIs nine times.

But the number "10" is what separates Schmidt from the other great power-hitting third basemen in baseball history. That's how many Gold Gloves he won, second only to Robinson's 16. He also captured a record-tying three N.L. Most Valuable Player awards.

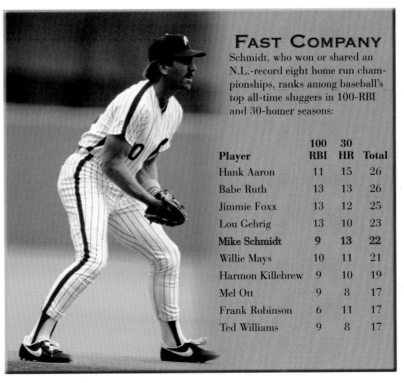

FAST COMPANY

Schmidt, who won or shared an N.L.-record eight home run championships, ranks among baseball's top all-time sluggers in 100-RBI and 30-homer seasons:

Player	100 RBI	30 HR	Total
Hank Aaron	11	15	26
Babe Ruth	13	13	26
Jimmie Foxx	13	12	25
Lou Gehrig	13	10	23
Mike Schmidt	9	13	22
Willie Mays	10	11	21
Harmon Killebrew	9	10	19
Mel Ott	9	8	17
Frank Robinson	6	11	17
Ted Williams	9	8	17

" Lajoie was one of the most rugged hitters I ever faced. He'd take your leg off with a line drive, turn the third baseman around like a swinging door and powder the hand of the left fielder."

Cy Young
The Sporting News, 1950

NAPOLEON LAJOIE  **29**

Stylish, graceful and handsome. Strong, intimidating and rugged. All of those seemingly contradictory descriptions applied to hard-hitting Napoleon Lajoie, a dark, bold-featured French-Canadian who made an indelible mark as the most important (and controversial) baseball star of the 20th century's first decade.

Lajoie's historic contribution was made in 1901, his sixth major league season, when he jumped from the Philadelphia Phillies of the established National League to Connie Mack's Philadelphia Athletics of the new American League, giving the rival circuit its first superstar and instant credibility. Lajoie punctuated his controversial move by winning the century's first Triple Crown and posting a remarkable .426 average—still the highest single-season mark in big-league history. When the Phillies obtained an injunction prohibiting Lajoie from playing for the other Philadelphia club in 1902, Mack dealt his star to the A.L.'s franchise in Cleve-land, where he spent the remainder of his 21-year career.

Cleveland fans formed a love affair with their big Frenchman, who reigned as the early dead-ball era's premier second baseman. The 6-1, 200-pounder with upturned collar and cap cocked stylishly to the side glided effortlessly on defense and third basemen lived in fear of the line drives he hit with amazing consistency. True to the dead-ball style he helped create, Lajoie stood deep in the box, hands choked and split on a thick-handled bat, and drove balls to all fields with a smooth, extended swing.

The result was a .338 career average and four A.L. batting titles. But Lajoie is best remembered for the disputed 1910 batting title he lost by a fraction to Detroit-rival Ty Cobb. A testimony to Lajoie's popularity was that the Indians were known as the "Naps" from 1905-09 when he was player/manager.

THE EXCLUSIVE .420 CLUB

Lajoie, in the American League's debut season, compiled an average that has withstood the challenge of 20th-century batters:

Year	Player	R	H	HR	RBI	Avg.
1901	Lajoie	145	232	14	125	.426
1924	Hornsby	121	227	25	94	.424
1911	Cobb	147	248	8	127	.420
1922	Sisler	134	246	8	105	.420

30 STEVE CARLTON

His overpowering fastball and sweeping curve were good enough to humble most major league hitters. But they were only complementary pitches in the Hall of Fame arsenal of Steve Carlton. When Lefty unleashed his primary weapon with all the force his 6-4, 210-pound frame could muster, the result was usually predictable and intimidating.

The Slider. Carlton went into his easy windup, right leg kicked forward and arm propelled the ball plateward from a three-quarters delivery. The batter, forced to think fastball, began his swing as the white blur moved ever closer. Suddenly, just before contact, the ball exploded—sideways and downward—as the batter realized his mistake, a split second too late.

The eccentric, intelligent Carlton, a martial arts practitioner whose outstanding conditioning and strength contributed to the force of his slider, was intensely focused and durable. He confounded hitters with his devastating pitches and pinpoint control over a 24-year career (1965 to 1988) that produced 329 victories, a record-tying four Cy Young Awards and 4,136 strikeouts—a total that ranks second all-time only to Nolan Ryan. Only once over a 17-season stretch (the strike-shortened 1981 campaign) did the 10-time All-Star selection work fewer than 229 innings.

Carlton, an intensely private man, resisted his celebrity status and waged a war of silence against the media over the final decade-plus of his career. The six-time 20-game winner preferred the satisfaction he gained on the mound for St. Louis Cardinals teams that won two National League pennants and one World Series and Philadelphia Phillies teams that won five East Division titles, two pennants and a World Series.

Carlton's signature season was 1972, his first in Philadelphia, when he finished 27-10 with a 1.97 ERA and 310 strikeouts for a weak Phillies team that won 59 times.

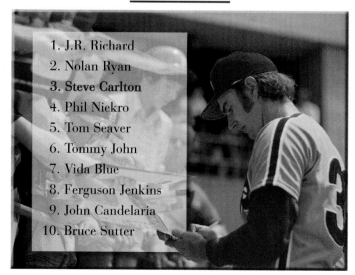

MOST-INTIMIDATING PITCHERS
SELECTED BY
OZZIE SMITH

1. J.R. Richard
2. Nolan Ryan
3. Steve Carlton
4. Phil Niekro
5. Tom Seaver
6. Tommy John
7. Vida Blue
8. Ferguson Jenkins
9. John Candelaria
10. Bruce Sutter

"CARLTON IS IN A CLASS BY HIMSELF AMONG LEFTHANDERS. IF YOU DON'T GET TO STEVE BY THE FIFTH INNING, YOU MIGHT AS WELL PUT YOUR BATS AWAY."

BILL MADLOCK
FOUR-TIME BATTING CHAMPION

THE SPORTING NEWS, 1982

31 BOB GIBSON

ob Gibson's fastball was filled with the same intense rage as the man who launched it past helpless hitters for the better part of two decades. So was the sharp-breaking slider that some observers called the best of all time for a righthander. When Gibson was at his dazzling best, he almost made pitching seem unfair.

Look at it from the batter's point of view. Gibson, cap pulled down low over a glowering face, sets his powerful jaw and stares at his newest worst enemy. Everything about him looks mean as he begins a three-quarters delivery that will propel the ball homeward. The full-body follow-through is the killer. It begins with right leg extended sideways and ends with a full running step forward and toward the first-base line. The man behind the scowl appears to be leaping toward you with hostile intent.

That intense, unfriendly style served Gibson well over the 17 seasons (1959 to 1975) he provided an anchor for the St. Louis Cardinals' rotation, posting a 251-174 career record. Teammates described a man with "pride, dedication and a must-win" demeanor on the mound; a man who would bury a fastball in the batter's rib when he wanted to make a point. But they described the off-field Gibson as eloquent, bright and fun-loving, although his barbs were delivered with a cutting edge.

Gibson always will be remembered for a 1968 performance that produced a 22-9 record, the lowest season ERA (1.12) for a pitcher with 300 or more innings and a National League MVP and Cy Young—the first of two he would win. He punctuated that effort with a dominating 17-strikeout performance against the Detroit Tigers in Game 1 of the World Series—his third fall classic and the only one his Cardinals would lose.

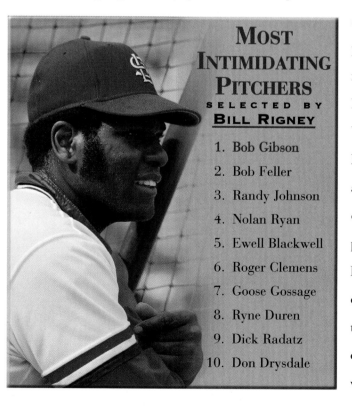

MOST INTIMIDATING PITCHERS
SELECTED BY BILL RIGNEY

1. Bob Gibson
2. Bob Feller
3. Randy Johnson
4. Nolan Ryan
5. Ewell Blackwell
6. Roger Clemens
7. Goose Gossage
8. Ryne Duren
9. Dick Radatz
10. Don Drysdale

"As long as I've been with him, I've never seen him smile on a day he's pitching. Whether he's winning or losing 1-0 or 12-0, he's all business."

RED SCHOENDIENST

THE SPORTING NEWS, 1972

32 TOM SEAVER

They billed him as the All-American boy and the image stayed with Tom Seaver throughout a successful 20-year career that took him to New York, Cincinnati, Chicago and Boston. Articulate, handsome and intelligent off the field, Tom Terrific transformed into an intense, take-no-prisoners pitching machine when he climbed onto the mound.

Seaver charmed the tough New York market from the moment he took to the hill as a 22-year-old Mets rookie in 1967 until he was sent to the Reds in a controversial 1977 trade. His principle weapons were the hopping fastball, sharp-breaking curve and wicked slider that he delivered with a powerful right arm and pinpoint control. But his secrets to success were the scientifically-crafted delivery that saved his arm from wear and tear and the detailed book he kept on the strengths and weaknesses of every major league hitter.

Seaver literally exploded off the mound, driving hard toward the hitter with powerful legs and a well-muscled 210-pound body. He looked like a locomotive bursting from a tunnel. The delivery was compact and so low that Seaver's right leg would drag the ground during his follow-through. He was overpowering, a strikeout pitcher who once fanned 19 batters in a game and topped 200 strikeouts in nine consecutive seasons. But he also was a craftsman who would set up hitters with different-speed fastballs and other well-placed off-speed pitches.

Seaver's signature performance in a career that produced 311 wins, five 20-victory seasons, three Cy Young Awards and 12 All-Star Game selections came in 1969, when he finished 25-7 and anchored a staff that pitched Gil Hodges' Amazin' Mets to a shocking National League pennant and World Series victory over powerful Baltimore.

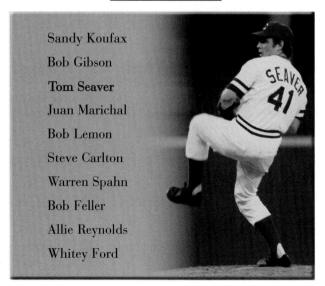

BEST BIG-GAME PITCHERS
SELECTED BY
WHITEY HERZOG

Sandy Koufax
Bob Gibson
Tom Seaver
Juan Marichal
Bob Lemon
Steve Carlton
Warren Spahn
Bob Feller
Allie Reynolds
Whitey Ford

"I'VE NEVER SEEN ANYONE SO
COMPLETELY PREPARED, PHYSICALLY
AND MENTALLY, SO AWARE OF HIMSELF
IN GAME SITUATIONS. IF NOT FOR HIS
HUMANNESS, I DON'T THINK ANYBODY
WOULD GET ANY HITS OFF HIM."

CARLTON FISK, 1985

" HE WAS A PROFESSIONAL WITH THE BAT IN HIS
HANDS. HE NEVER STOPPED THINKING. HE WAS A
MENACE EVERY TIME HE STEPPED TO THE PLATE.
IN THE FIELD, HE WAS THE PICTURE PLAYER, THE
ACME OF GRACE AND FLUENCY."

BRANCH RICKEY

THE SPORTING NEWS, 1953

GEORGE SISLER 33

He was the quiet man in an era that showcased Ty Cobb and Babe Ruth and a city that heaped its praise on St. Louis-rival Rogers Hornsby. But the backseat George Sisler took to those colorful personalities was not reflected in his remarkable 15-year major league record, most of which he fashioned while toiling for the lowly St. Louis Browns.

The 170-pound Sisler, who was Hall of Fame contemporary Frank Frisch's "perfect player," brought manners and gentility to a baseball era that was lacking in both. Modest and self-effacing, the University of Michigan grad played with a quiet self-confidence that was not lost on opponents and fans. He emerged on the big-league scene in 1915 as a lefthanded pitcher and quickly made the transition to first base, a position he graced with superior speed and quickness.

But Sisler's real magic could be found in the 42-ounce hickory bat he used like a wand to direct hits all over the park. In a remarkable three-year hitting exhibition from 1920-22, the choke-hitting lefty batted .407, .371 and .420 while collecting 719 hits and striking out only 60 times. The 257 hits Sisler recorded in 1920 still stand as a major-league record and the 41-game hitting streak he compiled in 1922 stood as a record until 1941, when Joe DiMaggio hit in 56 straight.

Sisler was forced to sit out the 1923 season with sinusitis, a disease that caused double vision, and he never hit with the same ferocious consistency. And he never even got a taste of postseason play, missing his only chance in 1922 when the Browns finished one game behind the New York Yankees.

THE HIT MAN COMETH

From 1920-22, Sisler posted hit totals of 257, 216 and 246. No player has come close to matching that three-season barrage.

Total	Player	Years
719	George Sisler	1920-22
703	Rogers Hornsby	1920-22
693	Bill Terry	1929-31
684	Joe Medwick	1935-37
678	Lloyd Waner	1927-29
676	Chuck Klein	1930-32
668	Ty Cobb	1910-12
664	Kirby Puckett	1986-88
660	Paul Waner	1927-29
659	Sam Rice	1924-26

"HE'S THE BEST PLAYER IN THE GAME,
AND IT'S NOT EVEN CLOSE."

DARREN DAULTON, 1994

FORMER PHILLIES CATCHER

BARRY BONDS 34

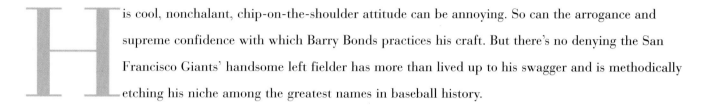

His cool, nonchalant, chip-on-the-shoulder attitude can be annoying. So can the arrogance and supreme confidence with which Barry Bonds practices his craft. But there's no denying the San Francisco Giants' handsome left fielder has more than lived up to his swagger and is methodically etching his niche among the greatest names in baseball history.

Start with the 400-400 club Bonds founded in 1998 when he became the game's first 400-home run, 400-steal superstar. Until that milestone homer, Barry and father Bobby had formed half of the membership in the elite 300-300 club that also included Willie Mays and Andre Dawson. Bonds also was a three-time National League MVP by age 29, a five-time Gold Glove winner by age 30 and a Hall of Fame-bound hitting machine by 1998, his 13th big-league season.

It's all in the genes for Bonds, who, like his father more than two decades ago, brings a superior combination of power, grace, agility and speed to every game. His lefthanded swing is fluid, with the ability to drive any pitch out of any section of the park. He is one of the most feared run-producers in the game, a three-time 40-homer man who has led the league in walks four times. Bonds also can take the extra base or ignite a rally by stealing, an aggressiveness he was asked to display often when he batted leadoff during his first seven seasons with Pittsburgh.

The only thing missing for the five-time 30-30 man is the immense popularity enjoyed by contemporary stars such as Cal Ripken and Tony Gwynn. It's a self-inflicted slight that could be erased as the career milestones continue to fall.

FAMILY MATTERS
The Bonds, Bobby and Barry, top the charts in most father/son offensive combinations:

HOME RUNS

Family	Tot.	Breakdown
*Bonds	706	(Bobby 332, Barry 374)
*Griffey	446	(Ken Sr. 152, Ken Jr. 294)
Bell	407	(Gus 206, Buddy 201)
Berra	407	(Yogi 358, Dale 49)
Averill	282	(Earl Sr. 238, Earl Jr. 44)

STOLEN BASES

Family	Tot.	Breakdown
*Bonds	878	(Bobby 461, Barry 417)
Wills	782	(Maury 586, Bump 196)
Sisler	381	(George 375, Dick 6)
*Griffey	323	(Ken Sr. 200, Ken Jr. 123)
Sullivan	128	(Billy Sr. 98, Billy Jr. 30)

Through the 1997 season

35 JOE JACKSON

His name will forever be associated with the messiest episode of baseball history. His lifetime ban and exclusion from Hall of Fame consideration are viewed by many as a travesty of justice. But there's one thing nobody can take away from Shoeless Joe Jackson: his reputation as the greatest natural hitter in the game's long history.

Ty Cobb thought he was. An impressed Babe Ruth copied his batting style. Other contemporaries, such as Tris Speaker, Nap Lajoie and Eddie Collins, marveled at the slashing line drives that whipped off his over-sized bat during the 13 years (1908-20) he starred for the Philadelphia Athletics, Cleveland Indians and Chicago White Sox.

The lefthanded-hitting, righthanded-throwing left fielder never met a pitcher he couldn't hit. Jackson stood well back in the box, feet close together, and unleashed his big, even swing—unlike the short, punching jabs of other top dead-ball hitters. The only thing missing from the 6-1, 200-pounder's offensive arsenal was the great speed that gave Cobb the additional hits he needed to win 12 batting championships. Jackson still batted .408 for the

Indians in 1911—losing the batting title to Cobb's .420—and .395 the following year en route to a whopping .356 career mark—third all-time behind Cobb and Rogers Hornsby.

Jackson's exact role in the 1919 Black Sox scandal will never be known. But there's no doubt the illiterate country kid from the Carolina hill country, perhaps caught up unwittingly in something he did not fully understand, enjoyed an outstanding World Series against Cincinnati (.375, a record 12 hits, no errors) while teammates were helping the Reds to victory.

One of eight White Sox players banned for life by then-commissioner Kenesaw Mountain Landis, Jackson never played another big-league game—a punishment, right or wrong, that continued long after his 1951 death.

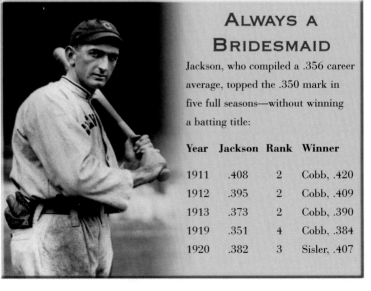

ALWAYS A BRIDESMAID

Jackson, who compiled a .356 career average, topped the .350 mark in five full seasons—without winning a batting title:

Year	Jackson	Rank	Winner
1911	.408	2	Cobb, .420
1912	.395	2	Cobb, .409
1913	.373	2	Cobb, .390
1919	.351	4	Cobb, .384
1920	.382	3	Sisler, .407

" I COPIED JACKSON'S BATTING STYLE
BECAUSE I THOUGHT HE WAS THE GREATEST HITTER
I HAD EVER SEEN. I STILL THINK THE SAME WAY."

BABE RUTH, 1942

36 BOB FELLER

He whirled into major league prominence in 1936 as a naive 17-year-old farmboy and retired two decades later as one of the most sophisticated strikeout machines in baseball history. Through most of his 18 seasons with the Cleveland Indians, Bob Feller must have seemed like a white blur to hitters trying to catch up with his 98-plus mph fastballs.

Feller, a 6-foot, high-kicking righthander who never played a minor league game, stepped off his Van Meter, Iowa, farm and struck out 15 St. Louis Browns in his first big-league start. Three weeks later, he tied Dizzy Dean's major league record with 17 strikeouts in a two-hit win over the Philadelphia Athletics. When his short rookie season ended, Feller returned home and finished high school.

Feller's pitching ledger is filled with strikeouts (2,581), no-hitters (3), one-hitters (12) and 20-win seasons (6). But those numbers and his 266-162 career record could have been a lot higher if not for the three-plus seasons he spent winning battle stars for the Navy during World War II. Baseball's

All-American boy, who could have avoided military duty because his father was dying of cancer, chose instead to serve his country at age 24—after three consecutive 20-win seasons.

That was typical Feller, who once insisted on taking a pay cut after what he considered a bad season. He was proud, outspoken, opinionated and self-promoting—but the strutting arrogance he displayed on the mound did not draw criticism from the hitters he dominated. The biggest void in Feller's career was his inability to record a post-season victory. The five-time All-Star was 0-2 in Cleveland's 1948 World Series win and, surprisingly, he did not pitch as the Indians were swept in the 1954 fall classic by the New York Giants.

TOUGHEST RIGHTHANDED PITCHERS
SELECTED BY
STAN MUSIAL
Bob Feller
Ewell Blackwell
Tom Seaver
Nolan Ryan
Bob Gibson
Don Drysdale
Robin Roberts
Bob Rush
Don Cardwell
Don Newcombe

"(WALTER) JOHNSON WAS TOPS.
FELLER ISN'T TOO FAR AWAY."

CY YOUNG, 1951

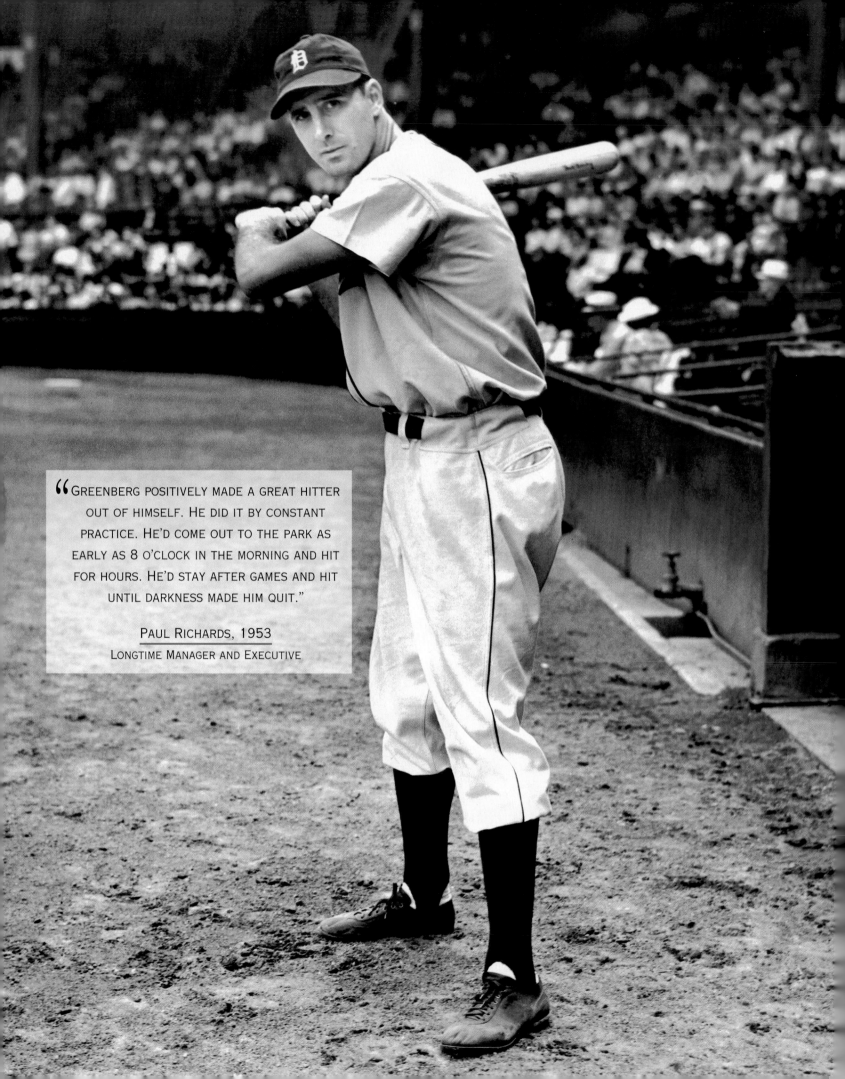

"GREENBERG POSITIVELY MADE A GREAT HITTER OUT OF HIMSELF. HE DID IT BY CONSTANT PRACTICE. HE'D COME OUT TO THE PARK AS EARLY AS 8 O'CLOCK IN THE MORNING AND HIT FOR HOURS. HE'D STAY AFTER GAMES AND HIT UNTIL DARKNESS MADE HIM QUIT."

PAUL RICHARDS, 1953
LONGTIME MANAGER AND EXECUTIVE

HANK GREENBERG 37

He was a self-made superstar, the big, clumsy New York City kid who transformed his ugly-duckling awkwardness into Hall-of-Fame grace. What Hank Greenberg lacked in natural talent he more than made up for with unyielding desire, gritty determination, hard work and intense dedication to his craft.

Nothing came easy for the 6-4 Greenberg, who made his major-league debut for the Detroit Tigers in 1930 as a stumbling first baseman. He wasn't fast, a shortcoming he never could overcome. But he worked hard to improve his quickness, spent hours mastering defensive fundamentals and learned to hit the curveball in early morning sessions with weary batting practice pitchers.

American League pitchers felt the crunch of Hank's mind-over-matter determination. His 215-pound body cut a menacing figure and his big arms and roundhouse swing pounded the ball with Ruthian-like frequency, power and run production. Six times he topped 30 home runs, including a 58-homer 1938 season that left him only two short of Babe Ruth's single-season record. Seven times he topped 100 RBIs, including seasons of 183 (1937), 170 (1935) and 150 (1940). Two times he earned MVP citations and his .313 career average defied the conventional profile of a power hitter. The outspoken, articulate Greenberg, who later put those qualities to use as a front-office executive, finished his career with 331 home runs—a figure that would have been considerably higher if he had not lost $4\frac{1}{2}$ seasons to World War II and another to a broken wrist, giving him a real career of about 11 years. His defining moment came in 1945, when he hit a dramatic final-day grand slam to clinch the A.L. pennant for the Tigers and complete his first half season back from military duty. He added two more homers in a World Series victory over Chicago.

RUN PRODUCING

If you combine the best five one-season RBI totals of baseball's top sluggers, only three players rank ahead of Greenberg. Numbers are through the 1997 season:

Tot.	Name/Seasons
857	Lou Gehrig (184, 175, 174, 165, 159)
806	Jimmie Foxx (175, 169, 163, 156, 143)
805	Babe Ruth (171, 164, 163, 154, 153)
788	Hank Greenberg (183, 170, 150, 146, 139)
730	Al Simmons (165, 157, 151, 129, 128)
721	Hack Wilson (190, 159, 129, 123, 120)
721	Joe DiMaggio (167, 155, 140, 133, 126)
695	Rogers Hornsby (152, 149, 143, 126, 125)
694	Ted Williams (159, 145, 137, 127, 126)
693	Chuck Klein (170, 145, 137, 121, 120)

" Do you know of a better way to earn a living than playing baseball? Baseball isn't work to me, it's a game. Everything in baseball is fun for me."

Ernie Banks, 1961

ERNIE BANKS 38

His smile lit up Wrigley Field and his quick bat lit up National League scoreboards. Everything about Ernie Banks was contagious, from the boundless enthusiasm he brought to long-suffering Chicago fans to the grace and flair with which he roamed his shortstop and first base positions for 19 major league seasons. Never has an athletic love affair been consummated with more devotion than the one between Mr. Cub and Chicago's North Side devotees.

The painfully shy Banks, who was plucked off the Kansas City Monarchs Negro All-Star roster in 1953, injected much-needed hope into a depressed franchise. His movement was quick and agile, his reflexes were magnificent, his eyesight was an exceptional 20/13 and his skinny 6-1, 180-pound frame packed a wallop that would inspire a new legion of "little man" power hitters. The secret was in his wrists and forearms, leading Hall of Fame pitcher Robin Roberts to marvel: "From the elbows down, he's got the muscles of a 230-pounder."

Banks also used a 31-ounce bat, proving that bat speed, not size, unlocked the secret to power-hitting success. He stood deep in the box, left foot crowding the plate, and stared blankly at the pitcher, fingers drumming rhythmically on the bat handle. Banks didn't swing at the ball; he lashed at it—with a deadly force that yielded spectacular results. Five times he topped 40 home runs en route to a career total of 512. He topped 100 RBIs eight times, played in 13 All-Star Games and captured consecutive MVPs (1958 and '59) while playing on weak teams.

But nothing captures the essence of Banks better than the "let's play two" enthusiasm he always brought to the park, win or lose—even though the Cubs never gave him the postseason opportunity that might have added a luster to his outstanding career.

STAYING HOME

Banks is one of nine players to hit more than 500 home runs with one team:

Player/Team	HRs
Hank Aaron, Braves	733
Babe Ruth, Yankees	659
Willie Mays, Giants	646
Harmon Killebrew, Twins	559
Mike Schmidt, Phillies	548
Mickey Mantle, Yankees	536
Ted Williams, Red Sox	521
Ernie Banks, Cubs	**512**
Mel Ott, Giants	511

"GREG MADDUX IS TRULY AN ARTIST. WHEN I WATCH GREG MADDUX, HE IS ALL I WISH I COULD HAVE BEEN."

DON SUTTON, 1996

GREG MADDUX 39

He's equal parts scientist, artist and magician, a professorial-looking righthander with the ability to dissect a lineup, paint a corner or make a good hitter disappear. Greg Maddux is a throwback. He's an efficiency expert, an old-style craftsman, who kills opponents softly with his masterful control, deceptive cunning and rally-stopping defense.

Every Maddux performance is a clinic. Cut fastball outside corner. Slider inside. Curveball, cut fastball, changeup—everything in its place, hitters always off balance. Maddux has the uncanny ability to throw any pitch anywhere he wants on any count. Hitters, seldom in sync with the pitch, usually reach or get handcuffed, resulting in a harmless grounder or fly ball.

Location and pitch movement—those are the magic words that give him status as ace of a dominating Atlanta Braves staff and as the best pitcher in the National League. A typical Maddux outing can end in less than two hours with him throwing fewer than 100 pitches. He seldom walks a hitter and sometimes plays with them like a cat with a

mouse. When in trouble, he helps himself with a defensive genius that has earned him eight straight Gold Gloves.

Maddux, pitching the last of seven years with the Chicago Cubs, began a string of sensational seasons in 1992 when he finished 20-11 and won the N.L. Cy Young. His 20-10 1993 season for Atlanta was followed by 16-6 (1.56 ERA) and 19-2 (1.63) records in the strike-interrupted 1994 and 1995 campaigns—and three more Cy Youngs, giving him an unprecedented four in a row. His inevitable march toward the 200-win barrier in 1998 coincided with the Braves' march toward their seventh division title of the decade and their hopes to win a second World Series championship.

BEST BIG-GAME PITCHERS
SELECTED BY
ROGER CRAIG

1. Bob Gibson
2. Don Drysdale
3. Sandy Koufax
4. Greg Maddux
5. Tom Seaver
6. Warren Spahn
7. Juan Marichal
8. Whitey Ford
9. Ferguson Jenkins
10. Early Wynn

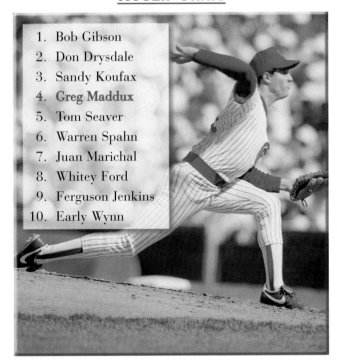

40 YOGI BERRA

The squat, gnome-like body, topped by a face locked in permanent caricature, inspired jokes and friendly barbs. But there was nothing funny about the surprising agility, fast feet and slashing bat that carried Yogi Berra to Hall of Fame heights as the backstop for one of the greatest dynasties in sports history. The lovable, fun-loving, gregarious personality defines Berra the man, but the 14 World Series in which he showcased his talents for the New York Yankees define his baseball legacy.

It was easy to dismiss the 5-8, 190-pound, barrel-chested Berra when he slipped into his baggy No. 8 Yankee uniform for the first time in 1946. But teammates and fans quickly learned to appreciate the boyish enthusiasm with which the knock-kneed youngster moved around behind the plate and the desire with which he enhanced his catching skills under the tutelage of fading star Bill Dickey. His quickness was deceptive, his arm was strong if occasionally erratic.

But the bat is what separated Yogi from other big-league catchers. A lefthanded hitter, he stood at the plate with a nervous air of expectancy and used his quick wrists to slash pitches, with power, to all fields. Berra, a notorious bad-ball hitter who seldom struck out, was tough to pitch to and especially dangerous when the game was on the line. Three A.L. MVP awards (in 1951, 1954 and 1955) are testimony to the respect he earned over a 19-year career that ended in 1965.

Berra, known for the charming malaprops he delivered with gravelly-voiced innocence, played for 10 World Series champions and holds fall classic records for games (75), at-bats (259) and hits (71) and ranks second in RBIs (39) and third in home runs (12). He also played in 15 All-Star Games.

BEST CLUTCH HITTERS
SELECTED BY
RALPH HOUK

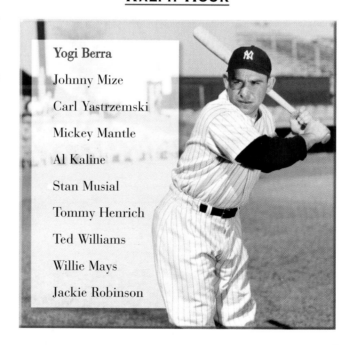

Yogi Berra
Johnny Mize
Carl Yastrzemski
Mickey Mantle
Al Kaline
Stan Musial
Tommy Henrich
Ted Williams
Willie Mays
Jackie Robinson

"MR. BERRA WAS SECOND ONLY TO JOE
DiMAGGIO IN ALL-AROUND ABILITY AMONG
THE PLAYERS I MANAGED."

CASEY STENGEL

THE SPORTING NEWS, 1971

"AT HIS AGE, THERE IS NO WAY A
MAN SHOULD BE ABLE TO THROW
THAT FINE AND THAT HARD."

WALT WEISS

MAJOR LEAGUE SHORTSTOP

THE SPORTING NEWS, 1990

NOLAN RYAN 41

The Nolan Ryan fastball made its first appearance on the radar guns in 1966 and was still being tracked in 1993, an amazing 27 years later. There was nothing subtle about it. At Ryan's peak, it shot to the plate at more than 100 mph. In Ryan's final season, it reached only 95—the man's one concession to age. The pitching legacy it helped produce might withstand the test of time.

Start with the strikeouts—5,714 of them, 1,578 more than second-place Steve Carlton produced. Then the no-hitters—seven, three more than second-place Sandy Koufax threw. Then the innings (5,386), the victories (324), the shutouts (61), the one-hitters (12) and the countless longevity records Ryan piled up over a career that started with the New York Mets and included long stints with the California Angels, Houston Astros and Texas Rangers.

Simply stated, Ryan was the master of the attention-getting performance—a no-hitter or a strikeout record waiting to happen. But unlike the great Walter Johnson, the 6-2, 210-pound Ryan was not a one-pitch wonder. Wild and erratic in the early years, Ryan's steady improvement

HARDEST THROWING PITCHERS
SELECTED BY
HARMON KILLEBREW

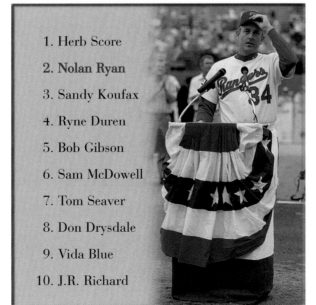

1. Herb Score
2. Nolan Ryan
3. Sandy Koufax
4. Ryne Duren
5. Bob Gibson
6. Sam McDowell
7. Tom Seaver
8. Don Drysdale
9. Vida Blue
10. J.R. Richard

drew a direct parallel to his mastery of a nasty curveball that mesmerized fastball-thinking hitters and a changeup that almost seemed unfair. Blessed with a bionic arm and an insatiable work ethic that stressed conditioning, Ryan simply got better with age.

Once criticized as a .500 pitcher with a million-dollar arm, Ryan's greatest popularity came in the 1990s, when he continued to dominate American League batters, recorded his 300th victory and added no-hitters Nos. 6 and 7— at the ages of 43 and 44. Ryan spent most of his years with weak teams as his 292 losses might suggest, but he did pitch for the 1969 Amazin' Mets in their World Series victory over Baltimore.

42 MEL OTT

He was a living, breathing oxymoron, a diminutive 5-9, 170-pound boy wonder who dared to challenge Babe Ruth for home run-hitting superiority in New York City. When Mel Ott lifted his famous right leg and lashed into another pitch, Giants fans stationed in the Polo Grounds' short right-field bleachers braced—a ritual they enjoyed for 22 glorious seasons.

A 16-year-old Ott and his impressive lefthanded swing showed up on the Giants' doorstep in 1925 and spent a season learning the game at the side of manager John McGraw. At age 17 he played his first big-league game, at 19 he belted 18 home runs and at 20 he vaulted into prominence with a 42-homer, 151-RBI season—the first of eight 30-homer efforts that would define Ott's career.

raised his right leg, about knee high, as the pitcher began his delivery. In one instantaneous motion, the bat pulled back, the foot planted and he swung. A high-kicking pitcher working to the high-kicking Ott looked like a scene right out of *Swan Lake*.

Ott, a dead-pull hitter, was tailor-made for the longball-friendly Polo Grounds (257 feet down the right field line), where he drilled 323 of his 511 career home runs. By the time he became the National League's first 500-homer man in 1945, he also was serving as player/manager, a role he filled for six seasons. Ott played on three New York pennant winners but only one World Series champion (1933).

TEAMWORK

Ott led the New York Giants in home runs for 18 straight seasons. No other player or pitcher can match that consecutive-season team domination in batting average, hits, home runs, RBIs or wins:

Yrs.	Player/Team/Years	Category
18	Mel Ott, Giants, 1928-45	Homers
15	Warren Spahn, Braves, 1949-63	Wins
12	Stan Musial, Cardinals, 1946-57	Hits
11	Hank Aaron, Braves, 1962-72	Homers
11	Walter Johnson, Senators, 1909-19	Wins
11	Pete Rose, Reds, 1968-78	Hits
10	Jack Morris, Tigers, 1979-88	Wins
10	Stan Musial, Cardinals, 1948-57	Homers
10	Kirby Puckett, Twins, 1985-94	Hits
10	Honus Wagner, Pirates, 1903-12	Average

Ottie, always smiling and personable, won over fans with defensive hustle that made him a better-than-average right fielder and his distinctive batting style. One former writer said that Ott, a .304 career hitter, squared away to the pitcher as if he was going to beat a rug. He crowded the plate with feet apart and

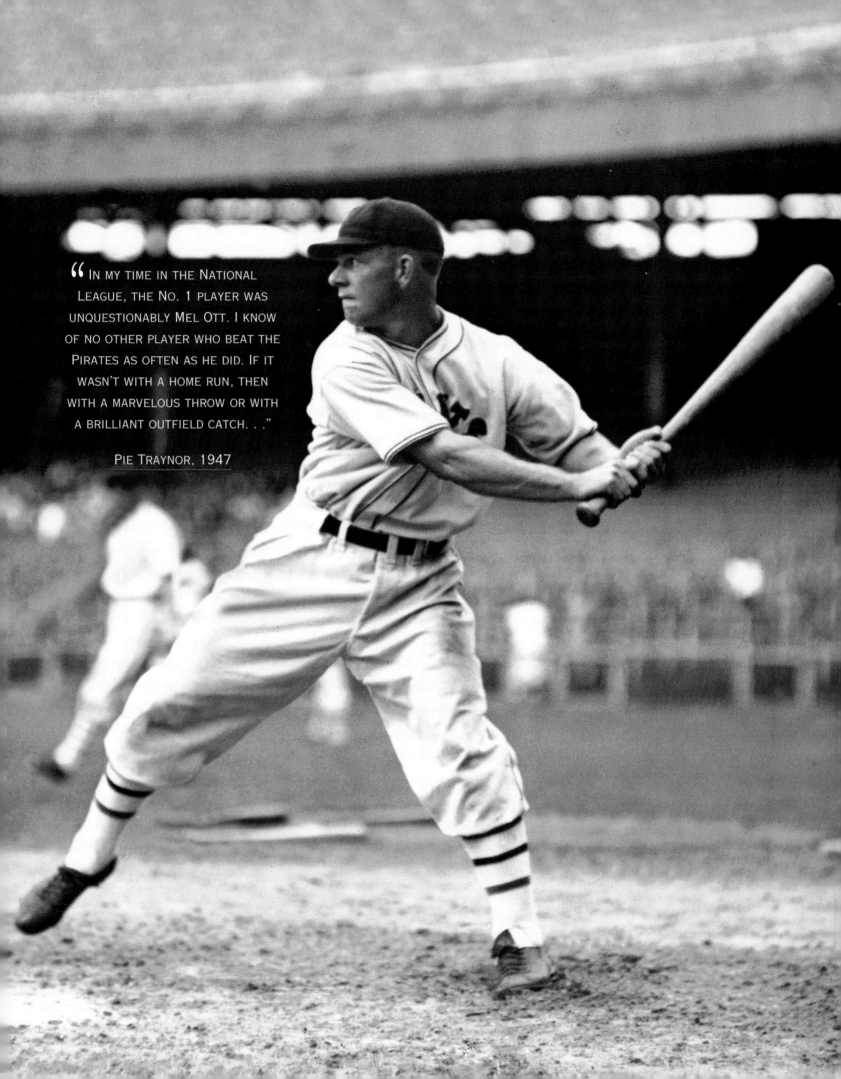

"IN MY TIME IN THE NATIONAL LEAGUE, THE NO. 1 PLAYER WAS UNQUESTIONABLY MEL OTT. I KNOW OF NO OTHER PLAYER WHO BEAT THE PIRATES AS OFTEN AS HE DID. IF IT WASN'T WITH A HOME RUN, THEN WITH A MARVELOUS THROW OR WITH A BRILLIANT OUTFIELD CATCH. . ."

PIE TRAYNOR, 1947

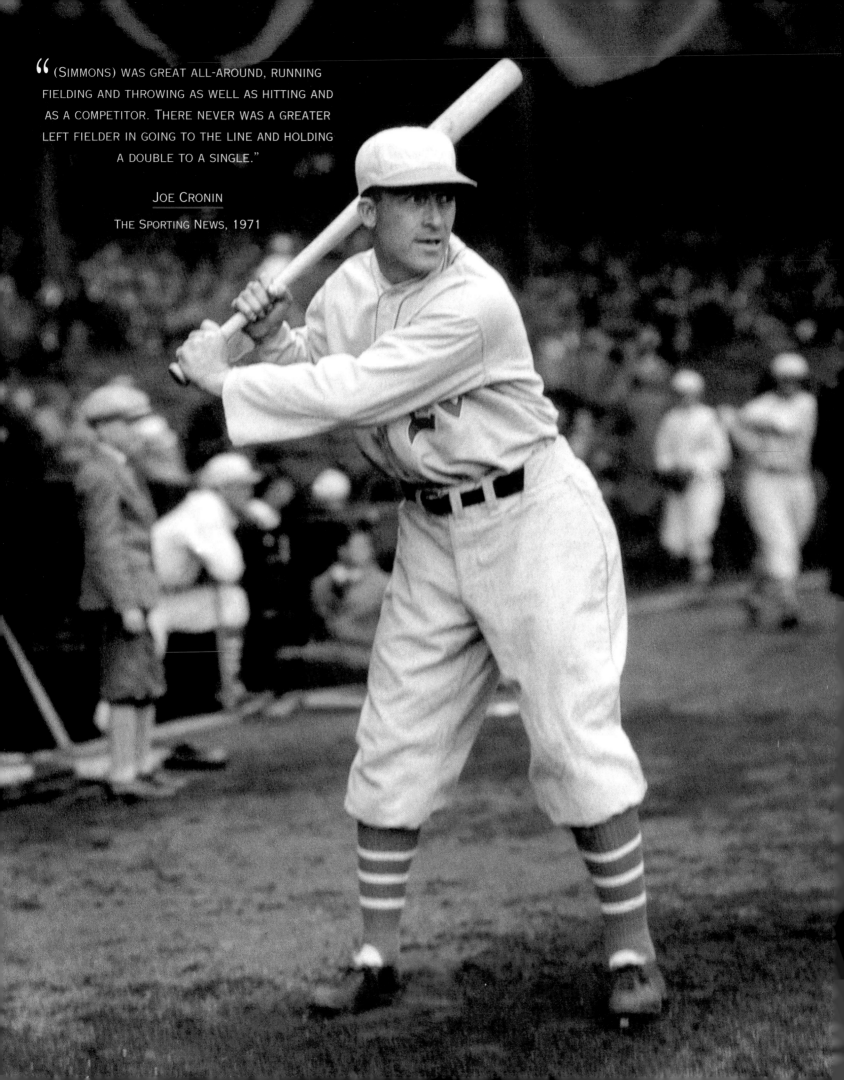

"(SIMMONS) WAS GREAT ALL-AROUND, RUNNING FIELDING AND THROWING AS WELL AS HITTING AND AS A COMPETITOR. THERE NEVER WAS A GREATER LEFT FIELDER IN GOING TO THE LINE AND HOLDING A DOUBLE TO A SINGLE."

JOE CRONIN

THE SPORTING NEWS, 1971

AL SIMMONS 43

A haughty swagger and defiance complemented his driving-force status for one of the greatest teams ever assembled. The vicious line drives Al Simmons slashed out for 20 big-league seasons emulated the ones stroked by his boyhood hero, Ty Cobb. Some Simmons watchers called him the second-best righthanded hitter behind Rogers Hornsby; others classified him as the second-best all-around player of his era behind Cobb himself.

Simmons' .334 career average, which included 2,927 hits and 307 home runs, says a lot. But it doesn't capture the quiet confidence with which he ran the bases, played left field and gunned down aggressive baserunners with a shotgun arm. He seldom made a mistake, a quality not lost on Philadelphia manager Connie Mack, who made him the centerpiece of his 1929, '30 and '31 pennant-winning Athletics—a star-studded team that captured two straight World Series.

Simmons' right-handed batting style was not the stuff of which instructional films are made. He stood deep in the box, feet close together, and took a long stride toward third base, as if bailing out. But Bucketfoot Al had the uncanny ability to keep his hips and weight in control, a discipline that allowed him to hit to the opposite field with unusual power. Seasons of .387, .392, .381 and .390 yielded two A.L. batting titles and cemented Simmons' status as one of the great hitters of his time.

But some of the luster was lost when Mack, strapped financially by the Great Depression, sold Simmons' contract after the 1932 season, sentencing his veteran star to wander from team to team over the next decade. Simmons served as a hired gun in such cities as Chicago, Detroit, Washington, Boston and Cincinnati, always hitting but never regaining the top form of his early Philadelphia years.

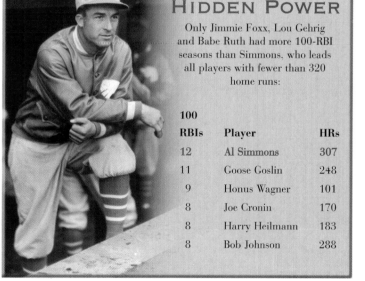

HIDDEN POWER

Only Jimmie Foxx, Lou Gehrig and Babe Ruth had more 100-RBI seasons than Simmons, who leads all players with fewer than 320 home runs:

100 RBIs	Player	HRs
12	Al Simmons	307
11	Goose Goslin	248
9	Honus Wagner	101
8	Joe Cronin	170
8	Harry Heilmann	183
8	Bob Johnson	288

44 JACKIE ROBINSON

Jackie Robinson will be remembered as a pioneer, the man who broke baseball's color barrier for Branch Rickey's Brooklyn Dodgers in 1947 and ushered in a second half-century of hope and opportunity. But sometimes lost in the shadow of Robinson's overwhelming achievement is the marvelous athletic ability that would have been enough to get him Hall of Fame recognition in a normal, integrated baseball society.

Any assessment of Robinson's career has to be made in the context of what he endured on the field—racial epithets, name-calling, threats, spikings and other cruel admonitions. Always, as demanded by Rickey, he bit his lip and turned the other cheek, letting his hitting, baserunning and fielding reap the only revenge he would be allowed. To say that Robinson, a four-sport athlete at UCLA, performed admirably under pressure was something of an understatement.

As a hitter, the righthanded swinger was always dangerous and unpredictable, whether using his great speed to beat out a bunt, driving a ball into the gap or hitting behind a runner with uncanny precision. As a baserunner he was aggressive and smart, distracting defenses and igniting the Dodgers' attack. As a second baseman, he was smooth, graceful and sure-handed. With Robinson providing a huge spark, the Dodgers captured six pennants and their only Brooklyn World Series victory over a 10-year career that produced a .311 average.

But more than anything else, Robinson's teammates marveled at the fierce pride and competitive spirit that allowed him to fight through the adversity. And it didn't take long for most opponents and writers to accord him the respect he commanded in the Brooklyn clubhouse. As a 28-year-old rookie, Robinson won the N.L. Rookie of the Year award. Two years later he was voted N.L. MVP.

MOST INTENSE PLAYERS
SELECTED BY DUKE SNIDER

1. Jackie Robinson
2. Joe DiMaggio
3. Tommy Henrich
4. Al Kaline
5. Pete Rose
6. Will Clark
7. Don Drysdale
8. Robin Roberts
9. Pee Wee Reese
10. Andre Dawson

"HE WAS A GREAT COMPETITOR WHO COULD DO IT ALL.
HE WAS A GREAT PLAYER, A MANAGER'S DREAM. ...
IF I HAD TO GO TO WAR, I'D WANT HIM ON MY SIDE."

LEO DUROCHER, 1972

45 CARL HUBBELL

Early century hitters called it the "fadeaway." Batters in the 1920s and '30s labeled it the "butterfly" or "reverse curve." By any name and by all accounts, the two kinds of screwballs Carl Hubbell delivered to National League hitters with uncanny accuracy from 1928-43 were downright nasty— and borderline unhittable.

Amazingly, the tall, Lincolnesque lefthander did not deliver his first screwie to a major leaguer until age 25, thanks to the common perception among coaches and managers that the pitch required an unnatural twisting motion that would destroy his arm. But Hubbell, who was blessed with exceptionally long and flexible wrists, refused to give in to cynics and rode his so-called "gimmick pitch" all the way to the Hall of Fame.

The high-kicking, fast-working Hubbell, the Meal Ticket for a New York Giants staff that produced three N.L. pennants and one World Series championship, undressed most of the game's top hitters with a sidearm screwball that faded down and away from righthanded batters and an overhand screwball that came in straight before

suddenly dropping into oblivion. King Carl was especially tough on righthanders and his outstanding control allowed him to throw the pitch on any count.

The mild-mannered Hubbell, the son of an Oklahoma pecan farmer, fashioned an impressive five-year run (1933-37) in which he was 115-50 and recorded three of baseball's most memorable feats: an 18-inning 1-0 victory over the Cardinals in 1933; consecutive strikeouts of Babe Ruth, Lou Gehrig, Jimmie Foxx, Al Simmons and Joe Cronin in the 1934 All-Star Game; and a major league-record 24 straight wins in the 1936 and 1937 seasons. Hubbell finally succumbed to the long-predicted arm trouble in 1943, but not before carving out 253 victories and a reputation as one of the great lefthanders in history.

GIANT STEPS

Hubbell is one of seven 20th-century pitchers to compile at least 250 wins with a .600 winning percentage, a below-3.00 ERA and 3,500 innings:

Pitcher	W	L	Pct.	ERA	IP
Cy Young	511	316	.618	2.63	7,356
Christy Mathewson	373	188	.665	2.13	4,780.2
Grover Alexander	373	208	.642	2.56	5,190
Eddie Plank	326	194	.627	2.35	4,495.2
Tom Seaver	311	205	.603	2.86	4,782.2
Jim Palmer	268	152	.638	2.86	3,948
Carl Hubbell	253	154	.622	2.98	3,590.1

> ❝He had the greatest screwball I ever looked at. He'd drop one in for a strike, then really explode one when you thought sure you had him.❞
>
> JOE CRONIN
>
> THE SPORTING NEWS, 1964

" (GEHRINGER) WAS ALWAYS NO. 1
(SECOND BASEMAN) IN MY BOOK.
CHARLEY MADE EVERY PLAY AND
HE MADE IT EFFORTLESSLY."

JOE DIMAGGIO, 1963

CHARLEY GEHRINGER 46

They called him The Mechanical Man. And indeed Charley Gehringer did everything with machine-like precision—an effortless, graceful consistency that belied the competitive spirit raging within. He was always stylish, polished and quiet, prompting former teammate Mickey Cochrane to observe, "He says hello opening day, goodbye closing day and, in between, hits .350."

All of Gehringer's in betweens came for Detroit, where he honed his picture-book batting style under the tutelage of manager Ty Cobb from 1924-26 and began his 19-year run as one of the smoothest second basemen the game has ever produced. The sad-faced former Michigan farm boy made everything look easy with his classy glove, whether ranging to his left, charging slow rollers or retreating to the outfield for short fly balls. What he lacked in showmanship he more than made up for with a sleep-inducing consistency that fit his expressionless demeanor.

At the plate, the lefthanded-hitting Gehringer stood erect and motionless, a cat preparing to pounce.

Ever patient, he worked the pitcher hard and drove the ball to all fields with extra-base power. The 6-foot Gehringer, one of the best two-strike hitters of his era, topped the .300 mark 13 times en route to a career .320 average and won an American League batting championship (.371) and MVP in 1937. He reached the magic 200-hit plateau seven times in a nine-season stretch.

The six-time All-Star was a middle-infield anchor for powerful Detroit lineups (featuring Cochrane, Hank Greenberg, Goose Goslin) that helped win two American League pennants and a World Series in the mid-1930s and another pennant in 1940.

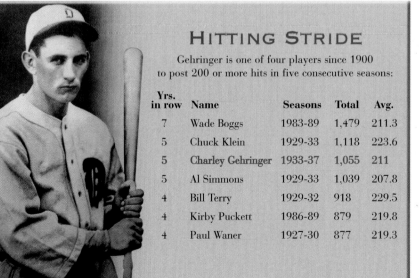

HITTING STRIDE

Gehringer is one of four players since 1900 to post 200 or more hits in five consecutive seasons:

Yrs. in row	Name	Seasons	Total	Avg.
7	Wade Boggs	1983-89	1,479	211.3
5	Chuck Klein	1929-33	1,118	223.6
5	Charley Gehringer	1933-37	1,055	211
5	Al Simmons	1929-33	1,039	207.8
4	Bill Terry	1929-32	918	229.5
4	Kirby Puckett	1986-89	879	219.8
4	Paul Waner	1927-30	877	219.3

" Satchel Paige and Josh Gibson got more publicity in the Negro Leagues, but Buck was just as good. Josh hit the ball farther, but Buck hit it just as often."

Monte Irvin
The Sporting News, 1972

BUCK LEONARD 47

As one-half of the greatest 1-2 hitting punch in Negro League history, Buck Leonard made an indelible impression on a baseball community he would never be allowed to inhabit. "He was major league all the way," said Hall of Fame catcher Roy Campanella. And nobody who saw him play—black or white—would argue the point.

Unfortunately, Leonard's only contact with major league players would be in offseason barnstorming exhibitions that filled out the exhaustive year-round schedule of the pre-World War II black player. For 23 years he competed in as many as three games per day and for 17 of those seasons he handled first-base duty for the Homestead Grays, a Pittsburgh-based power that also featured catcher Josh Gibson and pitcher Satchel Paige.

The combination of Gibson, the Babe Ruth of the Negro Leagues, and Leonard, the so-called Lou Gehrig of the Negro Leagues, was offensive mayhem. Gibson, renowned for his long home runs, batted third; Leonard, who hit his homers frequently if not as far, batted fourth. Pitchers who worked around Gibson had to deal with a lefthanded batter who uncoiled into their fastballs from a menacing crouch. He was a dead-pull hitter who posted averages in the high .300s.

At 5-10, 185 pounds, the stocky lefthander was not the prototypical first baseman. But nobody in any league could match Leonard's agility, powerful arm and ability to dig throws out of the dirt. Some observers called him quietly elegant. Others said his defense alone was worth the price of admission.

When baseball's color barrier fell in 1947, the unassuming Leonard was 39—past his prime and unwilling to pit diminishing talents against younger major-leaguers. He was forced to settle for Hall of Fame recognition, which came in 1972 at age 64.

THE BREAKTHROUGH

When the major leagues opened the door to Negro League players in 1947, Leonard was 39 and considered himself too old to represent his race in the national spotlight. The task of breaking baseball's color barrier went to Jackie Robinson and four other Negro League stars in a history-making season:

Player	Team/Position	Debut
Jackie Robinson	Dodgers/first base	April 15
Larry Doby	Indians/pinch hitter	July 5
Hank Thompson	Browns/second base	July 17
Willard Brown	Browns/outfield	July 19
Dan Bankhead	Dodgers/pitcher	August 26

"I LOVE COMPETITION. IT MOTIVATES ME, STIMULATES ME, EXCITES ME. I JUST LOVE TO HIT THE BASEBALL IN A BIG GAME."

REGGIE JACKSON

REGGIE JACKSON 48

He was charming and belligerent; cocky and self-effacing; articulate and crude; enigmatic and straightforward. You didn't just watch Reggie Jackson, you experienced him. The love/hate bond that fans, players and owners formed with the complex, often-contradictory kid from Wyncote, Pa., lasted 21 years, surviving 563 home runs and at least that many well-publicized tantrums.

Jackson, muscular and with an all-or-nothing corkscrew lefthanded swing, enjoyed several baseball lives. Jackson was the heart and soul of an Oakland team that won three straight World Series (1972, 1973 and 1974); the straw that stirred a Yankees team that won two straight Series (1977 and 1978); and Mr. October, who rose to his greatest heights in the 11 League Championship Series and five World Series in which he competed.

The bottom line on Jackson was drama—and emotion, which he kept upfront for all the paying customers to see. A Jackson home run was majestic and he exulted accordingly, with a slow, measured trot. Jackson strikeouts (all 2,597 of them) were exciting and he fumed with demonstrative vigor. Jackson's right-field defense was erratic, his baserunning was daring but sometimes careless and his battles with owners, teammates, fans and even himself were legendary.

But there's no denying the charisma, which the New York media devoured like hungry sharks. And there's no denying the talent, which produced at least a share of four American League home run titles, 12 All-Star Game appearances and one MVP (1973). Game 6 of the 1977 World Series was typical Jackson, who had endured a season of feuding with Yankees manager Billy Martin and several teammates, especially catcher Thurman Munson. Jackson dramatically powered a postseason-record-tying three home runs—on three consecutive pitches—in a Series-clinching victory over the Los Angeles Dodgers.

BEST PLAYERS I MANAGED
SELECTED BY
DICK WILLIAMS

1. Carl Yastrzemski
2. Catfish Hunter
3. Reggie Jackson
4. Nolan Ryan
5. Rollie Fingers
6. Tony Gwynn
7. Goose Gossage
8. Bert Campaneris
9. Jim Lonborg
10. Gary Carter

49 TONY GWYNN

He has been called the best pure hitter since Ted Williams. And his National League-record-tying eight batting championships put him in the exclusive company of Ty Cobb and Honus Wagner. Tony Gwynn's Hall of Fame stock continues to rise with every average-inflating line drive into the gap.

So does his reputation as baseball's consummate batsman of the 1990s, a Williams/Cobb-like connoisseur who has molded his crouching, lefthanded swing and studied his craft with a scientific fervor. Not only is Gwynn a superb two-strike hitter and a durable model of consistency, he is a feared clutch hitter who compiled a .417 average with runners in scoring position from 1995 through 1997.

He's also a team leader who promotes fun and chemistry in the San Diego locker room and attention to detail when the Padres take the field. Gwynn attacks his job with passion, whether playing solid right-field defense, moving runners with a grounder to the right side or delivering hits with assembly-line consistency. Like Cobb, the only player to win more batting championships, Gwynn has topped the .300 mark every year since his 1982 debut season and he carried a streak of five .350 seasons and a .340 average into 1998.

But that hitting prowess is only part of the legacy

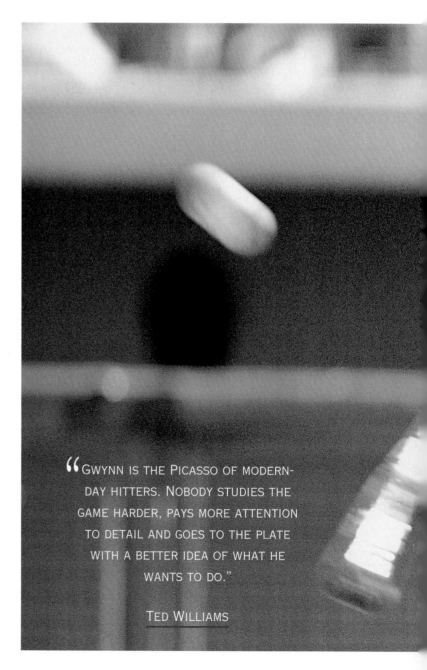

"GWYNN IS THE PICASSO OF MODERN-DAY HITTERS. NOBODY STUDIES THE GAME HARDER, PAYS MORE ATTENTION TO DETAIL AND GOES TO THE PLATE WITH A BETTER IDEA OF WHAT HE WANTS TO DO."

TED WILLIAMS

Gwynn will leave the city of San Diego when he retires sometime in the early 21st century. The 13-time All-Star selection was a big part of the Padres' only National League pennant in 1984 and their 1996 West Division championship. The most beloved player in franchise history, the man who ranks behind only Cal Ripken in one-team longevity among active players, also is one of the most enthusiastic, accessible and popular players in today's game.

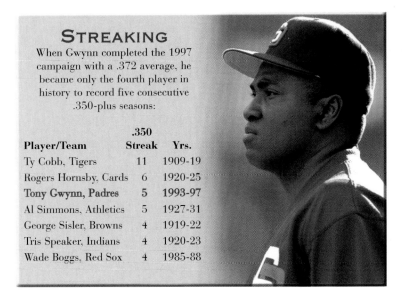

STREAKING

When Gwynn completed the 1997 campaign with a .372 average, he became only the fourth player in history to record five consecutive .350-plus seasons:

Player/Team	.350 Streak	Yrs.
Ty Cobb, Tigers	11	1909-19
Rogers Hornsby, Cards	6	1920-25
Tony Gwynn, Padres	**5**	**1993-97**
Al Simmons, Athletics	5	1927-31
George Sisler, Browns	4	1919-22
Tris Speaker, Indians	4	1920-23
Wade Boggs, Red Sox	4	1985-88

50 ROY CAMPANELLA

On one hand, the boyish enthusiasm that gushed from catcher Roy Campanella embodied the daffy, crazy Dodgers of the 1950s, Brooklyn's Boys of Summer. On the other hand, the same Campanella became the tragic symbol for a city's divorce from the team it had loved unconditionally for more than half a century. For 10 glorious seasons, Campy ruled the baseball world from his crouch behind home

plate. Then he spent the rest of his life in a wheelchair, the result of a crippling 1958 automobile accident.

The Campanella story is one of indomitable spirit. Following in the trail-blazing footsteps of Dodgers teammate Jackie Robinson, Campanella, who had started his professional career as a Negro Leaguer at age 15, reported for major league duty in 1948 and quickly won over baseball-crazy Brooklyn fans. The combination of Campy's thick-necked, roly-poly build and happy-go-lucky outlook was too much to resist.

So was the hustle, agility and cannon arm he displayed while rising to elite status among National League catchers. And the quick bat that consistently shot errant pitches into the left field stands at Ebbets Field. How good was Campy? Three times in a five-year period he walked away with N.L. MVP awards, one following an incredible .312, 41-homer, 142-RBI 1953 campaign. His Dodgers claimed five pennants and won their first Brooklyn World Series; he played in seven All-Star Games.

Campanella, whose easy-going personality was a

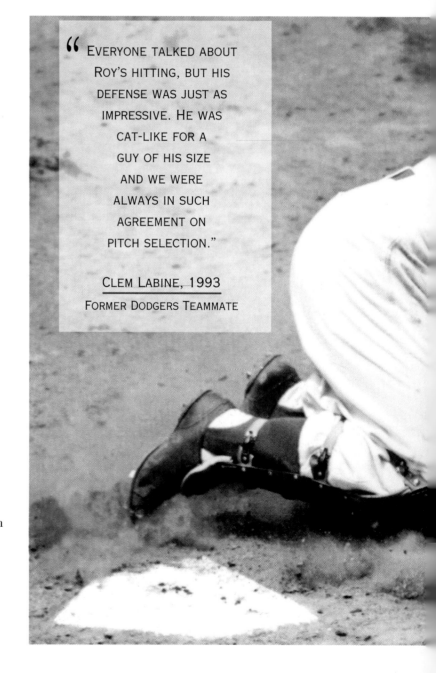

" EVERYONE TALKED ABOUT ROY'S HITTING, BUT HIS DEFENSE WAS JUST AS IMPRESSIVE. HE WAS CAT-LIKE FOR A GUY OF HIS SIZE AND WE WERE ALWAYS IN SUCH AGREEMENT ON PITCH SELECTION."

CLEM LABINE, 1993
FORMER DODGERS TEAMMATE

perfect fit for a difficult racial period, suffered a broken neck and paralysis in a January 1958 car accident—the off-season before the Dodgers would jilt Brooklyn fans with their cross-country move to Los Angeles. The wheelchair-confined Campy was elected to the Hall of Fame in 1969 and remained one of baseball's most gracious ambassadors until his death in 1993.

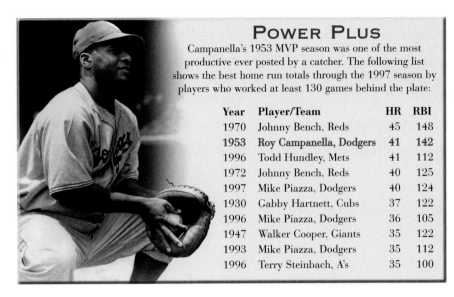

POWER PLUS

Campanella's 1953 MVP season was one of the most productive ever posted by a catcher. The following list shows the best home run totals through the 1997 season by players who worked at least 130 games behind the plate:

Year	Player/Team	HR	RBI
1970	Johnny Bench, Reds	45	148
1953	**Roy Campanella, Dodgers**	**41**	**142**
1996	Todd Hundley, Mets	41	112
1972	Johnny Bench, Reds	40	125
1997	Mike Piazza, Dodgers	40	124
1930	Gabby Hartnett, Cubs	37	122
1996	Mike Piazza, Dodgers	36	105
1947	Walker Cooper, Giants	35	122
1993	Mike Piazza, Dodgers	35	112
1996	Terry Steinbach, A's	35	100

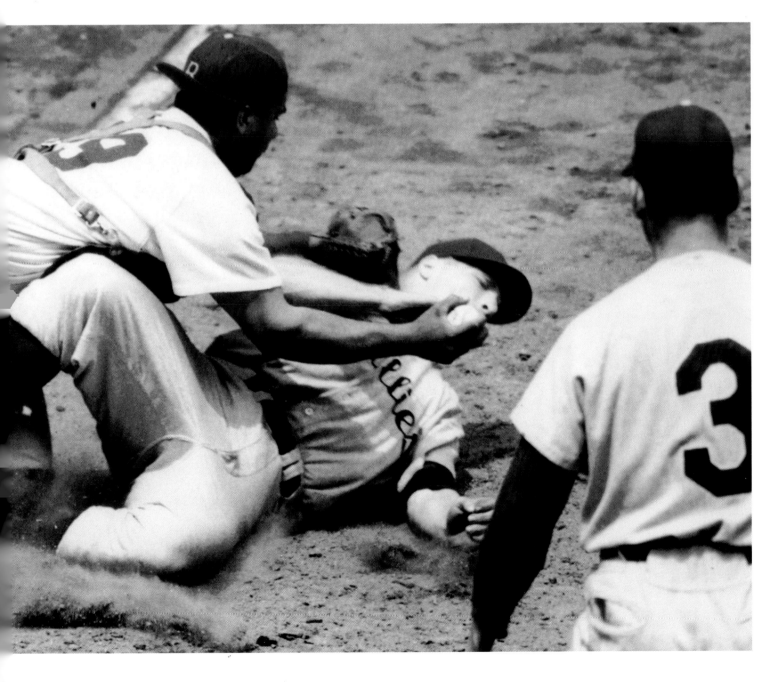

L iving members of the Top 100 list and a number of former managers and long-time baseball personalities were asked to select the 10 greatest players or pitchers they competed against or saw play before, during and after their careers. Note: Whitey Herzog, Ralph Houk and Stan Musial provided lists but did not rank their selections.

WADE BOGGS

1. Rod Carew
2. Pete Rose
3. Ted Williams
4. George Brett
5. Mike Schmidt
6. Johnny Bench
7. Paul Molitor
8. Eddie Murray
9. Carlton Fisk
10. Tom Seaver

BUCK RODGERS

1. Sandy Koufax
2. Ted Williams
3. Mickey Mantle
4. Willie Mays
5. Elston Howard
6. Joe DiMaggio
7. Eddie Mathews
8. Al Kaline
9. Vida Blue
10. Bob Gibson

ROGER CRAIG

1. Willie Mays
2. Hank Aaron
3. Stan Musial
4. Roberto Clemente
5. Juan Marichal
6. Bob Gibson
7. Don Drysdale
8. Greg Maddux
9. Warren Spahn
10. Sandy Koufax

OZZIE SMITH

1. George Brett
2. Mike Schmidt
3. Joe Morgan
4. Willie Stargell
5. Tony Perez
6. Johnny Bench
7. Keith Hernandez
8. Steve Carlton
9. Rollie Fingers
10. Ryne Sandberg

ALL-TIME TOP

CHUCK TANNER

1. Hank Aaron
2. Willie Mays
3. Eddie Mathews
4. Jackie Robinson
5. Willie Stargell
6. Dick Allen
7. Tony Oliva
8. Ted Williams
9. Stan Musial
10. Mickey Mantle

JIM FREY

1. Bob Feller
2. Joe DiMaggio
3. Ted Williams
4. Willie Mays
5. Mickey Mantle
6. Sandy Koufax
7. Stan Musial
8. Frank Robinson
9. Hank Aaron

HARMON KILLEBREW

1. Mickey Mantle
2. Ted Williams
3. Al Kaline
4. Brooks Robinson
5. Hank Aaron
6. Willie Mays
7. Stan Musial
8. Sandy Koufax
9. Frank Robinson
10. Yogi Berra

WILLIE McCOVEY

1. Hank Aaron
2. Jackie Robinson
3. Willie Mays
4. Ted Williams
5. Mickey Mantle
6. Stan Musial
7. Roberto Clemente
8. Frank Robinson
9. Sandy Koufax
10. Bob Gibson

BILL RIGNEY

1. Willie Mays
2. Ted Williams
3. Joe DiMaggio
4. Stan Musial
5. Al Kaline
6. Hank Aaron
7. Mickey Mantle
8. Roberto Clemente
9. Frank Robinson
10. Rod Carew
    Ken Griffey Jr.

DUKE SNIDER

1. Joe DiMaggio
2. Willie Mays
3. Mickey Mantle
4. Hank Aaron
5. Eddie Mathews
6. Willie Stargell
7. Roberto Clemente
8. Stan Musial
9. Ted Williams
10. Billy Williams

Stan Musial (left), Mickey Mantle

Eddie Mathews (left), Hank Aaron

ROLLIE FINGERS

1. Frank Robinson
2. Sandy Koufax
3. Brooks Robinson
4. Pete Rose
5. Mike Schmidt
6. Bob Gibson
7. Ernie Banks
8. Johnny Bench
9. Steve Carlton
10. Nolan Ryan

SPARKY ANDERSON

1. Roberto Clemente
2. Johnny Bench
3. Joe Morgan
4. Pete Rose
5. Sandy Koufax
6. Bob Gibson
7. Ken Griffey Jr.
8. Willie Mays
9. Mickey Mantle
10. Barry Bonds

BILL VIRDON

1. Willie Mays
2. Mickey Mantle
3. Hank Aaron
4. Warren Spahn
5. Frank Robinson
6. Sandy Koufax
7. Roberto Clemente
8. Billy Williams
9. Jackie Robinson
10. Bill Mazeroski

GENE MAUCH

1. Willie Mays
2. Frank Robinson
3. Hank Aaron
4. Roberto Clemente
5. Mickey Mantle
6. Stan Musial
7. Ted Williams
8. Sandy Koufax
9. Bob Gibson
10. Warren Spahn

DICK WILLIAMS

1. Willie Mays
2. Hank Aaron
3. Jackie Robinson
4. Stan Musial
5. Ted Williams
   Joe DiMaggio
7. Carl Yastrzemski
   Mickey Mantle
9. Bob Gibson
   Steve Carlton

DANNY OZARK

1. Ted Williams
2. Joe DiMaggio
3. Bob Feller
4. Hank Aaron
5. Sandy Koufax
6. Stan Musial
7. Luis Aparicio
8. Roberto Clemente
9. Babe Ruth
10. Mickey Mantle

TEN SELECTIONS

JIM FREGOSI

1. Mickey Mantle
2. Willie Mays
3. Hank Aaron
4. Roberto Clemente
5. Sandy Koufax
6. Bob Gibson
7. Roger Maris
8. Willie McCovey
9. Al Kaline
10. Harmon Killebrew

TOM SEAVER

1. Hank Aaron
2. Willie Mays
3. Mickey Mantle
4. Sandy Koufax
5. Steve Carlton
6. Bob Gibson
7. Joe Morgan
8. Mike Schmidt
9. Johnny Bench
10. Joe Morgan

RALPH HOUK

Mickey Mantle
Ted Williams
Willie Mays
Carl Yastrzemski
Yogi Berra
Sandy Koufax
Whitey Ford
Al Kaline
Roger Maris
Joe DiMaggio

STAN MUSIAL

Ted Williams
Jimmie Foxx
Willie Mays
Bob Feller
Joe DiMaggio
Hank Aaron
Mickey Mantle
Tom Seaver
Steve Carlton
Sandy Koufax

AL KALINE

1. Willie Mays
2. Mickey Mantle
3. Frank Robinson
4. Bob Gibson
5. Hank Aaron
6. Ted Williams
7. Joe DiMaggio
8. George Brett
9. Johnny Bench
10. Luis Aparicio

WHITEY HERZOG

Stan Musial
Ted Williams
Joe DiMaggio
Mickey Mantle
Yogi Berra
Willie Mays
Hank Aaron
Frank Robinson
Roberto Clemente
George Brett/
  Mike Schmidt

Jackie Robinson (left), Roy Campanella

51 RICKEY HENDERSON

H e's a terrorist in cleats, a merciless killer bent on the destruction of every pitcher he meets. It's nothing personal. Rickey Henderson just has this powerful obsession to get on base and score runs. When he achieves the first goal, the second usually follows, leaving a trail of frazzled opponents in his speedy wake.

Henderson is an instigator, a talented leadoff man who has changed the course of many games over his two decades in the major leagues. He hits from an exaggerated righthanded crouch, daring pitchers to penetrate his Eddie Gaedel-like strike zone with a hittable pitch. If they don't, he's perfectly happy with a walk that will allow him to exhibit his skills as the best basestealer in history. If they do, he's capable of launching the pitch 420 feet the other way.

The bottom line is that Henderson's career on-base percentage of .409 had generated 1,231 stolen bases entering the 1998 season, a record fueled by the incredible 130 he swiped in 1982. The speedy outfielder has led the American League in stolen bases 11 times, runs scored five times and walks on three occasions as the catalyst for five different teams—including four separate stints with Oakland and a five-year run with the New York Yankees. He also has won a Gold Glove while providing the spark for three World Series teams, including winners in Oakland and Toronto.

Henderson's offensive versatility does come with

some baggage, however. The 10-time All-Star and one-time MVP plays with a strutting arrogance that sometimes angers fans, opponents and even teammates. And he sometimes has to be prodded into giving his best effort or relinquishing his spot on the disabled list. But there's nothing unappealing about career numbers that include more than 2,500 hits and 1,900 runs and an average in the upper .280s.

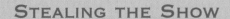

STEALING THE SHOW

Henderson has displayed his stolen base dominance by leading his league in that category a record 11 times. Here are players who have won or shared the most titles in several key offensive and pitching categories:

AVERAGE
Ty Cobb (12)

RUNS
Babe Ruth (8)

HITS
Ty Cobb (8)

HOME RUNS
Babe Ruth (12)

RBIs
Babe Ruth (6)

STEALS
Rickey Henderson (11)

WIN PERCENTAGE
Lefty Grove (5)

ERA
Lefty Grove (9)

STRIKEOUTS
Walter Johnson (12)

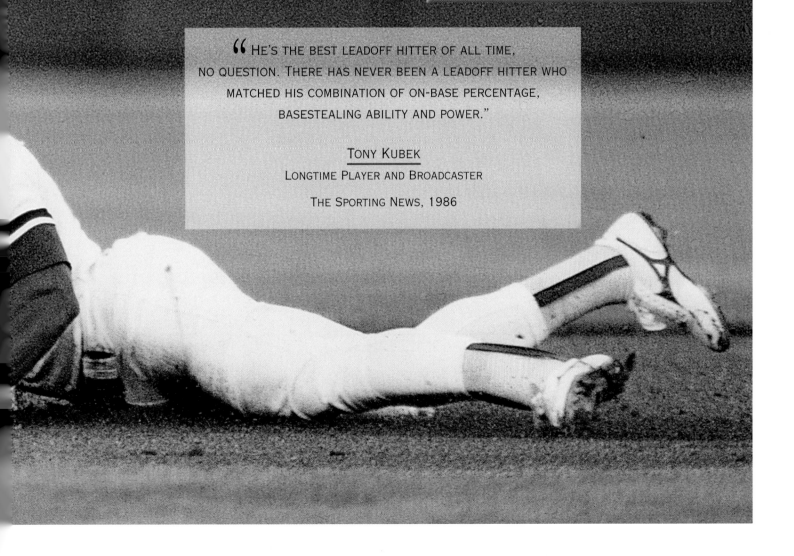

66 HE'S THE BEST LEADOFF HITTER OF ALL TIME, NO QUESTION. THERE HAS NEVER BEEN A LEADOFF HITTER WHO MATCHED HIS COMBINATION OF ON-BASE PERCENTAGE, BASESTEALING ABILITY AND POWER."

TONY KUBEK

LONGTIME PLAYER AND BROADCASTER

THE SPORTING NEWS, 1986

52 WHITEY FORD

He may not have been baseball's original "crafty little lefthander," but Whitey Ford sure fit the description as well as anybody who pitched before or after him. The blond-headed 5-10, 180-pound New Yorker also was the ace for a New York Yankees winning machine that captured 11 American League pennants and six World Series with him at the controls between 1950 and 1964.

What Ford's left arm lacked in power his head made up for with guile, determination and instinct. He delivered his fastball, curve, sinker and slider with overhand, three-quarters and sidearm motions, rarely giving the hitter the same look on consecutive pitches. His control was outstanding; his confident demeanor never wavered; his pickoff move froze embarrassed baserunners. He was a bulldog who seemed to get tougher as the situation warranted.

Supported by a series of powerful Yankee lineups, Ford parlayed his pitching prowess into an incredible .690 career winning percentage, the best in major league history for a 200-game winner. His 25-4 record earned him a 1961 Cy Young Award and he posted ERA titles in 1956 and 1958. His 236-106 career record could have been even better if not for the two peak seasons (1951 and 1952) he lost to military service during the Korean War.

Ford, a six-time All-Star performer who posted World Series records of 22 starts, 10 victories and $33\frac{2}{3}$ consecutive scoreless innings, was known for his humorous one-line quips, which brought back memories of Hall of Famer Lefty Gomez among longtime Yankees fans. He also was known for the nightlife he enjoyed with longtime friends and former teammates Mickey Mantle and Billy Martin.

BEST BIG-GAME PITCHERS
SELECTED BY
BILL VIRDON

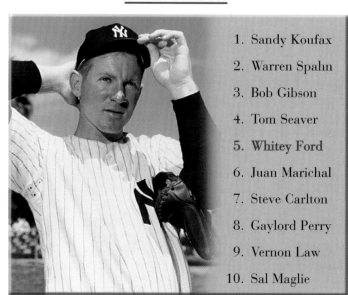

1. Sandy Koufax
2. Warren Spahn
3. Bob Gibson
4. Tom Seaver
5. Whitey Ford
6. Juan Marichal
7. Steve Carlton
8. Gaylord Perry
9. Vernon Law
10. Sal Maglie

" You go up to the plate thinking confidently that this is the time I'm going to do well against (Ford). Trouble is, you never seem to do it."

Brooks Robinson

The Sporting News, 1964

"IF (CLEMENS) IS NOT THE BEST, I'D HATE TO SEE WHO IS.
WHEN THEY MADE THE MOLD FOR PITCHERS, THEY MADE HIM.
HE'S THE PERFECT PITCHER."

DAN PLESAC

MAJOR LEAGUE PITCHER

THE SPORTING NEWS, 1988

ROGER CLEMENS 53

He's cocky, intensely focused and the master of his American League universe. And he's explosive, much like the fastball he has blown past hitters for 15 seasons. When the sometimes-volatile, always-confident Roger Clemens pitches, everybody listens—and that sound they hear is another pitch whistling through the strike zone and into the catcher's mitt.

Finesse is not a quality associated with the 6-4, 230-pound righthander who embraces the very essence of his "Rocket" nickname. Clemens is raw power, a finely-tuned strikeout machine driven by strong legs, a resilient arm and an intense competitive fire. When the big Texan is at his best with an 84-mph curveball and a forkball complementing the 96-mph hummer, he is close to unhittable.

Seattle batters found that out in 1986 when Clemens mowed them down in a record-setting 20-strikeout masterpiece; Detroit hitters felt the same way 10 years later when he matched his own remarkable strikeout feat against them. Four 20-win sea-sons, a record-tying four Cy Young Awards and four league-leading strikeout totals have added to the Clemens mystique, which was built around 13 outstanding years in Boston and two more as ace of a rebuilding Toronto staff.

Clemens, a five-time All-Star, posted his signature season in 1986—the year after he underwent shoulder surgery. He swept A.L. Cy Young and MVP honors while finishing 24-4 and leading the Red Sox to a pennant. He also enjoyed 20-9 and 21-6 seasons for Boston before signing a free-agent contract with Toronto in 1996. His first season with the Blue Jays produced a 21-7 record and 2.05 ERA.

HARDEST-THROWING PITCHERS
SELECTED BY
GENE MAUCH

1. Nolan Ryan
2. Ryne Duren
3. Bob Feller
4. Roger Clemens
5. Steve Dalkowski
6. Ewell Blackwell
7. Sandy Koufax
8. Jim Maloney
9. Rex Barney
10. J.R. Richard

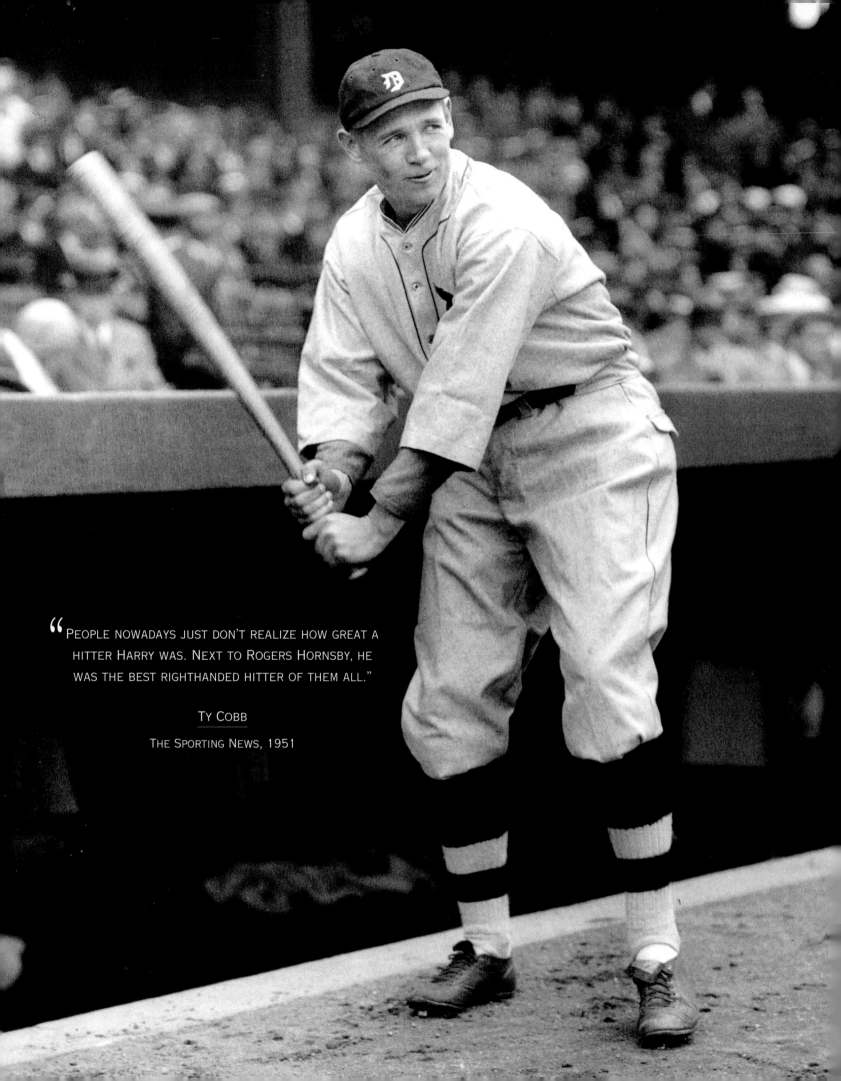

"PEOPLE NOWADAYS JUST DON'T REALIZE HOW GREAT A HITTER HARRY WAS. NEXT TO ROGERS HORNSBY, HE WAS THE BEST RIGHTHANDED HITTER OF THEM ALL."

TY COBB

THE SPORTING NEWS, 1951

HARRY HEILMANN 54

He was slow afoot, his defense was sometimes suspect and his personality was overshadowed by Detroit outfield partner Ty Cobb. But, oh, could Harry Heilmann hit. He proved that over 17 major-league seasons, competing with the likes of Cobb, Rogers Hornsby, George Sisler, Babe Ruth, Tris Speaker and Lou Gehrig for batting superiority in the 1920s.

Old Slug, a nickname bestowed by Heilmann's Detroit teammates because of his lack of speed, was a righthanded hitter who slashed line drives around A.L. ballparks. He attacked the pitch from a slight crouch and moved his hands up and down the bat, a trick he learned from Cobb. Heilmann never ranked high on the home run charts, but he consistently showed up among the leaders in doubles and triples, despite his slow footspeed. He topped the 100-RBI plateau eight times in a nine-season span.

But Heilmann's legacy will be the four American League batting titles he captured in the decade of the hitter—with lofty averages of .403,

.398, .394 and .393. His career .342 average, which ranks among the top 10 all-time, was compiled on 2,660 hits, the final 161 of which he collected with the Cincinnati Reds over his last two seasons.

The personable, outgoing Heilmann was a favorite of Detroit fans, who had endured a long-standing love/hate relationship with the controversial Cobb. Long after retirement in 1932, Heilmann remained a close personal friend of both Cobb and Ruth, two of the game's most colorful and divergent personalities. Heilmann's Hall of Fame election was announced in 1952, seven months after he died of lung cancer.

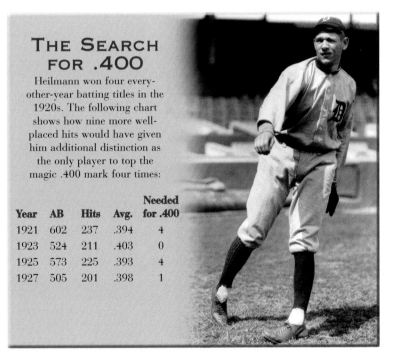

THE SEARCH FOR .400

Heilmann won four every-other-year batting titles in the 1920s. The following chart shows how nine more well-placed hits would have given him additional distinction as the only player to top the magic .400 mark four times:

Year	AB	Hits	Avg.	Needed for .400
1921	602	237	.394	4
1923	524	211	.403	0
1925	573	225	.393	4
1927	505	201	.398	1

55 GEORGE BRETT

The first thing pitchers noticed about George Brett was the concentration, the intense eye contact that suggested he was up for any challenge. The second was a line drive plugging the gap or nestling into either corner, a likely occurrence whenever a game was on the line. Brett was known for many magical moments during his 21-season run with the Kansas City Royals, but his reputation as one of the

most feared clutch hitters in baseball history will transcend the 20th century.

He broke into the major leagues in 1973 as a sure-handed but scatter-armed third baseman and finished his career 3,154 hits later as a first baseman. The sandy-haired, free-spirited Californian often credited his offensive prowess, which produced three American League batting titles and a spectacular .390 average in 1980, to hitting guru Charley Lau, who changed him from a Carl Yastrzemski-type free swinger into a controlled, weight-shifting machine.

The sight of the lefthanded-hitting Brett crouching, weight shifted to the back leg and bat resting comfortably on his shoulder, suggested confidence and relaxed control. His focus was unbreakable, his swing was picture-perfect and he always was a step ahead of the pitcher. He could drive the ball with home run power to any section of the park and his flair for dramatics was uncanny.

Numerous big-game home runs and a career .305

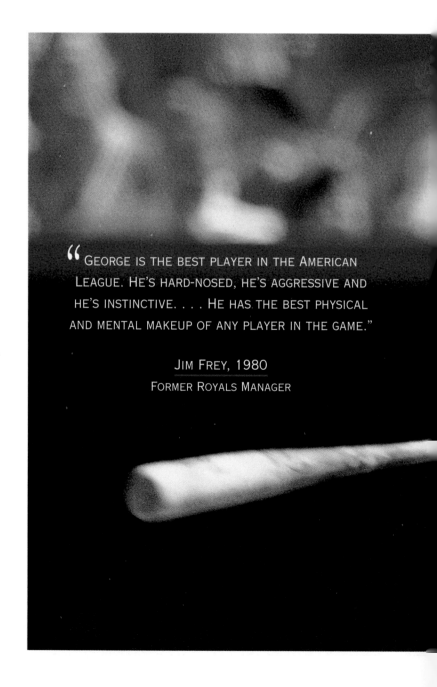

“ GEORGE IS THE BEST PLAYER IN THE AMERICAN LEAGUE. HE'S HARD-NOSED, HE'S AGGRESSIVE AND HE'S INSTINCTIVE. . . . HE HAS THE BEST PHYSICAL AND MENTAL MAKEUP OF ANY PLAYER IN THE GAME.”

JIM FREY, 1980
FORMER ROYALS MANAGER

average would attest to that. So would a post-season passion that allowed him to produce numerous slugging records in six American League Championship Series and a .373 average in two World Series. Brett, a 13-time All-Star selection and 1985 Gold Glove winner, could have posted even better numbers if not for a series of nagging injuries, the product of the aggressive, hustling intensity he always brought to the field.

MOST INTIMIDATING HITTERS
SELECTED BY
ROGER CRAIG

1. Willie Mays
2. Hank Aaron
3. Stan Musial
4. Mark McGwire
5. Duke Snider
6. Mickey Mantle
7. Willie McCovey
8. George Brett
9. Ken Griffey Jr.
10. Eddie Mathews

"You've got to fear McCovey more than you do a .340 or .350 hitter when he's in position to bat in the winning or tying run. I think you could hurt the Giants if you walked McCovey every time he came up."

SPARKY ANDERSON

THE SPORTING NEWS, 1973

WILLIE McCOVEY 56

C incinnati Reds manager Sparky Anderson once called him "the most awesome man I've ever seen." Pitchers shuddered and an expectant hush enveloped the ballpark every time he stepped into the batter's box. Intimidation really wasn't Willie McCovey's style, but you couldn't tell that just by watching him.

In reality, the 6-4, 220-pound San Francisco first baseman was a gentle Giant, amiable, soft-spoken and always respectful. But at the plate, the towering lefthanded hitter was the epitome of intimidation— massive arms sweeping a toothpick-like bat back and forth, dipping it menacingly low, as the pitcher released the ball. He didn't just hit home runs; he launched them with a whiplash swing that produced 521 over a 22-year major league career that started in 1959 and touched four decades.

McCovey is best remembered as the enforcer who protected Willie Mays for 13-plus seasons in the Giants' lineup and the man who hit the blistering line drive that New York Yankees second baseman Bobby Richardson snared for the final out in Game 7 of the 1962 World Series. But the man teammates called Stretch also was a solid first baseman, a six-time All-Star and a .270 career hitter who earned a National League MVP award in 1969. That was the season he was walked intentionally an N.L-record 45 times.

But the most remarkable thing about McCovey might have been the physical traits nobody could see. He played his entire career without complaint on arthritic, surgically-repaired knees that hindered his running and quick movement and he later battled other injuries and intense back problems that might have hindered his Hall of Fame offensive production.

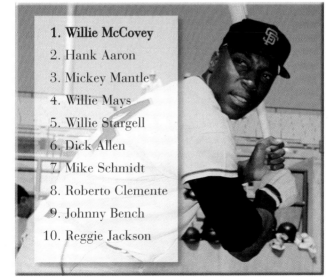

MOST INTIMIDATING HITTERS
SELECTED BY
TOM SEAVER

1. **Willie McCovey**
2. Hank Aaron
3. Mickey Mantle
4. Willie Mays
5. Willie Stargell
6. Dick Allen
7. Mike Schmidt
8. Roberto Clemente
9. Johnny Bench
10. Reggie Jackson

"THERE IS ONLY ONE BILL DICKEY. BILL ISN'T FAST. BUT HE IS THE BEST HANDLER OF PITCHERS I EVER SAW. BEYOND WHICH, HE IS THE GREATEST CLUTCH HITTER I EVER SAW, NOT ONLY FOR A CATCHER BUT FOR ANYONE ELSE IN BASEBALL."

ROGER BRESNAHAN

HALL OF FAME CATCHER

BILL DICKEY 57

He fit into his catching gear as naturally as a turtle into its shell. When Bill Dickey crouched behind the plate, all was right in Yankeeland and pennant-crazy New York fans could thank the baseball gods their pitching staff was in good hands. Dickey lived up to his part of that bond for 17 major league seasons as a link between the Ruth/Gehrig/Lazzeri champions of the late 1920s and the DiMaggio/Keller/Gordon winning machines of the early 1940s.

Before heading off to war in 1944, Dickey backstopped eight New York pennant winners and seven World Series champs, a legacy he passed on in 1946 to rookie Yogi Berra, who would catch 14 pennant winners and 10 champions of his own. The stately Dickey provided an interesting contrast as tutor to the roly-poly Berra, but both men moved around behind the plate with similar cat-like quickness, authority and agility. No one, however, could match Dickey's tactical genius and ability to keep pitchers on an even keel.

Few catchers, before or since, have been able to match Dickey's dangerous bat, either. He sprayed hits all over the park from his upright lefthanded stance and was especially dangerous in the clutch. Not surprisingly, the four consecutive 100-RBI seasons he strung together from 1936 to 1939 coincided with the first four-straight World Series run in history.

Dickey will be remembered for a rugged durability that allowed him to catch more than 100 games in 13 consecutive seasons and a surprising 1932 incident in which the quiet, mild-mannered Dickey delivered a one-punch knockout to Washington's Carl Reynolds after a home-plate collision, breaking his jaw and drawing a 30-day suspension. More significant was his introduction of a smaller, lightweight catcher's mitt that helped revolutionize the position.

HIGH SOCIETY

Dickey ranked among the top 10 all-time Yankee players in numerous offensive categories through 1997:

Category	Rank	Total
Games	6th	1,789
At-Bats	9th	6,300
Hits	7th	1,969
Doubles	6th	343
Triples	T9th	72
Home Runs	10th	202
Total Bases	7th	3,062
RBIs	6th	1,209
Extra-Base Hits	7th	617
Batting Average	7th	.313

"You look at Lou's career and you envy it. I do. I think most players do."

Ted Simmons
Brock's longtime teammate

The Sporting News, 1979

LOU BROCK 58

His big smile, soft voice and slow, graceful movements belied the thievery in Lou Brock's heart. His thoughtful, analytical mind meticulously planned the controlled mayhem he would perpetrate on helpless pitchers and defenses. The stolen base was Brock's weapon and he dominated baseball games throughout the 1960s and '70s without even touching a bat, ball or glove.

Brock, 5-11 and 170 pounds, was the ultimate leadoff man and driving force for the St. Louis Cardinals in an era that featured long-ball hitters, one-base-at-a-time strategy and dominant pitchers. He was a dangerous left-handed batter who slashed out 3,023 hits, but the real damage Brock inflicted came after he had reached base. Using his outstanding speed like a club, he pounded away at distracted pitchers and defenses while setting a new course for baseball strategy.

If the stolen base was Brock's artform, then the 1974 season was his masterpiece. His .306 average and 194 hits set the tone for a startling 118-stolen base performance—14 steals better than the record-setting Maury Wills total

of 1962. Brock taking a short lead, sprinting for second and arriving safely with a quick pop-up slide was a familiar sight throughout National League cities.

It wasn't as easy as it looked. Brock spent hours studying pitchers, timing their deliveries to the plate and their moves to first base. He approached hitting in the same meticulous manner. The six-time All-Star selection, who helped the Cardinals to three National League pennants and two World Series championships in the 1960s, made his final signature on a Hall of Fame career in 1979, when he became baseball's 14th 3,000-hit man and its all-time leading basestealer—a plateau he reached with then-record-setting steal No. 938.

STOLEN MEMORIES

When Brock stole his record-setting 118 bases in 1974, Davey Lopes, his nearest major league competitor, checked in with half that total. That's the second-biggest first/second differential in baseball's eight 100-steal seasons:

Year	Leader/Total	2nd/Total
1962	Maury Wills, 104	Willie Davis, 32
1974	Lou Brock, 118	Davey Lopes, 59
1982	Rickey Henderson, 130	Tim Raines, 78
1987	Vince Coleman, 109	Harold Reynolds, 60
1985	Vince Coleman, 110	Rickey Henderson, 80
1986	Vince Coleman, 107	Rickey Henderson, 87
1983	Rickey Henderson, 108	Tim Raines, 90
1980	Rickey Henderson, 100	Ron LeFlore, 97

"BILL MANAGED LIKE HE PLAYED.
IT WAS BUSINESS TO HIM, NOT FUN,
AND HE WAS SUCCESSFUL."

CARL HUBBELL, 1948

BILL TERRY 59

The first thing you noticed about Bill Terry was the hard-edged bluntness, a glassy-eyed, no-nonsense attitude that made it perfectly clear he was about business, not pleasure. Baseball was a means to Terry's end and he pulled no punches in his legendary duels with strong-willed New York Giants manager John McGraw, his hard-edged battles with members of the press and his no-mercy plundering of National League pitchers.

Terry grew up in poverty, the victim of a broken home in Jacksonville, Fla., and his silent rage and obsession to succeed were magnified with every line drive he slashed into the left and right center field gaps at New York's Polo Grounds. His aloofness in the locker room transformed into competitive passion when he took the field and that passion was documented by the .341 career average the graceful 6-2, 200-pound first baseman carved out over a 14-year major league career.

Terry's icy glare and savage line drives through the box unnerved many pitchers, who had to deal with a powerfully built, shoulder-hunching lefthanded hitter with straightaway gap power. His third New York season in 1925 pro- duced a .319 average and he failed to top the .300 plateau only once over the next 11 years. Terry's signature performance came in 1930, when he posted an eye-catching .401 average that still stands as the last .400 season in National League history.

The Terry-McGraw personality clashes were legendary—they once went a year and a half without speaking to each other. But when McGraw ended his brilliant 33-year managerial run in 1932, he handpicked Terry as his successor. As player/manager, Terry guided the Giants to two National League pennants and a 1933 World Series victory over the Washington Senators. He retired from active duty after the 1936 season, but continued in his managerial capacity until 1941.

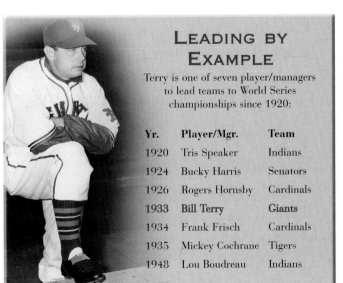

LEADING BY EXAMPLE

Terry is one of seven player/managers to lead teams to World Series championships since 1920:

Yr.	Player/Mgr.	Team
1920	Tris Speaker	Indians
1924	Bucky Harris	Senators
1926	Rogers Hornsby	Cardinals
1933	**Bill Terry**	**Giants**
1934	Frank Frisch	Cardinals
1935	Mickey Cochrane	Tigers
1948	Lou Boudreau	Indians

"WHEN HE'S HEALTHY, HE'S THE FINEST BALLPLAYER I
EVER PLAYED WITH. HE COULD WIN MORE BALLGAMES
IN MORE WAYS THAN ANYBODY."

JOHNNY BENCH, 1980

JOE MORGAN 60

He was an equal-opportunity assassin. Joe Morgan could kill you softly with his glove, speed and quick mind. Or he could kill you savagely with a vicious line drive into the gap or a heart-piercing home run. Either way, you always would end up dead and Morgan would end up another step closer to the Hall of Fame.

That lofty height must have seemed out of reach for a 5-7, 155-pound second baseman when he made his major league debut with the Houston Astros in 1963. But Morgan used his quick hands, his scientific, analytical approach and his game-turning speed to wreak a special kind of havoc over a 22-year career with five teams.

Little Joe, who was called "the strongest little guy I've ever been around" by former manager Sparky Anderson, was at his best when he helped fuel Cincinnati's Big Red Machine from 1972 through 1977. He won five Gold Gloves and averaged .301 with 157 hits, 113 runs scored, 118 walks, 21.7 home runs, 84 RBIs and 60 stolen bases over that six-year stretch and he was the N.L.

MVP for Reds teams that captured consecutive World Series in 1975 and '76. The articulate, quick-to-laugh Morgan, one of the smartest players ever to put on a uniform, simply did whatever it took to win—no matter what effect it would have on his personal statistics.

Morgan, a lefthanded hitter who distinctively flapped his left elbow before every pitch, showed a Ted Williams-like patience that allowed him to set a National League career record for walks with 1,865. But he swung often enough to rap out 2,517 hits and 268 home runs, 266 as a second baseman. The eight-time All-Star also scored 100 runs eight times and stole 689 bases, even though he played eight seasons in one of the most powerful lineups ever assembled.

SMARTEST PLAYERS
SELECTED BY
GENE MAUCH

1. Al Dark
2. Billy Herman
3. Eddie Stanky
4. Ted Williams
5. Tim Foli
6. Jim Gilliam
7. Don Hoak
8. Joe Morgan
9. Cookie Rojas
10. Tony Taylor

"I'VE NEVER SEEN ANYONE QUITE LIKE THIS FELLOW. I SAW TED WILLIAMS DO THINGS WITH A BASEBALL BAT I'D NEVER SEEN DONE BEFORE. I NEVER THOUGHT I'D SEE BETTER, BUT THAT WAS BEFORE I SAW CAREW."

GENE MAUCH, 1977

ROD CAREW 61

He handled the bat with the same efficiency Merlin coaxed from his wand. Rod Carew was a baseball magician with the power to make well-placed pitches disappear into every conceivable outfield gap. Carew was to the 1970s what Ty Cobb was to the 1910s and Rogers Hornsby to the 1920s—a bat-control artist, the keeper of batting titles and an annual threat to hit .400.

Carew's magic was performed with a 32-ounce bat and a natural inside-out lefthanded swing that allowed him to stay back until the last possible second and spray line drives to all fields with seeing-eye consistency. He also was fast, which allowed him to beat out infield hits, and former manager Billy Martin said "he could bunt .330 if he tried," which helped him stay out of slumps. Selective and smart, Carew was an outstanding two-strike hitter and instinctive baserunner.

Such efficiency allowed him to win seven batting titles in his 12 seasons with the Minnesota Twins, the first in his third big-league season (1969) and the other six in a seven-year period beginning in 1972. Carew, a career .328 hitter, never quite reached the .400 plateau that many predicted, but he did pull off a .388, 239-hit 1977 performance that earned him the American League MVP.

Carew was a moody, sometimes-difficult locker room loner when he captured Rookie of the Year honors as an erratic second baseman in 1967. But he was a well-respected veteran first baseman when he collected his 3,000th career hit in 1985, his seventh and final season with the California Angels. The only thing missing from Carew's Hall of Fame ledger was a World Series appearance, although he did play in four American League Championship Series—two each with the Twins and Angels.

BEST PURE HITTERS
SELECTED BY
WADE BOGGS

1. Rod Carew
2. George Brett
3. Pete Rose
4. Paul Molitor
5. Tony Gwynn

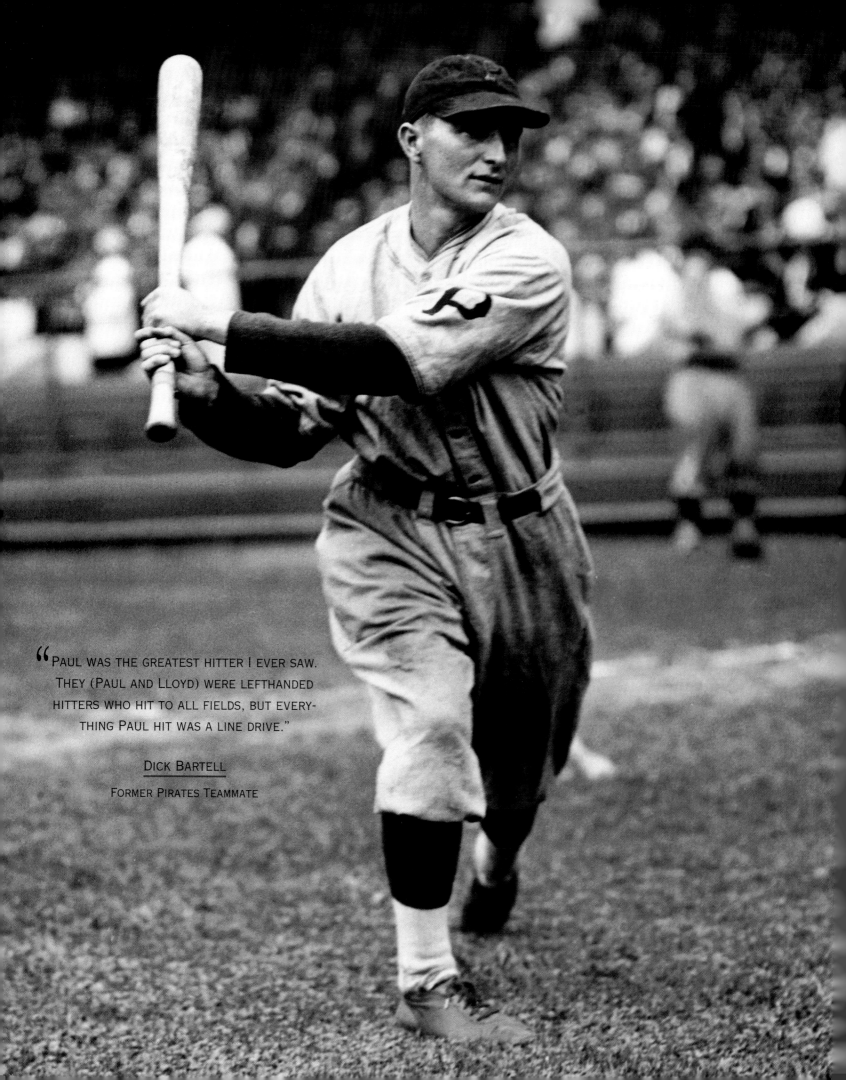

"Paul was the greatest hitter I ever saw. They (Paul and Lloyd) were lefthanded hitters who hit to all fields, but everything Paul hit was a line drive."

Dick Bartell

Former Pirates Teammate

PAUL WANER

He was the marquee half of the most offensive brother act ever to take the baseball stage. Hits simply oozed out of Paul Waner's oversized bat, and all the leftovers he passed on to brother Lloyd. The sprightly Waner brothers, Paul in right and Lloyd in center, were like gnats buzzing the faces of National League pitchers for the 14 incredible seasons (1927 to 1940) they spent together as speedy flychasers in Pittsburgh's outfield.

The 5-8 1/2, 153-pound Paul (Big Poison) was a better hitter than his 5-8 1/4, 150-pound younger brother (Little Poison), but not by much. Lloyd, the Pirates' leadoff hitter, would slap a single and Paul, who compiled 3,152 hits and a .333 average over a 20-year career, would shoot a drive down the line or into a gap, scoring his brother or sending him to third. That combination helped carry the Pirates to the 1927 World Series, a classic they lost in four games to the greatest New York Yankees team ever assembled.

Paul was a lefthanded-swinging bat-control artist who stepped into the pitch from a close-footed stance,

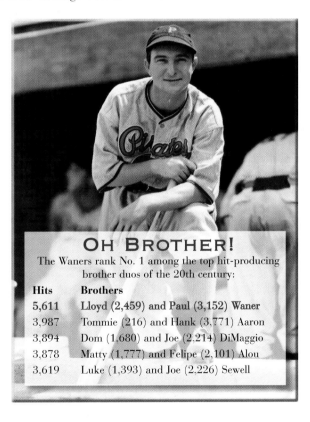

OH BROTHER!
The Waners rank No. 1 among the top hit-producing brother duos of the 20th century:

Hits	Brothers
5,611	Lloyd (2,459) and Paul (3,152) Waner
3,987	Tommie (216) and Hank (3,771) Aaron
3,894	Dom (1,680) and Joe (2,214) DiMaggio
3,878	Matty (1,777) and Felipe (2,101) Alou
3,619	Luke (1,393) and Joe (2,226) Sewell

driving some balls to the opposite field, tomahawking others to right. He was fast enough to beat out infield rollers and quick enough to fend off the nastiest of pitches. Waner seldom struck out (34 times in his worst season) and managed eight 200-hit seasons, third all-time behind Pete Rose and Ty Cobb. His three N.L. batting titles were the result of .380, .362 and .373 efforts.

Waner's only weakness was an affinity for the carousing nightlife that kept Yankees contemporary Babe Ruth in hot water. But it never seemed to affect Waner's performance or the scientific hitting approach he later passed on to Ted Williams and numerous other players who sought his batting instruction.

63 EDDIE MATHEWS

The apple cheeks, dark, handsome features and Texas country-boy shyness belied the fiery intensity Eddie Mathews brought to a baseball diamond. The short sentences he fed reporters stood in stark contrast to the long home runs he powered 512 times over a 17-year career; the boyish charm contrasted his quick temper and no-nonsense toughness; the 6-1, 200-pound, rock-solid body contrasted

the quickness and speed that put him in company of the game's best all-around players.

The quickness was fundamental to Mathews' development as a solid third baseman and the near-perfect swing that made him one of the most feared hitters in the major leagues. The speed, often overshadowed by his power achievements, was documented in 1953, Mathews' second season with the Braves, when he was timed from home to first base in 3.5 seconds.

Early career observers saw a lot of Ted Williams in Mathews' batting style. He used a slightly open stance to

attack pitches with a quick, Williams-like, buggy-whip swing that shot line drives into the distant stands. A dead-pull hitter who powered home runs in bunches, he formed a lethal 13-season (from Milwaukee to Atlanta) combination in the Braves' lineup with Hank Aaron—a tandem that helped Milwaukee capture consecutive pennants and the city's only World Series championship in 1957.

The sometimes-moody Mathews, a four-time 40-homer man and two-time N.L. home run champion, was feared beyond his hitting feats. His fiery temper was exhibited in several celebrated baseball fights—none of

which he lost. But former teammates cited the never-say-die hustle, the personal expectations and the demands he made on others as the real bottom line on Eddie Mathews.

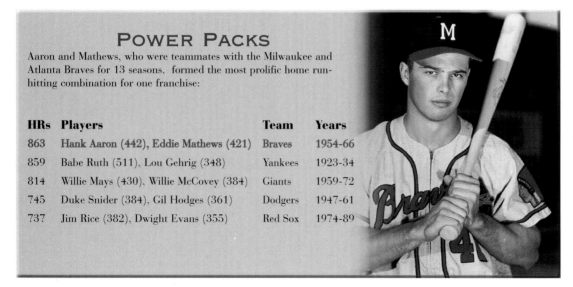

POWER PACKS

Aaron and Mathews, who were teammates with the Milwaukee and Atlanta Braves for 13 seasons, formed the most prolific home run-hitting combination for one franchise:

HRs	Players	Team	Years
863	Hank Aaron (442), Eddie Mathews (421)	Braves	1954-66
859	Babe Ruth (511), Lou Gehrig (348)	Yankees	1923-34
814	Willie Mays (430), Willie McCovey (384)	Giants	1959-72
745	Duke Snider (384), Gil Hodges (361)	Dodgers	1947-61
737	Jim Rice (382), Dwight Evans (355)	Red Sox	1974-89

"I'VE SEEN THREE OR FOUR PERFECT
SWINGS IN MY TIME. THIS LAD HAS
ONE OF THEM. BARRING A BAD
INJURY, HE CAN GO AS FAR AS
HE WANTS."

TY COBB, 1953

"JIM HAD ONE OF THE MOST BEAUTIFUL DELIVERIES I'VE EVER SEEN. IT WAS ALMOST LIKE WATCHING BALLET."

RAY MILLER, 1990
PALMER'S FORMER PITCHING COACH

JIM PALMER 64

Every Jim Palmer pitch was a poetic revelation, from the perfectly fluid motion, traditional high leg kick and effortless delivery right down to its explosive conclusion. But everything else about the big righthander was delivered with a rough edge, from his outspoken, candid and articulate views on life in general to his frustrating complaints and verbal exchanges with Baltimore manager Earl Weaver.

On the field, the strikingly handsome New Yorker was the American League's most dominating pitcher of the 1970s, a 268-game winner over a 19-season career that started with the Orioles in 1965. Off the field, he was impetuous and unpredictable, a sometimes-aloof perfectionist who frustrated Weaver, teammates and fans with a never-ending stream of mysterious ailments that sometimes kept him off the mound.

Palmer's pitching style was determined by a rotator-cuff injury that cut him down after the 1966 World Series and cost him almost two full seasons. When he returned in 1969, he had transformed from a straight power pitcher into a power/finesse artist who could paint the corners with his still

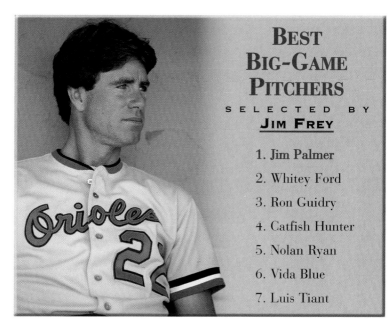

dominant fastball, a sharp-breaking curve and a nasty changeup. Armed and dangerous once more, Palmer proceeded to carve out eight 20-win seasons over a nine-year stretch while winning three Cy Young Awards and six All-Star selections. He was the ace of a powerful 1971 Orioles staff that featured a record-tying four 20-game winners.

Palmer's ledger also included an 8-3 postseason record in six A.L. Championship Series and six World Series, three of which the Orioles won. But success didn't stop the verbal war with Weaver, who prodded Palmer about imagined injuries. "The only thing Weaver knows about pitching is that he couldn't hit it," Palmer would quip in typical response.

BEST BIG-GAME PITCHERS

SELECTED BY **JIM FREY**

1. Jim Palmer
2. Whitey Ford
3. Ron Guidry
4. Catfish Hunter
5. Nolan Ryan
6. Vida Blue
7. Luis Tiant

65 MICKEY COCHRANE

The first thing you noticed about Mickey Cochrane was his ears, ham-size protrusions with funny little points that had to tempt baseball's hard-core bench jockeys. The second thing was the respect he commanded—ears and all—as one of the grittiest and smartest leaders the game has produced. Cochrane was equal parts fascinating, contradictory and puzzling in his never-wavering dedication to—and obsession for—winning.

Baseball old-timers remember him as the best of the Depression-era catchers, the heart and soul of a Connie Mack Philadelphia Athletics machine that captured three straight American League pennants and consecutive World Series titles from 1929 to 1931. Others recall the intense, driven player/manager of a Detroit team that won two straight pennants and one World Series in 1934 and 1935.

Cochrane, both player and manager, was a whirling dervish, a savvy student who never stopped looking for an edge that could mean the difference between winning and losing. Nobody took defeat harder and that was reflected by the way he played, the caged-tiger manner in which he prowled the dugout and

the demands he made on teammates. The emotion he invested in every game, every pitch, was complemented by a defensive genius, an outstanding lefthanded bat that produced a .320 career average and surprising speed that allowed him to perform occasional leadoff duties.

The emotional peaks and valleys took their toll on Cochrane in 1936 when, two years after winning the A.L. MVP award, he suffered a mid-season nervous breakdown. In the spring of 1937, a pitch from New York's Bump Hadley beaned Cochrane, fracturing his skull in three places and prematurely ending his playing career in its 13th season. Cochrane's on-field association ended in August of 1938 when he was replaced as manager.

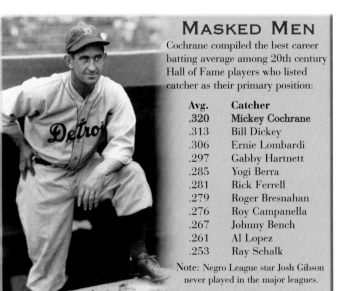

MASKED MEN

Cochrane compiled the best career batting average among 20th century Hall of Fame players who listed catcher as their primary position:

Avg.	Catcher
.320	**Mickey Cochrane**
.313	Bill Dickey
.306	Ernie Lombardi
.297	Gabby Hartnett
.285	Yogi Berra
.281	Rick Ferrell
.279	Roger Bresnahan
.276	Roy Campanella
.267	Johnny Bench
.261	Al Lopez
.253	Ray Schalk

Note: Negro League star Josh Gibson never played in the major leagues.

" HE HAD CATCHING INTUITION,
A FLAIR FOR OUTGUESSING THE OTHER SIDE.
TY COBB WEARING A MASK."

CONNIE MACK

66 COOL PAPA BELL

N o, Cool Papa Bell could not hit the wall switch and hop into bed before the light went out. And, no, he never hit a ball through the pitcher's legs and got hit by it while sliding into second base. But the point of these exaggerations should not be lost on the modern baseball fan: Bell was fast, very fast, possibly faster than any player in history.

Like fellow Negro League stars Josh Gibson, Buck Leonard and Oscar Charleston, however, Bell never got to show how fast at the major league level. But he did perform in enough barnstorming games against big-league players to make an impression. "He could run like a deer," marveled Frank Frisch. "The smoothest center fielder I've ever seen," said Paul Waner. Said Pie Traynor: "He'd steal the pitcher's pants."

Bell, a stringbean 6-footer who weighed only 143 pounds, wielded his speed like a club over a two-decade-plus career that started in 1922. The switch hitter slashed and poked balls through the infield and placed bunts as if he had the ball on a string.

Legend has it Bell never batted below .308 and most of his averages were in the .350-plus range. But the real damage came after Bell got on base and the embellishments range from the almost-believable 175 steals in one season to two steals on one pitch.

Bell's aggressive play for the St. Louis Stars, Pittsburgh Crawfords and Homestead Grays belied the laid-back, affable personality that made him one of the most popular players on the Negro League circuit. His baserunning drew comparisons to the reckless daring of Ty Cobb, his hitting style favored Willie Keeler and his shallow-playing, go-get-'em defensive prowess reminded many of Tris Speaker. Such lofty comparisons helped Bell gain Hall of Fame recognition in 1974.

STAR POWER

When Major League Baseball staged its first All-Star Game in 1933, the American and National league teams featured 17 players who would go on to Hall of Fame distinction. When the Negro Leagues staged their first All-Star Game that same season in the same park—14 years before the modern color line would be broken—six future Hall of Famers competed for the East and West squads, including Bell, who was the first batter in the inaugural classic:

East

Player	Team	Pos.
Cool Papa Bell	Pittsburgh	CF
Oscar Charleston	Pittsburgh	1B
Josh Gibson	Pittsburgh	C
Judy Johnson	Pittsburgh	3B

West

Player	Team	Pos.
Willie Wells	Chicago	SS
Bill "Willie" Foster	Chicago	P

"COOL PAPA WAS ONE OF THE
MOST MAGICAL PLAYERS I'VE EVER SEEN."

BILL VEECK

67 OSCAR CHARLESTON

His name rolled off the tongue and his game rolled off the memory of everybody who saw him play. Oscar McKinley Charleston was considered by many the greatest all-around player in Negro League history. John McGraw, the managerial brain behind the New York Giants for more than a quarter century, disagreed. McGraw called Charleston the greatest player he had ever seen—in any league.

McGraw did not offer such praise freely. What he saw in Charleston was a five-tool star who combined the speed, savvy and baserunning meanness of Ty Cobb, the hitting and center field defense of Tris Speaker and the magnetic showmanship of Babe Ruth. One minute he was clowning for the kids and women who flocked to see him play; the next he was performing with a savage determination and obsession for winning.

Charleston even was built like Ruth—a 5-11, 190-pound body with a barrel chest, sizable paunch and spindly legs. He hit for both power and average from a left-handed stance, seldom dipping under the .350 mark. He could be borderline cruel when running the bases, his spikes cutting a bloody path through anybody who stood in his way. But he was at his entertaining best when playing defense, stationing himself behind second base and daring anybody to hit a ball over his head.

When opportunities arose, Charleston would turn a back flip before making a catch or take an acrobatic tumble—anything to please the crowd. Charleston brought that zest to the Negro League product for more than 30 seasons in a career that began in 1915 and touched four decades with 11 different teams. He retired as a player/manager at age 48 in 1944, three years before Jackie Robinson broke the major league color barrier.

OVERDUE RECOGNITION

In 1976, Charleston took his place among the 14 former Negro League stars and officials who have been added to the Hall of Fame since 1971. Jackie Robinson and Larry Doby, who spent most of their careers in the major leagues after short Negro League stints, are not included on the list:

Name	Induction Year
Satchel Paige	1971
Josh Gibson	1972
Buck Leonard	1972
Monte Irvin	1973
Cool Papa Bell	**1974**
Judy Johnson	1975
Oscar Charleston	1976
Martin Dihigo	1977
John Henry Lloyd	1977
Rube Foster	1981
Ray Dandridge	1987
Leon Day	1995
Bill Foster	1996
Joe Rogan	1998

"I COULD OUTRUN CHARLESTON A BIT
AND MAYBE OTHERS MIGHT DO THIS
OR THAT BETTER THAN HIM. BUT
PUTTING IT ALL TOGETHER—THE
ABILITY TO HIT, RUN, FIELD, THROW
AND HIT FOR POWER—HE WAS THE
BEST I EVER SAW."

COOL PAPA BELL

THE SPORTING NEWS, 1976

"EDDIE WAS ONE OF THE SMARTEST LEFT-HANDED PITCHERS IN BASEBALL. HE WAS A MASTER OF THE CROSSFIRE DELIVERY AND THAT WAS ONE OF HIS BIG ASSETS."

CONNIE MACK
THE SPORTING NEWS, 1926

EDDIE PLANK

68

atching Eddie Plank work was like watching grass grow. He was a frustrating anomaly in the fast-paced baseball world of the early 20th century. In an era of no-wasted-motion efficiency and two-hour games, Plank fought a war of attrition that helped him post 326 victories, most of them for Connie Mack-coached Philadelphia Athletics teams that won six American League pennants from 1901 to 1914.

The somber-looking lefthander would hitch his cap, tug at his belt, inch forward, inch backward, step off the rubber and fidget in numerous other ways before delivering a pitch to the waiting batter. Hitters facing Plank, not familiar with such brazen delay tactics, would fume and fret before chasing an intentionally bad pitch with predictable results. Plank also talked to himself in a distinctive nasal tone that could be heard in both dugouts.

But Plank was much more than psychological gamesmanship. He also was a fierce competitor who attacked hitters with a better-than-average fastball, a good curve and uncanny control that allowed him to work to spots, making them chase the pitches he wanted. Plank also went after lefthanded batters with a devastating crossfire pitch—a wicked sidearm delivery that appeared to be coming from first base—and further helped his cause with a runner-freezing pickoff motion.

The strong-jawed, no-nonsense Plank, who graduated from Gettysburg College before pitching his first major league game at age 25, converted his unusual pitching style into eight 20-victory seasons, including a 21-win 1915 campaign for St. Louis in the outlaw Federal League. He also carved out an impressive 1.15 ERA over seven games and 54 $^2/_3$ innings in four World Series, even though his hard-luck record was only 2-5. Plank still owns many pitching records in the long history of the Athletics franchise.

STRAIGHT A'S

Anybody who wonders where Plank rates in the long history of Athletics baseball needs only check out the numbers through 1997:

Category	Rank	Total
Wins	1st	284
Losses	1st	162
Innings	1st	3,860.2
ERA	3rd	2.39
Strikeouts	1st	1,985
Walks	1st	913
Games	2nd	524
Shutouts	1st	59

"EVERY TIME HARMON COMES TO THE PLATE, HE IS DANGEROUS.
HE IS AS GOOD A CLUTCH HITTER AS THERE IS IN THE LEAGUE.
I HAVE MORE RESPECT FOR HIM THAN ANYONE."

BOOG POWELL
FORMER ORIOLES SLUGGER

THE SPORTING NEWS, 1969

HARMON KILLEBREW 69

He was raw power, 210 pounds of muscle crammed into a 5-11 frame. The thick legs supported a barrel chest and shoulders that looked like something right out of a blacksmith's shop. Harmon Killebrew was the prototypical baseball slugger, the kind of all-or-nothing home run hitter who found acclaim in the power-crazy 1950s and '60s.

As a home run hitter, Killebrew was very successful. He hit 573, fifth on the all-time list, topped the 40 plateau eight times and captured six American League homer titles over a 22-year career, 21 of which were spent with a Minnesota Twins franchise that shifted from Washington in 1961. The balding, round-faced Killebrew did not hit many line drives—most of his home runs were towering fly balls that seemed to soar into the stands anywhere from the right center-field gap to the left-field line.

Killebrew, a right-handed hitter with a big swing, was slow afoot and that was a factor in his .256 career average. It also contributed to his inability to settle into a defensive position. Killebrew shuttled throughout his career among first base, third base and left field, but always performed solidly and without complaint.

That was typical for the gentle giant who started his career as a painfully shy rookie in 1954 and retired more than two decades later as a Minnesota icon. In between, Killebrew performed cleanup duty for strong Twins teams that lost to Los Angeles in the 1965 World Series and claimed West Division titles in 1969 and '70. With Cesar Tovar, Rod Carew and Tony Oliva hitting in front of him, Killebrew also claimed three RBI titles and 1969 A.L. MVP distinction after a 49-homer, 140-RBI performance.

LONGEST HITTERS
SELECTED BY WILLIE McCOVEY

1. Willie Stargell
2. Dick Allen
3. Mickey Mantle
4. Luke Easter
5. Jim Ray Hart
6. Frank Howard
7. Dick Stuart
8. Harmon Killebrew
9. Jimmy Wynn
10. Jim Gentile

70 PIE TRAYNOR

He was tall, rangy and broad in the shoulders, an unlikely candidate for baseball immortality. But anybody who watched Pie Traynor perform his third base magic was overpowered by the experience. Lightning-quick reflexes, long, supple arms and an unfailingly accurate throw helped him set the lofty standard by which future generations of defensive third basemen would be judged.

Traynor drew his first defensive raves when he took over as Pittsburgh's regular third baseman in 1922. National League players and managers had never seen anybody quite like him. Traynor would range far to his left, cutting off balls that normally skipped past overextended shortstops, or he would discourage bunters with his hard-charging gracefulness. But he was at his best on balls hit over the bag, making lunging stops and equally acrobatic throws from awkward positions. He occasionally snared potential doubles with his bare hand, making an amazing play look easy.

"Hornsby doubled down the left field line, but Traynor threw him out," was the joke that circulated through N.L. cities. And long-time New York manager John McGraw,

moved by Traynor's incredible defense against his Giants, called him the greatest team player he had ever seen. But Traynor was more than just a pretty glove. He was a dangerous righthanded hitter who compiled a .320 career average, including a 1923 season in which he batted .338 with 208 hits, 101 RBIs and 108 runs scored.

Traynor, though easy-going and affable, often complained that his hitting was overshadowed by his fielding, but that might have been because he played in an offensive-minded era and seldom hit home runs. His 17-year career, which ended as a player/manager in 1937, included two World Series rings, one from the Pirates' 1925 winner over Washington.

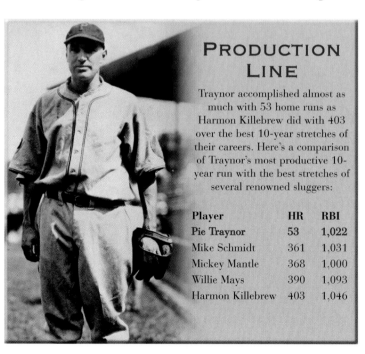

PRODUCTION LINE

Traynor accomplished almost as much with 53 home runs as Harmon Killebrew did with 403 over the best 10-year stretches of their careers. Here's a comparison of Traynor's most productive 10-year run with the best stretches of several renowned sluggers:

Player	HR	RBI
Pie Traynor	53	1,022
Mike Schmidt	361	1,031
Mickey Mantle	368	1,000
Willie Mays	390	1,093
Harmon Killebrew	403	1,046

"IF I WERE TO PICK THE GREATEST TEAM PLAYER IN BASEBALL TODAY—AND I HAVE SOME OF THE GREATS ON MY OWN CLUB—I WOULD HAVE TO PICK PIE TRAYNOR."

JOHN McGRAW

THE SPORTING NEWS, 1929

"PUT YOUR CLUB A RUN AHEAD IN THE LATER INNINGS
AND MARICHAL IS THE GREATEST PITCHER I EVER SAW."

ALVIN DARK, 1963

FORMER GIANTS MANAGER

JUAN MARICHAL 71

His left leg rose up ... up ... up, until his foot was suspended over his head. Then the real fun began: His leg, his right arm, his entire body swept forward in a blur and the ball swept toward home plate with unpredictable velocity and movement. Hitting against Juan Marichal was like trying to grab a fish out of a stream.

That's what it must have been like for the Philadelphia Phillies when the 22-year-old Dominican righthander made his major league debut in 1960 with a one-hit shutout. And that's what it must have been like throughout the 1960s as Marichal won 191 games, more than any other major league pitcher. He was the ace for a San Francisco Giants team that won one pennant and annually battled the Los Angeles Dodgers and St. Louis Cardinals for N.L. superiority.

The name of Marichal's game was confidence and control. He would throw five basic pitches, but never at the same speed or with the same motion. The count was inconsequential because Marichal had the uncanny knack for painting the corner with everything. Batters could not guess and their frustration was exacerbated by the impish grin that lit up his cherubic face and the child-like playfulness that always accompanied him to the mound.

Marichal's only weakness was an emotional fire that burned just under the surface of his outwardly calm demeanor. That emotion erupted in a 1965 bat-swinging brawl during which Marichal clubbed Dodgers catcher John Roseboro and put an indelible black mark on his image. But nothing could tarnish the .631 winning percentage (243-142) and 2.89 ERA he compiled over a 16-year career that included six 20-win seasons before ending in 1975.

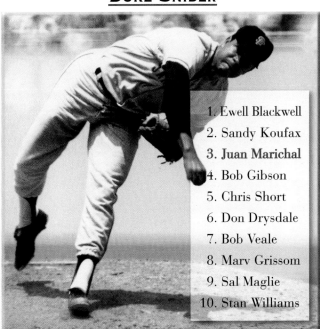

MOST-INTIMIDATING PITCHERS
S E L E C T E D   B Y
DUKE SNIDER

1. Ewell Blackwell
2. Sandy Koufax
3. Juan Marichal
4. Bob Gibson
5. Chris Short
6. Don Drysdale
7. Bob Veale
8. Marv Grissom
9. Sal Maglie
10. Stan Williams

" I'M A TED WILLIAMS GUY, BUT I THINK YAZ WILL GO DOWN
AS THE BEST PLAYER IN RED SOX HISTORY."

JOHNNY PESKY, 1979
WILLIAMS' LONGTIME TEAMMATE

CARL YASTRZEMSKI 72

His career was filled with Hall of Fame accomplishments. But nobody had to work harder for his rewards than Carl Yastrzemski. As keeper of the left field tradition at Boston's Fenway Park for 23 seasons, Yaz was equal parts hero and goat—and he never seemed to have the fun that should have accompanied his considerable accomplishments.

Yastrzemski's often-strained relationship with Red Sox fans could be traced directly to 1961, when he accepted the left field baton passed to him by Boston icon Ted Williams. The Fenway faithful were skeptical when Yaz produced, quick to boo when he didn't. The 5-11 New Yorker didn't understand their reluctance to embrace a player who would claim among his career achievements 3,419 hits, 452 home runs, a Triple Crown, an American League MVP award, seven Gold Gloves, 18 All-Star selections and three batting titles.

Unlike the more natural hitters of the 1960s and '70s, Yaz was a grinder who spent hours in the batting cage and studied the game with a dedication few players could claim. As a left-handed batter with an upright stance and a corkscrew swing that slashed line drives to any section of the park, he was devastating in the clutch. When things were going right, Yaz was easy to live with; when they weren't, he was moody and distant. But he never stopped working—especially on his defense as protector of Fenway's Green Monster left-field wall.

Yaz's pinnacle season came in 1967, when he helped fuel Boston's Impossible Dream pennant with the last Triple Crown in baseball history—a .326, 44-homer, 121-RBI masterpiece. He retired in 1983 with a .285 career average and distinction as the first A.L. player to amass 400 home runs and 3,000 hits.

BEST CLUTCH HITTERS
SELECTED BY
DICK WILLIAMS

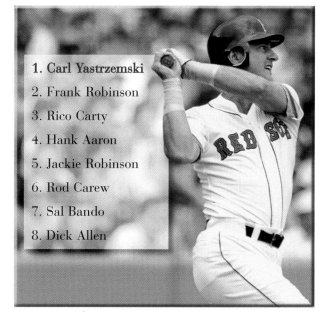

1. Carl Yastrzemski
2. Frank Robinson
3. Rico Carty
4. Hank Aaron
5. Jackie Robinson
6. Rod Carew
7. Sal Bando
8. Dick Allen

73 LEFTY GOMEZ

His fastballs zipped across the plate with the same accuracy his one-liners zipped across the locker room. Lefty Gomez was masterful, whether serving as court jester or pitching ace for the New York Yankees' World Series machine of the 1930s. Equal parts humorist and pitcher, El Goofy brought fun and personality to a sport that sometimes took itself too seriously.

Gomez was a high-kicking 6-2 lefthander who joined the Yankees as a 150-pound beanpole in 1930 and never weighed more than 175. But his fastball, powered by well-developed shoulder muscles, was one of the best in the game and he mesmerized hitters with a slow curve that served as his strikeout pitch. Backed by a lineup featuring Babe Ruth, Lou Gehrig and later Joe DiMaggio, he powered his way to four 20-win seasons, including a 26-5, 2.33-ERA masterpiece in 1934.

But the Gomez legend was built around the happy-go-lucky atmosphere he brought to the field. He had a special rapport with Ruth, who kidded and prodded Gomez relentlessly about his weak hitting. The high-strung Gomez, who drove manager Joe McCarthy batty with his dugout pacing and nervous energy, was famous for his one-line quips, locker-room pranks and goofy on-field antics, such as the tense World Series moment in 1936 when he stepped off the mound to watch a plane fly overhead.

But he also was known as one of the best big-game pitchers in the game, a reputation enhanced by his 6-0 record in five World Series and 3-1 record in seven All-Star Games. Gomez's Hall of Fame career was cut short by a series of arm problems that limited him to 24 victories over his final four seasons and a 189-102 final mark.

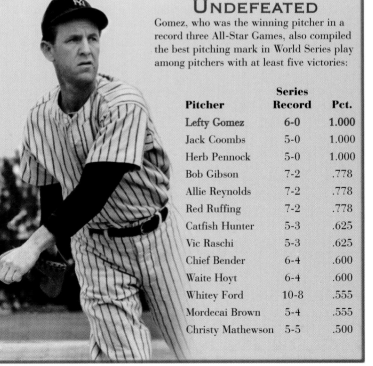

UNDEFEATED

Gomez, who was the winning pitcher in a record three All-Star Games, also compiled the best pitching mark in World Series play among pitchers with at least five victories:

Pitcher	Series Record	Pct.
Lefty Gomez	6-0	1.000
Jack Coombs	5-0	1.000
Herb Pennock	5-0	1.000
Bob Gibson	7-2	.778
Allie Reynolds	7-2	.778
Red Ruffing	7-2	.778
Catfish Hunter	5-3	.625
Vic Raschi	5-3	.625
Chief Bender	6-4	.600
Waite Hoyt	6-4	.600
Whitey Ford	10-8	.555
Mordecai Brown	5-4	.555
Christy Mathewson	5-5	.500

"GOMEZ SHOWED ME MORE SPEED THAN ANY MAN I EVER HAD CAUGHT BEFORE. HE MADE THAT BALL BURN INTO MY MITT. I WONDER WHERE THAT SKINNY GUY GETS ALL OF HIS SPEED."

BILL DICKEY, 1932

74 ROBIN ROBERTS

he first distressing signs came in 1956, the year Robin Roberts became a baseball mortal. The strong right arm that had produced six consecutive 20-win, 300-inning seasons couldn't deliver fastballs with quite the same gusto or quite the same control. The legs tired quicker, the once-durable body just would not cooperate. What had started as a race for Hall of Fame glory suddenly became a struggle for survival.

It's safe to say that Roberts was remarkable—perhaps as good as any pitcher over the second half century—for that six-season stretch: 138 wins, 1,937 $^2/_3$ innings, 161 complete games in 232 starts. And the temptation to regain the World Series spotlight was too strong for a downtrodden Philadelphia Phillies franchise that had not qualified for postseason play in 35 years. Roberts appeared to be a savior in 1950 when the Whiz Kids finally ended that jinx and his stature rose even more two years later when he posted a dazzling 28-7 record.

The key to Roberts' success was an overpowering fastball delivered with pinpoint control from a smooth, almost-effortless motion. It was difficult for batters to time the speed of a ball that literally slid across the plate. A so-so curve was merely window dressing and a cool, calculating demeanor masked an intense competitive fire. Roberts was ready and willing to take the mound at a moment's notice, even out of the bullpen between starts.

Roberts paid for that work ethic over the second half of a 19-year career that ended with a 286-245 record—179 of those victories coming before age 30. He also ended up with the dubious all-time record of 505 home runs allowed, a mark that can be attributed to the outstanding control that allowed confident hitters to dig in at the plate.

HARDEST-THROWING PITCHERS
SELECTED BY
STAN MUSIAL

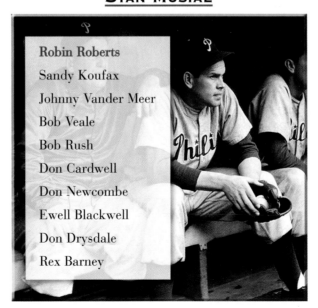

Robin Roberts
Sandy Koufax
Johnny Vander Meer
Bob Veale
Bob Rush
Don Cardwell
Don Newcombe
Ewell Blackwell
Don Drysdale
Rex Barney

"Robby's fastball seems to get up to the plate an inviting appetizer, and then suddenly skids across the strike zone as if on a cake of ice."

Red Schoendienst, 1956

" KEEP YOUR EYE CLEAR AND HIT 'EM WHERE THEY AIN'T."

WILLIE KEELER

WHEN ASKED HIS SECRET TO GREAT HITTING

WILLIE KEELER

75

He was a 5-4 $^1/_2$, 140-pound package of baseball dynamite. Light Willie Keeler's fuse and watch him run around the bases. What Wee Willie lacked in size and brawn he more than made up for with an explosive style that frustrated opposing pitchers and endeared him to fans of the dead-ball era.

Keeler's game was speed and he quickly recognized the adjustments he would need to keep up with the big boys. While others were trying to drive the ball into the outfield, Wee Willie developed a style that would make him the scourge of the National League. He choked up midway on his 29-ounce bat and used it expertly while placing bunts, tapping Baltimore-chop grounders over charging infielders and dropping shallow fly balls into the outfield. When outfielders played shallow to stop that strategy, Keeler had enough power to drive the ball over their head.

Off the field, Keeler was painfully shy, quiet and always polite, obviously embarrassed by his diminutive size. But on the field, he was an aggressive pioneer,

maybe baseball's first scientific hitter. And when he reached base, he used his speed like a club against distracted defenses. Not only did he steal 495 bases over his 19-year career, he combined with Baltimore leadoff man John McGraw to invent the hit-and-run play.

Keeler's greatest seasons were spent as a go-get-'em right fielder on the Orioles' pennant-winning teams of the late 1890s, but he remained a force well into the 20th century—first for the N.L.'s Brooklyn team, then for the New York Highlanders of the new American League. Keeler, who completed his career in 1910 with a .341 average, was the first real superstar for a Highlanders franchise that went on to later and greater fame as the Yankees.

HOMEWARD BOUND

Through 1997, Keeler and Lou Gehrig shared the career record for most seasons with 200 or more hits AND 100 or more runs scored:

No.	Player
8	Lou Gehrig
8	Willie Keeler
7	Wade Boggs
7	Ty Cobb
7	Charley Gehringer
7	Paul Waner
6	Rogers Hornsby
6	Stan Musial
6	Pete Rose

1900s

	N.L.		A.L.
1B	Frank Chance	1B	Harry Davis
2B	Johnny Evers	2B	Nap Lajoie
3B	Tommy Leach	3B	Jimmy Collins
SS	Honus Wagner	SS	Bobby Wallace
OF	Ginger Beaumont	OF	Ty Cobb
OF	Fred Clarke	OF	Sam Crawford
OF	Cy Seymour	OF	Willie Keeler
C	Roger Bresnahan	C	Ossee Schreckengost
LHP	Noodles Hahn	LHP	Eddie Plank
RHP	Christy Mathewson	RHP	Cy Young
P	Joe McGinnity	P	Ed Walsh

1910s

	N.L.		A.L.
1B	Jake Daubert	1B	Stuffy McInnis
2B	Larry Doyle	2B	Eddie Collins
3B	Heinie Zimmerman	3B	Home Run Baker
SS	Honus Wagner	SS	Buck Weaver
OF	Max Carey	OF	Ty Cobb
OF	Sherry Magee	OF	Joe Jackson
OF	Wildfire Schulte	OF	Tris Speaker
C	Chief Meyers	C	Ray Schalk
LHP	Rube Marquard	LHP	Eddie Plank
RHP	Grover Alexander	RHP	Walter Johnson
P	Christy Mathewson	P	Ed Cicotte

1920s

	N.L.		A.L.
1B	Jim Bottomley	1B	George Sisler
2B	Rogers Hornsby	2B	Eddie Collins
3B	Pie Traynor	3B	Joe Dugan
SS	Rabbit Maranville	SS	Joe Sewell
OF	Ross Youngs	OF	Harry Heilmann
OF	Zack Wheat	OF	Babe Ruth
OF	Edd Roush	OF	Al Simmons
C	Jimmie Wilson	C	Mickey Cochrane
LHP	Eppa Rixey	LHP	Herb Pennock
RHP	Burleigh Grimes	RHP	Walter Johnson
P	Dazzy Vance	P	Waite Hoyt

TSN'S ALL-DE

1930s

	N.L.		A.L.
1B	Bill Terry	1B	Lou Gehrig
2B	Frank Frisch	2B	Charley Gehringer
3B	Pepper Martin	3B	Jimmie Foxx
SS	Arky Vaughan	SS	Joe Cronin
OF	Joe Medwick	OF	Joe DiMaggio
OF	Mel Ott	OF	Goose Goslin
OF	Paul Waner	OF	Al Simmons
C	Gabby Hartnett	C	Bill Dickey
LHP	Carl Hubbell	LHP	Lefty Grove
RHP	Dizzy Dean	RHP	Red Ruffing
P	Paul Derringer	P	Lefty Gomez

Ted Williams (left), Joe DiMaggio

1940s

	N.L.		A.L.
1B	Johnny Mize	1B	Rudy York
2B	Eddie Stanky	2B	Bobby Doerr
3B	Bob Elliott	3B	George Kell
SS	Pee Wee Reese	SS	Lou Boudreau
OF	Ralph Kiner	OF	Joe DiMaggio
OF	Stan Musial	OF	Tommy Henrich
OF	Enos Slaughter	OF	Ted Williams
C	Ernie Lombardi	C	Birdie Tebbetts
LHP	Harry Brecheen	LHP	Hal Newhouser
RHP	Rip Sewell	RHP	Bob Feller
P	Bucky Walters	P	Dizzy Trout

1950s

	N.L.		A.L.
1B	Stan Musial	1B	Mickey Vernon
2B	Jackie Robinson	2B	Nellie Fox
3B	Eddie Mathews	3B	Al Rosen
SS	Ernie Banks	SS	Harvey Kuenn
OF	Hank Aaron	OF	Larry Doby
OF	Willie Mays	OF	Mickey Mantle
OF	Duke Snider	OF	Ted Williams
C	Roy Campanella	C	Yogi Berra
LHP	Warren Spahn	LHP	Whitey Ford
RHP	Robin Roberts	RHP	Early Wynn
P	Lew Burdette	P	Bob Lemon

1960s

	N.L.		A.L.
1B	Willie McCovey	1B	Harmon Killebrew
2B	Pete Rose	2B	Bobby Richardson
3B	Ron Santo	3B	Brooks Robinson
SS	Maury Wills	SS	Luis Aparicio
OF	Hank Aaron	OF	Mickey Mantle
OF	Roberto Clemente	OF	Frank Robinson
OF	Willie Mays	OF	Carl Yastrzemski
C	Joe Torre	C	Bill Freehan
LHP	Sandy Koufax	LHP	Whitey Ford
RHP	Bob Gibson	RHP	Dean Chance
P	Juan Marichal	P	Hoyt Wilhelm

1970s

	N.L.		A.L.
1B	Willie Stargell	1B	George Scott
2B	Joe Morgan	2B	Rod Carew
3B	Mike Schmidt	3B	George Brett
SS	Dave Concepcion	SS	Mark Belanger
OF	Lou Brock	OF	Reggie Jackson
OF	Cesar Cedeno	OF	Jim Rice
OF	Pete Rose	OF	Carl Yastrzemski
C	Johnny Bench	C	Thurman Munson
LHP	Steve Carlton	LHP	Vida Blue
RHP	Tom Seaver	RHP	Jim Palmer
P	Don Sutton	P	Rollie Fingers

CADE TEAMS

1980s

	N.L.		A.L.
1B	Keith Hernandez	1B	Eddie Murray
2B	Ryne Sandberg	2B	Lou Whitaker
3B	Mike Schmidt	3B	George Brett
SS	Ozzie Smith	SS	Cal Ripken
OF	Tony Gwynn	OF	Rickey Henderson
OF	Dale Murphy	OF	Dave Winfield
OF	Tim Raines	OF	Robin Yount
C	Gary Carter	C	Carlton Fisk
LHP	Fernando Valenzuela	LHP	Ron Guidry
RHP	Nolan Ryan	RHP	Jack Morris
P	Lee Smith	P	Roger Clemens

1990s

	N.L.		A.L.
1B	Jeff Bagwell	1B	Frank Thomas
2B	Craig Biggio	2B	Roberto Alomar
3B	Matt Williams	3B	Paul Molitor
SS	Barry Larkin	SS	Cal Ripken
OF	Barry Bonds	OF	Joe Carter
OF	Tony Gwynn	OF	Juan Gonzalez
OF	Sammy Sosa	OF	Ken Griffey Jr.
C	Mike Piazza	C	Ivan Rodriguez
LHP	Tom Glavine	LHP	Randy Johnson
RHP	Greg Maddux	RHP	Roger Clemens
P	Randy Myers	P	Mike Mussina

76 AL KALINE

He guarded the right field tradition at Tiger Stadium like a jealous lover, much as former Detroit icon Ty Cobb had done more than four decades earlier. What Al Kaline might have lacked in color and charisma he more than made up for with hard work, persistence and all-around consistency. Kaline was the battery that juiced the Tigers' attack for 22 seasons and one of the premier defensive outfielders of the 1950s and 1960s.

Kaline was a graceful stylist who made the game look easy. Shy and unsmiling off the field, Kaline spoke volumes with an aggressive, always-heady performance that reflected an intense desire to succeed. The consistency that became a Kaline trademark was best reflected by the way he cut down runners with a strong, accurate arm and the diving, wall-banging defense that earned him 10 Gold Gloves and numerous stays on the disabled list.

Kaline, a righthanded hitter who made his big-league debut at the tender age of 18, used a feet-apart, Joe DiMaggio-like stance and lightning-quick wrists to slash line drives to all fields. He provided himself a lofty career standard in 1955 when, at age 20, he hit .340 and became the youngest batting champion in history. That early success saddled Kaline with great expectations he struggled throughout his career to fulfill, but a final .297 average, 399 home runs and 3,007 hits would suggest he more than succeeded. So would his reputation as one of the most-feared clutch hitters of his era.

Kaline, who achieved career success despite a childhood operation that forced him to compete with a deformed left foot, played in his only World Series in 1968, batting .379 in the Tigers' seven-game victory over the St. Louis Cardinals.

BEST CLUTCH HITTERS
SELECTED BY JIM FREGOSI

1. Mickey Mantle
2. Roy Sievers
3. Elston Howard
4. Al Kaline
5. Don Baylor
6. Willie Mays
7. Tommy Davis
8. Barry Bonds
9. Ken Griffey Jr.
10. Frank Robinson

"I'LL TAKE KALINE OVER MANTLE OR ANY OTHER YOUNG OUTFIELDER YOU CAN NAME. THIS KID IS GOING DOWN WITH THE GREAT ONES OF ALL TIME."

FRED HUTCHINSON, 1960

FORMER TIGERS MANAGER

"FOR MY MONEY, HE'S THE BEST PLAYER IN THE GAME TODAY. OTHER PEOPLE MAY DISAGREE, BUT IF YOU'RE ASKING ME WHAT PLAYER I'D WANT UP THERE TO WIN A GAME FOR ME, IT'S EDDIE MURRAY."

SPARKY ANDERSON, 1986

EDDIE MURRAY 77

It was easy to dismiss Eddie Murray as a secondary player in baseball's superstar cast. That's just the way the quiet, brooding first baseman wanted it. But Murray's seeming indifference couldn't mask the outstanding numbers he compiled over 21 major league seasons and his reign as the only switch hitter to achieve both 3,000 hits and 500 home runs probably will be a long one.

Murray, shy and distrustful, played the game with a perpetual scowl, a facade that only teammates and close friends were allowed to penetrate. But those who did discovered a warm, hard-working, no-nonsense craftsman with a disdain for the spotlight, a smooth glove and a lethal swing from either side of the plate. What the 6-2, 210-pound Los Angeles kid lacked in media-friendly charisma he more than made up for with an intense desire to succeed and his ability to perform in the clutch.

The intimidating demeanor helped Murray thrive for 12 seasons in a Good Oriole, Bad Oriole combination with Baltimore shortstop Cal Ripken. While the clean-shaven Ripken won the hearts of Orioles fans with his durable consistency,

Murray played the role of enforcer—an image perpetuated by his crouched, uncoiling lefthanded stance. The Ripken-Murray-led Orioles won a World Series championship in 1983.

Murray, a three-time Gold Glove winner and seven-time All-Star selection before leaving Baltimore after the 1988 season, made hired-gun stops in Los Angeles, New York, Cleveland and Anaheim before retiring in 1997 as one of the two best switch hitters in history. Murray's 3,255 career hits rank No. 1 all-time among switch hitters and only former New York Yankees great Mickey Mantle hit more than Murray's 504 homers. Murray hit home runs from both sides of the plate in the same game 11 times, another record.

SWITCHING CHANNELS

Only Mickey Mantle hit more switch-hit home runs than Murray. Totals are through the 1997 season:

HR	Player
536	Mickey Mantle
504	Eddie Murray
328	Chili Davis
314	Reggie Smith
262	Bobby Bonilla
248	Ted Simmons
246	Ken Singleton
245	Mickey Tettleton
235	Ruben Sierra
228	Howard Johnson

"He loves to play. He loves to compete. And you can't compete from the dugout."

MIKE FLANAGAN
ORIOLES PITCHING COACH

THE SPORTING NEWS, 1995

CAL RIPKEN 78

The graying hair is a result of age and the intense media scrutiny he has endured. It's also a byproduct of the incredible 14-year endurance test that will forever be the measure of Cal Ripken's career. As Ripken's consecutive-games record continues to grow and he inches methodically toward 3,000 hits, his claim as one of the best all-around shortstops to play the game becomes more secure.

Nobody could have envisioned Ripken as a threat to Lou Gehrig's 2,130 consecutive-games record when he broke in as an oversized shortstop in 1981. But a Rookie of the Year 1982 season was followed by a 27-homer, 102-RBI, MVP-winning 1983 and the quiet, no-nonsense Baltimore infielder was on his way.

As the long-expected shift to third base was put off season after season, Ripken moved gracefully around his shortstop position, never flashy but making every play look easy and even winning a pair of Gold Gloves. Mr. Dependable also was a constant threat at the plate, where he changed from stance to stance but still posted power and production numbers not associated with a middle infielder.

The line drive-hitting righthander topped 20 home runs in 10 straight seasons and 100 RBIs four times, combining with Eddie Murray to power the Orioles to a World Series championship in 1983.

But the Ripken legacy revolves around the Gehrig streak he shattered in 1995 when, before a national television audience and under the intense spotlight that had been focused on his every move for several years, he played in consecutive game No. 2,131. As the streak continued on past 2,500, the classy 15-time All-Star and two-time American League MVP finally made the defensive switch to third while taking his place atop most of Baltimore's key all-time statistical categories.

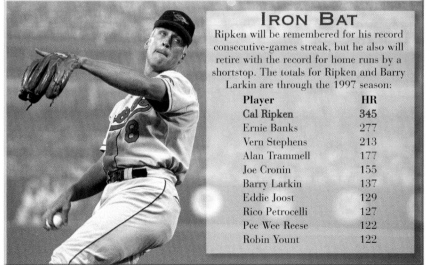

IRON BAT

Ripken will be remembered for his record consecutive-games streak, but he also will retire with the record for home runs by a shortstop. The totals for Ripken and Barry Larkin are through the 1997 season:

Player	HR
Cal Ripken	345
Ernie Banks	277
Vern Stephens	213
Alan Trammell	177
Joe Cronin	155
Barry Larkin	137
Eddie Joost	129
Rico Petrocelli	127
Pee Wee Reese	122
Robin Yount	122

79 JOE MEDWICK

I f Dizzy Dean was the heart of St. Louis' Gashouse Gang, Joe Medwick was its soul. He also was the enforcer for the colorful Cardinals who battled fate, opponents and each other during a raucous 1934 season that ended with a World Series championship. What the hard-edged left fielder couldn't conquer with his lusty bat, he often challenged with his equally dangerous fists.

Medwick was a perfect fit for baseball's rugged Depression-era style. Quick-tempered, he competed with an aggressive intensity that angered opponents and often befuddled his own teammates. "If you want to be a clown, join the circus," he told his cut-up teammates, and stories abound about his dugout and locker room battles with Dean, Rip Collins, Pepper Martin and other Gashouse buddies. But Medwick was at his dangerous best when slashing line drives with the big righthanded swing that spread terror throughout the National League.

The pitch didn't have to be good; it just had to be within reach. Medwick was like a machine in a four-season stretch from 1935-38, piling up 874 hits, leading the league in doubles and RBIs three times and capturing

an MVP. His .374, 31-homer, 154-RBI 1937 effort produced the last Triple Crown in N.L. history. Ducky—the nickname spoofed his duck-like walk—remained an offensive madman until 1940 when, shortly after he was traded to Brooklyn because of a salary dispute, former Cardinals teammate Bob Bowman drilled him in the head with a pitch, almost ending his career. Medwick came back to post solid numbers, but he never hit with the old passion.

Medwick is best remembered as the left fielder who had to be removed from the seventh game of the 1934 Series by commissioner Kenesaw Mountain Landis because he was being pelted with garbage by outraged Detroit fans in the Cardinals' 11-0 title-clinching win.

UP AND DOWN

Before he was beaned in 1940, Medwick ranked among the great hitters of Depression-era baseball. After the beaning, he wandered from team to team posting mediocre statistics:

Pre-Beaning (1932-39)

G	AB	R	H	HR	RBI	Avg.
1,084	4,420	771	1,492	145	873	.338

Post-Beaning (1940-48)

G	AB	R	H	HR	RBI	Avg.
900	3,215	427	979	60	510	.305

"He was the meanest, roughest guy you could imagine. He just stood up there and whaled everything within reach. Doubles, triples, home runs; he sprayed 'em all over every park. ..."

Leo Durocher, 1949

"FROM KANSAS CITY TO KANKAKEE AND BACK AGAIN, I AIN'T NEVER SEEN NOTHING LIKE (ROBINSON). AND THEN, WHEN YOU SEE HIM YOU DON'T BELIEVE IT."

CASEY STENGEL, 1974

BROOKS ROBINSON 80

The hunched shoulders and loping run made Brooks Robinson easy to spot. But it took a hot ground ball within hailing distance of third base to give him perspective. The eyes would flash, the reflexes would kick in and the glove would streak toward a white blur barely discernible to the human eye. Another accurate throw would complete another masterful play by baseball's "human vacuum cleaner."

Robinson's 23-year legacy was built around the scores of potential hits he stole from frustrated Baltimore opponents. And his record-tying 16 Gold Gloves are testimonials to the routine plays he always made and the tumbling, acrobatic gyrations he often pulled off with dramatic flair. Robinson, who made his Orioles debut in 1955 at age 18, was slow afoot and his arm was only average, but his reflexes and dexterity were exceptional and his quick release and throwing accuracy were uncanny.

Robinson will be remembered for his defense, but the righthanded punch and even-keeled leadership he added to the powerful Orioles' lineups of the 1960s and 1970s cannot be overlooked. A disciplined hitter with a team-first attitude, Robinson topped 20 home runs six times and earned an American League MVP with a .317, 118-RBI performance in 1964. He was especially dangerous in the clutch and a gracious demeanor lifted him to icon status among Baltimore fans.

The R&R combination of Brooks and Frank Robinson led the Orioles to four World Series and two championships. Brooks, an 18-time All-Star, put on a defensive clinic and claimed MVP honors in a five-game 1970 World Series, when he stole hit after hit from the disbelieving Reds. "The guy can field a ball with a pair of pliers," Cincinnati star Pete Rose grumbled, expressing the frustration felt by Robinson contemporaries for almost a quarter century.

BEST DEFENSIVE PLAYERS
SELECTED BY
DANNY OZARK

1. Gil Hodges
2. Luis Aparicio
3. **Brooks Robinson**
4. Willie Mays
5. Roberto Clemente
6. Mickey Mantle
7. Bill Mazeroski
8. Johnny Bench
9. Roger Maris
10. Jim Kaat

81 WILLIE STARGELL

The towering drives that registered 7s and 8s on baseball's richter scale provided a stark contrast to the gentle manner in which Willie Stargell practiced his craft. As a lumbering 6-3, 225-pound, bat-waving slugger, Stargell could be frightening. As the easy-going leader of Pittsburgh's clubhouse, he could be inspiring. Nobody combined these seemingly divergent qualities more effectively than the man young Pirates players came to know affectionately as "Pops."

Stargell was a classic power hitter. He stood deep in the box with feet spread far apart and attacked the pitch with a long, hard swing. The ball left his bat like a bazooka shot and he quickly gained a reputation for long home runs—two balls out of Dodger Stadium, seven out of Forbes Field, four into the upper deck at Three Rivers Stadium. In between his 475 career home runs and 1,936 strikeouts (No. 2 all-time), the seven-time All-Star collected enough hits to compile a solid .282 average over a 21-year career that began in 1962.

But the Stargell legacy is about much more than long homers and numbers. The fun-loving, quick-to-smile first baseman learned from early-career mentor Roberto Clemente and eventually became one of the most influential team leaders of the modern era. The Pirates captured the 1971 World Series with Clemente leading the charge, but the 1979 championship, fueled by Stargell's "We Are Family" approach, belonged to Pops.

First the 39-year-old Stargell claimed the National League co-MVP award with a 32-homer, 82-RBI performance. Then he earned NLCS MVP honors with a .455 average and two home runs in Pittsburgh's victory over Cincinnati. He completed his MVP triple when he batted .400 and hit a World Series-deciding home run in Game 7 against Baltimore.

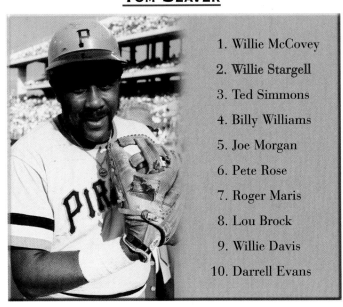

TOUGHEST LEFTHANDED HITTERS
SELECTED BY
TOM SEAVER

1. Willie McCovey
2. Willie Stargell
3. Ted Simmons
4. Billy Williams
5. Joe Morgan
6. Pete Rose
7. Roger Maris
8. Lou Brock
9. Willie Davis
10. Darrell Evans

"I NEVER HAVE SEEN
A BATTER WHO HITS THE
BALL ANY HARDER.
FOR SHEER CRASH OF BAT
MEETING BALL, STARGELL
SIMPLY IS THE BEST."

HARRY WALKER
FORMER PIRATES MANAGER
THE SPORTING NEWS, 1965

82 ED WALSH

He was strong, cocky and confident, qualities that served him well as one of the most prolific workhorse pitchers of the early 1900s. But a little less swagger and considerably more restraint might have prolonged Ed Walsh's fleeting moment in the spotlight and allowed him to challenge the career numbers posted by Christy Mathewson, Walter Johnson and other turn-of-the-century greats.

Walsh was a rubber-arm righthander and king of the legal spitballers. He also was a dapper, fun-loving, happy-go-lucky charmer who approached his work with youthful exuberance and defiance. An above-average fastball and mediocre curve got him to the major leagues in 1904, but it wasn't until he unleashed his devastating spitter in 1906 that he joined the baseball elite. His 17-13 record helped the Hitless Wonder White Sox defeat the powerful Cubs in the World Series.

Buoyed by that success and a spitball that broke sharply down, Walsh became a pitching machine, working his scheduled starts and providing between-start relief. The more work the better, and Walsh upped his win total to 24 in 1907 and

his innings count to 422$\frac{1}{3}$. That set the stage for one of the most prolific seasons in history, a 40-15, 42-complete game 1908 campaign in which he worked a modern-record 464 innings. Despite Walsh's yeoman effort, the White Sox could finish no better than third in the American League.

Walsh never reached that height again, but he did post consecutive 27-win records and completed a 168-112 seven-year run that included 2,526$\frac{1}{3}$ innings—an average of 361. Big Ed battled a tired arm for five more seasons, winning only 13 times and never again topping 100 innings. Walsh's 195-126 career mark was impressive, but the 1.82 ERA he posted over 14 seasons was the best in modern history.

FIVE-YEAR PLANS

Walsh, who delivered his spitball with gripping success, ranks among baseball's pitching elite when comparing top five single-season win totals:

Total	Name/Seasons
158	Christy Mathewson (37, 33, 31, 30, 27)
149	Grover Alexander (33, 31, 30, 28, 27)
149	Walter Johnson (36, 33, 28, 27, 25)
147	Joe McGinnity (35, 31, 28, 27, 26)
140	Cy Young (33, 32, 28, 26, 21)
136	**Ed Walsh (40, 27, 27, 24, 18)**
134	Jack Chesbro (41, 28, 23, 21, 21)
132	Lefty Grove (31, 28, 25, 24, 24)
128	Mordecai Brown (29, 27, 26, 25, 21)
124	Bob Feller (27, 26, 25, 24, 22)

" I COULD MAKE (THE SPITBALL) BREAK FOUR DIFFERENT WAYS—IN, OUT, UP OR DOWN. IT JUST DEPENDED ON HOW I DELIVERED THE BALL. I'D THROW EIGHT SPITBALLS OUT OF EVERY 10 PITCHES. A SPITBALL IS SO MUCH MORE EFFECTIVE THAN A CURVE BECAUSE IT BREAKS MORE SHARPLY."

ED WALSH, 1956

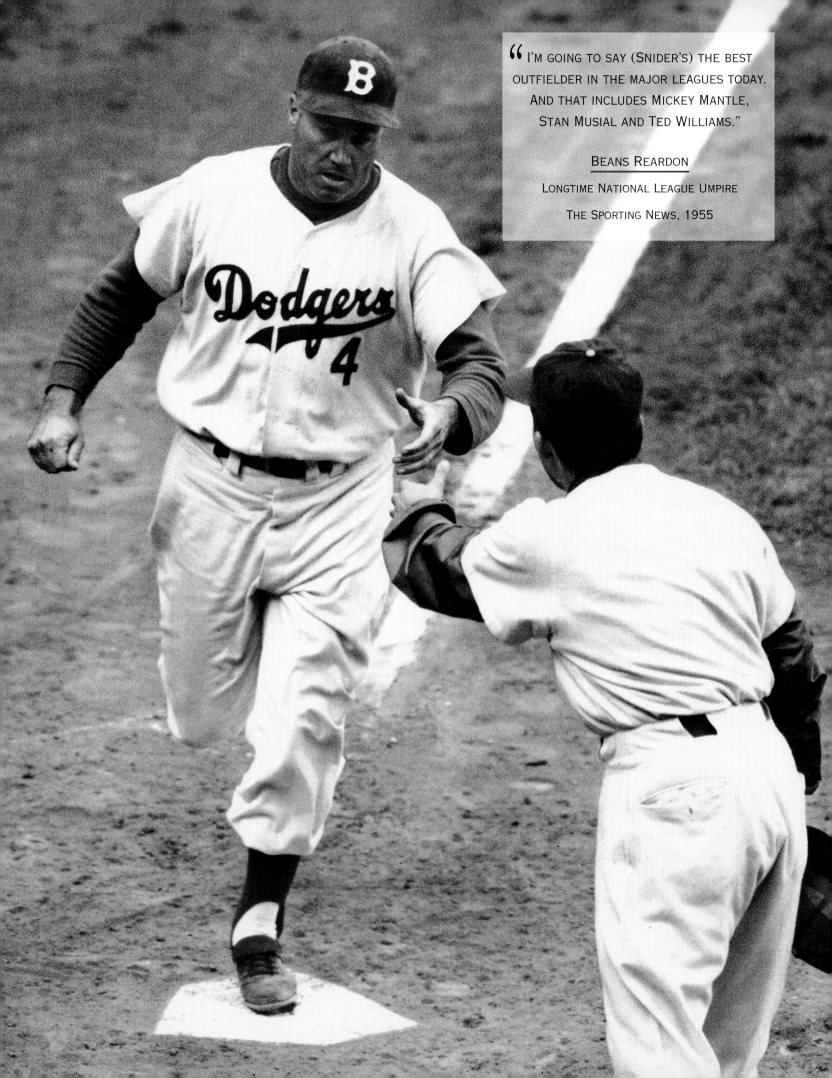

" I'M GOING TO SAY (SNIDER'S) THE BEST
OUTFIELDER IN THE MAJOR LEAGUES TODAY.
AND THAT INCLUDES MICKEY MANTLE,
STAN MUSIAL AND TED WILLIAMS."

BEANS REARDON
LONGTIME NATIONAL LEAGUE UMPIRE
THE SPORTING NEWS, 1955

DUKE SNIDER 83

He was the Duke of Flatbush, a Boy of Summer and a charter member of the Dem Bums fraternity that graced Brooklyn's Ebbets Field in the late 1940s and 1950s. And the image of a graceful, handsome young Duke Snider patrolling center field and driving pitches onto Bedford Avenue still burns deep in the Borough of Churches. Snider was the unofficial enforcer and most critically ana-lyzed enigma for a franchise that dominated the National League standings through most of his career.

The prematurely gray, free-swinging Snider, a speedy lefthanded pull hitter tailored for tiny Ebbets Field, was a power source who topped 40 home runs from 1953 to 1957 and averaged more than 100 RBIs over the same five-year stretch. He also was one of the best defensive outfielders in the game. But no matter how Snider pro-duced, he never could fully please demanding Brooklyn fans who thought he lacked the passion of his more intense Dodgers team-mates.

Part of the image problem resulted from Snider's tell-it-like-it-is bluntness and the inner rage he directed at his own failings. It also stemmed from a sensitivity fueled by constant compar-isons to two contemporary New York center fielders— Mickey Mantle and Willie Mays. But it's hard to knock Snider's .295 career average, 407 home runs and big-game efficiency—11 homers and 26 RBIs in six World Series, two of which resulted in Dodgers championships.

Snider, an eight-time All-Star, was a force through his Brooklyn career, but his hitting dropped off in 1958 when the Dodgers moved to his hometown of Los Angeles. Frustrated by the vast right center field dimensions of the Coliseum and playing without most of his Brooklyn teammates, Snider never topped 23 home runs or 88 RBIs again.

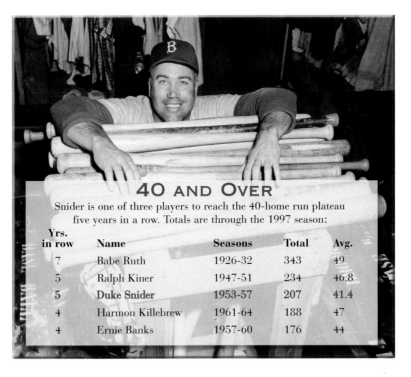

40 AND OVER

Snider is one of three players to reach the 40-home run plateau five years in a row. Totals are through the 1997 season:

Yrs. in row	Name	Seasons	Total	Avg.
7	Babe Ruth	1926-32	343	49
5	Ralph Kiner	1947-51	234	46.8
5	Duke Snider	1953-57	207	41.4
4	Harmon Killebrew	1961-64	188	47
4	Ernie Banks	1957-60	176	44

"A TREMENDOUS HITTER. HARDLY ANY PITCHERS
WHO PITCHED AGAINST (CRAWFORD) ARE STILL
ALIVE. HALF OF 'EM DIED OF HEART ATTACKS."

CASEY STENGEL, 1957

SAM CRAWFORD

84

Sam Crawford stood out like a sore thumb. The enormous shoulders, the muscular, well-conditioned body and the hard, menacing swing were futuristic illusions in a turn-of-the-century era that glorified its speedy contact hitters. Wahoo Sam (he was born and raised in Wahoo, Neb.) was more typical of the sluggers who would thrive after the 1920s and his contemporaries claimed he could have posted Babe Ruth-like home run totals if he had been born 20 years later.

So Crawford had to settle for a reputation as the hardest hitter of the dead-ball era. He stood erect in his lefthanded stance, feet spread, and whaled away at the offerings of pitchers he often intimidated. Many of his vicious line drives ended up in outfielders' gloves just short of the fence, but many others whistled into the gaps—and beyond. Crawford was not fast, but outstanding baserunning instincts allowed him to leg out an all-time record 309 triples, 14 more than longtime Detroit teammate Ty Cobb.

Center fielder Crawford and left fielder Cobb formed a formidable combination that fueled the Tigers to three consecutive American League pennants from 1907 to1909. But Crawford, the cleanup man, was overshadowed for most of his career by the fiery Cobb, who in turn resented Crawford's emotional connection with the fans of Detroit. But they performed well in tandem, Cobb as the instigator and Crawford as one of the most dangerous clutch hitters in the game.

Crawford, who began his career in 1899 with Cincinnati, became the first player to lead both leagues in home runs when he connected for 16 with the Reds in 1901 and seven in 1908 for the Tigers. He also was a .309 career hitter over a 19-year career that ended in 1917.

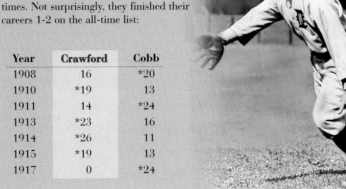

TRIPLE TROUBLE

From 1905 through 1917, their 13 seasons as Detroit outfield mates, either Crawford or Ty Cobb led the A.L. in triples seven times. Not surprisingly, they finished their careers 1-2 on the all-time list:

Year	Crawford	Cobb
1908	16	*20
1910	*19	13
1911	14	*24
1913	*23	16
1914	*26	11
1915	*19	13
1917	0	*24

85 DIZZY DEAN

He was the lovable, colorful, cornpone-spewing righthander who helped fuel the Gashouse Gang's success in the Depression-wracked 1930s. Dizzy Dean had the stuff of which legends are made, whether dazzling National League hitters with his powerful arm or sportswriters, teammates and fans with his braggadocio and glib tongue. Dean's supreme confidence could be annoying, but he backed up his boasts in a short-but-sweet career that ended all too prematurely because of an arm injury.

Ol' Diz, the self-ascribed moniker that reflected his poor Arkansas roots, was a baseball character. But he also was a strong-armed, iron-willed strikeout pitcher with a blazing fastball, a good curve and a nasty changeup. The always-smiling Dean fired his pitches with a smooth, fluid delivery and he fired barbs and gibes at hitters who let the good-natured ribbing add to their frustration.

Dean was the class of the N.L. from 1932, his first full big-league season, through 1936, a five-year stretch in which he won 120 games. He was a magnificent 30-7 in 1934 and combined with brother Paul, a 19-game winner, to lead the St. Louis Cardinals to a pennant and World Series victory over Detroit. The "Me 'n' Paul" Dean combination won four games in the World Series.

But Dizzy, who added 28 wins in 1935, saw his career turn dramatically in the 1937 All-Star Game when he was hit on the foot by a line drive. Trying to pitch with a broken toe, Dean altered his delivery and suffered an arm injury that limited him to 29 wins over his final six seasons with the Cardinals and Cubs.

Out of work at age 31, Dean went on to wow a second generation of baseball fans with the distinctive, fractured rhetoric he unleashed from the broadcast booth.

BROTHERLY LOVE

When Dizzy and Paul Dean combined for 49 wins in 1934, they set a single-season record no brother combination has been able to match. Here are the best seasons for 10 different brother duos through 1997:

Year	Brothers/Wins	Total
1934	Dean, Dizzy (30), Paul (19)	49
1970	Perry, Jim (24), Gaylord (23)	47
1979	Niekro, Phil (21), Joe (21)	42
1916	Coveleski, Harry (21), Stan (15)	36
1924	Barnes, Virgil (16), Jesse (15)	31
1995	Martinez, Ramon (17), Pedro (14)	31
1982	Forsch, Bob (15), Ken (13)	28
1977	Reuschel, Rick (20), Paul (5)	25
1907	Mathewson, Christy (24), Henry (0)	24
1988	Perez, Melido (12), Pascual (12)	24
1995	Maddux, Greg (19), Mike (5)	24

"GOING ANYWHERE WITH (DIZZY) WAS LIKE GOING WITH A BRASS BAND. HE HAD A GREAT SENSE OF HUMOR AND WAS JUST A VERY INTERESTING CHARACTER."

PHIL WRIGLEY

THE SPORTING NEWS, 1974

"I JUST LOVE WATCHING PUCKETT
PLAY. YOU CAN JUST SENSE HOW
MUCH HE ENJOYS THE GAME. IT OOZES
FROM HIM. BASEBALL NEEDS A LOT
MORE KIRBY PUCKETTS."

DICK WILLIAMS, 1987

LONGTIME MAJOR LEAGUE MANAGER

KIRBY PUCKETT 86

His smile brightened Minneapolis and his blazing bat lit up the American League for 12 enjoyable seasons. Charisma oozed out of Kirby Puckett's Smurfian 5-8 body like water out of a sponge. He brought effervescence, personality and success to a downtrodden Twins franchise while charming his way through a productive career cut short by a serious eye problem in 1996.

It was easy to love the barrel-chested, thick-necked Puckett, who signed autographs with the same enthusiasm that he drove line drives into the gap and chased down fly balls hit into his center-field domain. Fans and teammates were swept away by the quick smile; opposing pitchers were swept away by the quick righthanded swing that whipped through the ball from a crouching stance. Puckett was a classic bad-ball hitter who always seemed to drive the ball with authority.

He was at his defensive best when scaling the Metrodome's center-field fence to rob opposing hitters of home runs, a feat he pulled off with amazing regularity. He had the speed to cover the gaps and run the bases and the arm to throw out aggressive runners.

At his best, Puckett produced with machine-like precision from his No. 3 spot in the order. He topped 200 hits four years in a row and five times in seven years, winning a batting title in 1989. He was the offensive catalyst for Twins teams that won World Series titles in 1987 and 1991. But just before the 1996 season, Puckett woke up one morning with blurred vision in his right eye, a condition that later was diagnosed as glaucoma. He never played again. The 10-time All-Star finished with a .318 average and 2,304 hits—and status alongside Harmon Killebrew as the most popular players in Minnesota history.

A SMASH HIT

Puckett ranks among the all-time best batsmen when you add up hits recorded in the first 10 full seasons of their careers:

Player	Hits
Willie Keeler	2,065
Paul Waner	2,036
George Sisler	2,016
Stan Musial	2,003
Kirby Puckett	**1,996**
Al Simmons	1,996
Joe Medwick	1,967
Wade Boggs	1,965
Lou Gehrig	1,949
Pete Rose	1,922

"So many times I'll see the ball leave the bat and say, 'OK, that's a base hit.' And then somehow Ozzie will come up with it. A lot of the time I feel like standing out there and applauding with the rest of the fans. He's head and shoulders above every other shortstop."

Tommy Herr, 1987

Cardinals second baseman

OZZIE SMITH 87

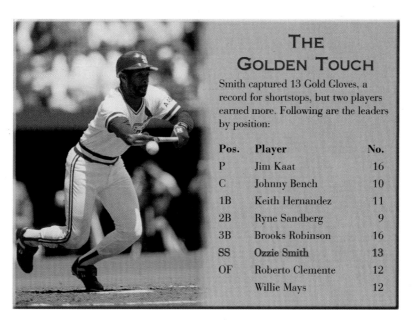

The "Oz-zie! Oz-zie! Oz-zie!" chants started the instant he raced to his shortstop position at St. Louis' Busch Stadium. He didn't even have to earn his daily ovations. The very thought of another sensational Ozzie Smith play was enough to electrify Cardinals fans, who have a history of tender relationships with the superstars they embrace.

Smith certainly qualified for that status. Supporters claim he was the best defensive shortstop in history; critics argue he was only one of the best. Suffice it to say few games were played without the Wizard of Oz flashing the acrobatic quickness that generated oohs and aahs usually reserved for offensive feats. Smith, who won 13 Gold Gloves, was the master at throwing on the run, whether racing behind second base or deep into the hole. He also had an uncanny knack for snaring balls with a dive, scrambling to his knees and throwing out startled runners. His range was incredible.

So was the work and determination Smith put into improving his offense. A low-.200 switch hitter in his first four seasons in San Diego, he raised his average consistently after a 1982 trade to St. Louis and finished his career as a consistent .280 threat—with 2,460 hits. Smith's ability to handle the bat and run the bases prompted promotion to the No. 2 slot in the order.

A big part of Smith's game was image, and he was as articulate in the locker room as he was with the glove. He was a dapper dresser with a ready smile and soft-spoken charm; he promoted himself well and was showered with adulation. The 14-time All-Star also was a leader for Cardinals teams that won four division titles, three National League pennants and one World Series before he retired after the 1996 season.

THE GOLDEN TOUCH

Smith captured 13 Gold Gloves, a record for shortstops, but two players earned more. Following are the leaders by position:

Pos.	Player	No.
P	Jim Kaat	16
C	Johnny Bench	10
1B	Keith Hernandez	11
2B	Ryne Sandberg	9
3B	Brooks Robinson	16
SS	Ozzie Smith	13
OF	Roberto Clemente	12
	Willie Mays	12

"MAYBE THERE NEVER WAS AND NEVER WILL BE A PERFECT BALLPLAYER. BUT LET ME ASK YOU THIS: WHAT WAS THERE FRANK FRISCH COULDN'T DO?"

JOE McCARTHY, 1962

FRANK FRISCH 88

He was the heart of the New York Giants' 1920s pennant-winning machine and the soul of St. Louis' Gashouse Gang in the 1930s. Frank Frisch was addicted to winning, a craving he filled with eight World Series appearances. As a hard-nosed second baseman and one of baseball's original switch hitters, he was a throwback to the intense, aggressive, daring, reckless style of baseball practiced at the turn of the century.

The stocky, strong-armed Frisch, a speedy three-sport star at Fordham University, never played a minor league game before stepping into a Giants lineup that produced four consecutive National League pennants—and two World Series championships—from 1921 to 1924. Frisch brought leadership to the field, whether knocking down hot grounders with his thick chest, diving in the dirt for balls hopelessly out of reach, running the bases with flawless instinct or baiting umpires and opponents with a razor-edged tongue.

Hitting from his natural left side, Frisch, his bat wagging, was aggressive and unpredictable. He was equally capable of dragging a bunt, punching an outside pitch into left field or driving a bases-loaded double into the gap. From the right side, Frisch had more power but was less aggressive.

Frisch was center stage in the shocking 1926 trade that sent him to St. Louis for Rogers Hornsby, one of the best hitters in the game. Frisch overcame fan resentment over the departure of the popular Hornsby to become the leader of Cardinals teams that won pennants in 1928 and 1930 and the player/manager of colorful Gashouse Gang crews that won World Series titles in 1931 and 1934.

Frisch, who compiled a .316 career average and 2,880 hits, was the first winner of the N.L. MVP award presented by the Baseball Writers' Association of America in 1931.

SERIES BUSINESS

Former Giants and Cardinals star Frisch ranks first among non-Yankees in six World Series categories and among the top 5 in four others:

First		Top 5	
Category	No.	Category	No.
Series	8	Triples	3
Games	50	Total bases	74
At-bats	197	Extra-base hits	13
Hits	58	Stolen bases	9
Singles	45		
Doubles	10		

"GOSLIN IS NOT ONLY OUR BEST HITTER,
BUT HE'S ONE OF THE GREATEST
NATURAL HITTERS IN THE LEAGUE."

BUCKY HARRIS, 1924
FORMER SENATORS PLAYER/MANAGER

GOOSE GOSLIN 89

He crowded the plate with a mocking defiance, daring pitchers to take their best shot. When they did, Goose Goslin would dust himself off, lean back over the plate and invite them to do it again. The fearless, hard-swinging lefthanded hitter believed that a fastball—anybody's fastball—was worth the inconvenience and he knew what to do when he got one to hit.

Goslin was first and foremost a hitter. He attacked the ball with vengeance, playing the role of enforcer for five World Series teams in an 18-year career that started in 1921 at Washington. He was a gap hitter with power, an extraordinary run-producer who topped the 100-RBI plateau 12 times. His .316 career average was highlighted by an American League-leading .379 mark in 1928.

The Goose, who ran with a palms-down sway that gave his stride the appearance of a duck-like waddle, was a night-life proponent and one of the more flamboyant players of the 1920s and '30s. His swing was so hard that he often ended up sitting in the dirt when he missed connections. A bulbous nose added to his colorful personna and he sometimes treated fly balls like hand grenades. Goslin worked hard and improved his defense over the years but, despite an outstanding arm, he never was known as a good left or right fielder.

He was, however, one of the most popular players in Washington and a World Series hero in Detroit, where he played from 1934 to 1937. Goslin hit seven home runs for the Senators in their three World Series (1924, '25 and '33) and his World Series-winning hit gave Detroit a 1935 championship.

SCORING POINTS

Goslin ranks among baseball's greatest run producers in an RBI-per-at-bat comparison based on 1,600 or more career RBIs:

Player	At-Bats	RBIs	Ratio
Babe Ruth	8,399	2,213	3.80
Lou Gehrig	8,001	1,995	4.01
Ted Williams	7,706	1,839	4.19
Jimmie Foxx	8,134	1,922	4.23
Al Simmons	8,759	1,827	4.79
Mel Ott	9,456	1,860	5.08
Goose Goslin	8,656	1,609	5.38
Hank Aaron	12,364	2,297	5.38
Frank Robinson	10,006	1,812	5.52
Stan Musial	10,972	1,951	5.62

"I TRY TO HIT THE BALL AS HARD
AS I CAN EVERY TIME I SWING."

RALPH KINER, 1949

RALPH KINER 90

The full, lusty swing told you everything you needed to know about Ralph Kiner's intentions. Hit the ball hard and trot slowly around the bases before it touched asphalt or concrete. Kiner was a 6-2, 195-pound baseball enforcer who brought the home run back into vogue during a short-but-productive 10-year career in the late 1940s and early 1950s.

Everything about Kiner suggested power. The broad shoulders, the fullback-like arms and legs, the quick wrists. Long-suffering Pittsburgh fans embraced their young slugger and Kiner reciprocated, enhancing his fearsome image with torrid home run binges that left opponents shaking their heads. Five in two games. Six in three games. Four in a doubleheader. And, incredibly, eight in one four-game stretch of unrelenting destruction.

The image of a smiling, wavy-haired Kiner spread quickly through the National League as he either won or shared home run titles in each of his first seven seasons. Twice he topped the 50 plateau and in five of those campaigns he topped 100 RBIs for weak teams.

And thanks to the early-career tutoring of Hank Greenberg, Kiner never topped 100 strikeouts after his 1946 rookie season.

Kiner's left field defense was suspect and he was one of the slowest runners in the game, but he more than made up for those deficiencies with his intelligent, low-key, one-of-the-guys personality and amazingly consistent run production. The six-time All-Star's final .279 average was respectable and his total of 369 home runs (an average of 36.9 per season) could have been considerably higher if not for the three prime seasons he missed during World War II and the back problems that forced a premature retirement at the still-productive age of 33.

LEADING MAN

Not only did Kiner win or share more consecutive home run titles than any other player, he did it over the first seven years of his career. The leaders of consecutive titles:

No.	Player/Team	Years
7	Ralph Kiner/Pirates	1946-52
6	Babe Ruth/Yankees	1926-31
4	Harry Davis/Athletics	1904-07
4	Frank Baker/Athletics	1911-14
4	Babe Ruth/Yankees	1918-21

"I DON'T CHASE MARK MCGWIRE'S SHOTS—
I ADMIRE THEM."

STEVE FINLEY
PADRES CENTER FIELDER

THE SPORTING NEWS, 1997

MARK McGWIRE

91

The swing is short and compact, hitting reduced to its simplest term. The bat speed that fuels Mark McGwire's growing mystique is generated by massive shoulders and tree trunk-like biceps that accentuate his 6-5, 245-pound frame. The big St. Louis Cardinals first baseman presents a menacing figure as he stands in the box, slightly crouched and unflinchingly focused, and slowly swooshes his bat back and forth across the plate with obviously devious anticipation.

McGwire, whether entertaining the early-arriving masses during batting practice or locking in his radar during a game, is a home run waiting to happen. He doesn't just hit the ball out of the park with quiet consistency—he hits seat-seeking missiles that generally register 450-feet or more on baseball's tape measure. He is frustratingly selective, unwavering in his commitment to waiting for the perfect pitch, and when he gets it he hits the ball farther with less effort than anybody in the game.

The big redhead seems oblivious to his incredible popularity, which seems to surge with every home run

he cranks into the outer limits of parks around the majors. But he's an unwitting victim of his own accomplishments—49 home runs in his Rookie of the Year 1987 season with Oakland, three consecutive 50-plus homer performances with the A's and Cardinals in 1996, '97 and '98, six 100-RBI campaigns—and uncomfortable with the Babe Ruth-like aura he has acquired.

The 10-time All-Star selection also is a solid first baseman, with soft hands and surprising agility around the bag. McGwire's six-year combination with Oakland bash brother Jose Canseco helped spark the A's to three American League pennants and a World Series championship.

ACTIVE PLAYERS I ADMIRE
SELECTED BY
ROLLIE FINGERS

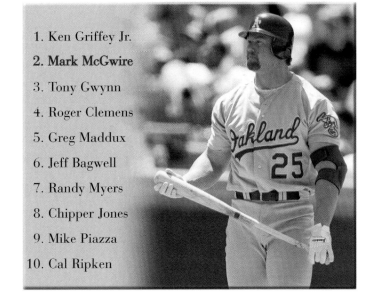

1. Ken Griffey Jr.
2. **Mark McGwire**
3. Tony Gwynn
4. Roger Clemens
5. Greg Maddux
6. Jeff Bagwell
7. Randy Myers
8. Chipper Jones
9. Mike Piazza
10. Cal Ripken

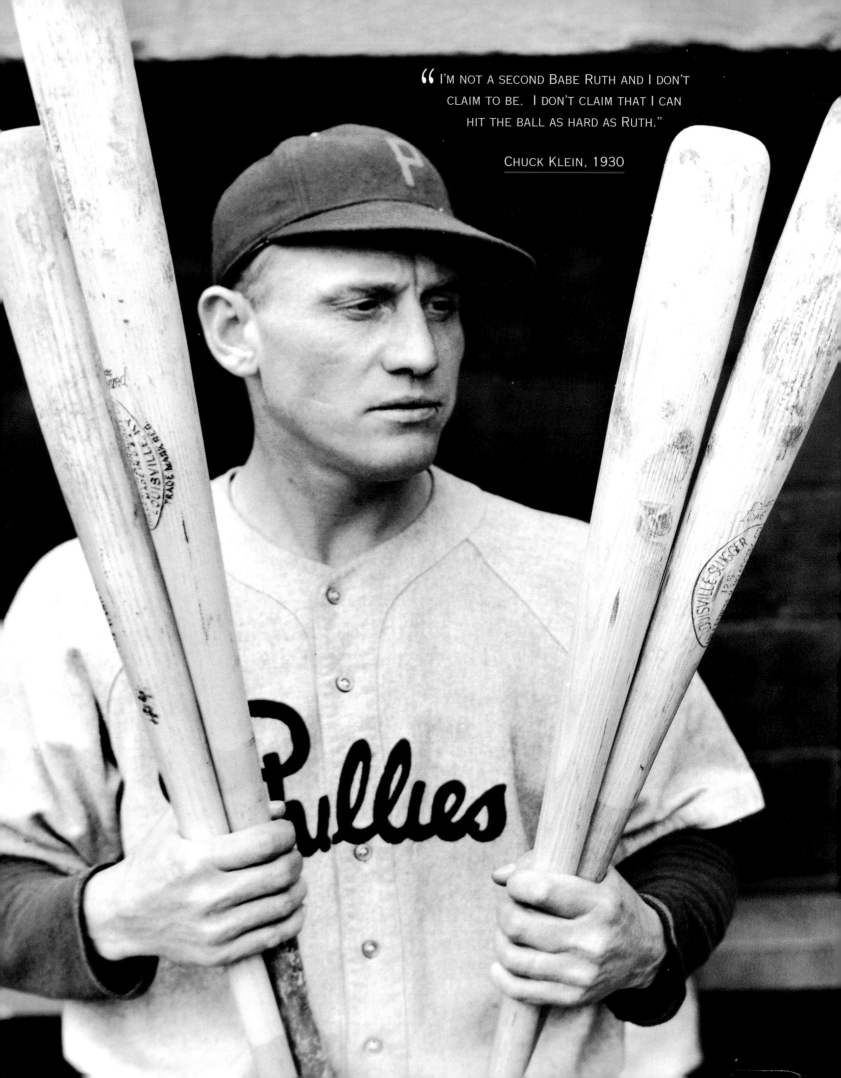

" I'M NOT A SECOND BABE RUTH AND I DON'T
CLAIM TO BE. I DON'T CLAIM THAT I CAN
HIT THE BALL AS HARD AS RUTH."

CHUCK KLEIN, 1930

CHUCK KLEIN 92

He clawed his way from an Indianapolis steel mill to the top of the baseball world. Over a five-year stretch with the Depression-era Philadelphia Phillies, Chuck Klein was as good as it gets. He belted, bashed and even threw his way into the record books with a consistency that earned him comparisons to Babe Ruth. Then, just as suddenly as he had risen, Klein faded out of the spotlight he had worked so hard to claim.

To get perspective on Klein, you start with the broad-shouldered, deep-chested body that was supported by relatively thin legs. It was all muscle, especially the powerful forearms that swung a 42-ounce bat from the left side like a toothpick. Klein had home run power, but fans were more likely to see his vicious drives bouncing into the gaps or off the 30-foot right-field wall at tiny Baker Bowl.

The quiet, sometimes-withdrawn Klein jumped into the spotlight with a .356 effort in 1929 and through 1933 he never batted lower than .337 or posted fewer than 200 hits, 28 home runs or 120 RBIs. His 1932 MVP performance was a warmup for the .368, 28-homer, 120-RBI Triple Crown he won a year later. He even set a still-standing 20th century defensive record in 1930 when he recorded 44 assists from his right field position.

But the numbers dropped sharply in 1934 when Klein was sent to Chicago by the financially-strapped Phillies and he never rediscovered the stroke over an 11-season finish that took him back to Philadelphia, to Pittsburgh and back to Philly. He did have his moments, such as a 1935 World Series appearance with the Cubs and a record-tying four-home run explosion for the Phillies a year later. Klein finished his Hall of Fame career in 1944 with a .320 average, 300 home runs and 2,076 hits.

NO DEPRESSION

Klein's lusty hitting from 1929-33, his first five full major league seasons, averaged out nicely against the other top sluggers of the same period:

Player	H	R	HR	RBI	Avg.
Chuck Klein	224	132	36	139	.359
Jimmie Foxx	188	124	41	145	.341
Lou Gehrig	201	142	38	155	.341
Babe Ruth	170	127	43	142	.345
Al Simmons	208	120	28	144	.355

93 KEN GRIFFEY JR.

H is mouth-watering swing is worth the price of admission to the American League ballparks he lights up with his effervescent smile. Ken Griffey Jr. is a real-life version of "The Natural," a multi-dimensional center fielder who can charm you with his boyish enthusiasm, kill you softly with his glove or ravage you violently with his bat.

When Junior swings, everybody watches—and his burgeoning success has carried him to the fringes of Jordanesque popularity.

Some of it's in the genes for Griffey, whose father, Ken Griffey Sr., was the right fielder for Cincinnati's Big Red Machine of the 1970s. But mostly it's in the personality and all-around athletic abilities the 6-3, 205-pound Seattle Mariners star brings to the field. Pegged by many as the next Triple Crown candidate, Junior has fluttered around .300, sacrificing average for recognition as one of the great power hitters of his generation—a reputation he enhanced with 300 career home runs by age 28.

Griffey's homers are usually the high floaters that sail convincingly into the right-field stands, the result of a smooth, slightly-uppercut lefthanded swing driven by quick hands and the quickest hips in the West. The swing and the stride are short, allowing him to identify breaking pitches and keep his hands back until the last possible instant.

Everything looks effortless for Junior, who patrols center field with a gliding, just-try-to-get-one-past-me attitude that has helped him win eight Gold Gloves— one every year since his 1989 rookie season. The eight-time All-Star selection also won the 1997 A.L. MVP after a 56-homer, 147-RBI rampage that helped the once-lowly Mariners win their second West Division title of the 1990s and second postseason berth of their history.

BEST OUTFIELDERS
SELECTED BY
OZZIE SMITH

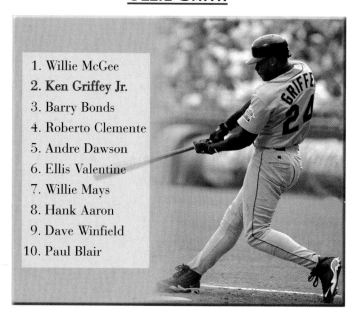

1. Willie McGee
2. **Ken Griffey Jr.**
3. Barry Bonds
4. Roberto Clemente
5. Andre Dawson
6. Ellis Valentine
7. Willie Mays
8. Hank Aaron
9. Dave Winfield
10. Paul Blair

"EVERY MISTAKE I THROW, (GRIFFEY) HITS
A HOME RUN. THAT DOESN'T SEEM FAIR.
HE CAN AT LEAST MIX IN A DOUBLE EVERY
ONCE IN A WHILE."

DAVID CONE

THE SPORTING NEWS, 1998

94 DAVE WINFIELD

The gap-toothed smile and the soft, easy-listening voice created a false sense of security. Then Dave Winfield stood up, all 6 feet 6 inches of him, and began swinging a bat that looked like a toothpick in his massive hands. The tall, lean body, with broad shoulders anchoring long arms, was enough to intimidate any pitcher with hopes of living through another day.

But Winfield was more than just another burly home run hitter. He was an athlete—a superior athlete—who could run, hit, throw and perform just about any other baseball skill imaginable. A college athlete at Minnesota who was drafted in three professional sports, Winfield could cover plenty of ground with his long, loping stride as a left or right fielder and end rallies with his powerful arm. He was an instinctive baserunner who got plenty of practice because of his ability to put bat on ball.

Winfield's big righthanded swing produced 3,110 hits over a 22-year career, most of which was divided between San Diego and New York. After eight productive seasons for weak Padres teams from 1973 to 1980, he took his slugging act to the Big Apple, reeled off an eight-plus-season string of 25-homer, 100-RBI performances and began feuding publicly with hard-to-satisfy owner George Steinbrenner. The articulate, image-conscious Winfield kept his cool through difficult times while remaining productive and continuing to fund the off-field charities that were an important part of his legacy.

Much of Steinbrenner's dissatisfaction stemmed from Winfield's less-than sterling performance and .045 average in the 1981 World Series. But it's hard to criticize the 12 All-Star selections, 465 career home runs and 1,833 RBIs (13th on the all-time list) he collected before retiring in 1995 after short stints in California, Toronto, Minnesota and Cleveland.

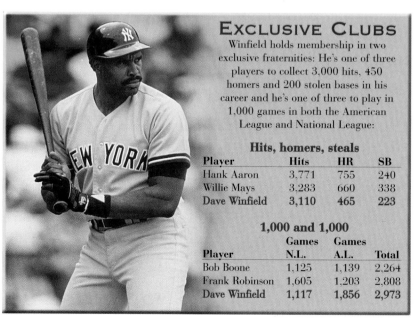

EXCLUSIVE CLUBS

Winfield holds membership in two exclusive fraternities: He's one of three players to collect 3,000 hits, 450 homers and 200 stolen bases in his career and he's one of three to play in 1,000 games in both the American League and National League:

Hits, homers, steals

Player	Hits	HR	SB
Hank Aaron	3,771	755	240
Willie Mays	3,283	660	338
Dave Winfield	3,110	465	223

1,000 and 1,000

Player	Games N.L.	Games A.L.	Total
Bob Boone	1,125	1,139	2,264
Frank Robinson	1,605	1,203	2,808
Dave Winfield	1,117	1,856	2,973

"YEAR AFTER YEAR, (WINFIELD)
GOES OUT THERE, DRIVES IN HIS
100 RUNS, NEVER FAILS TO
HUSTLE IN EVERY PHASE OF THE
GAME AND BEATS YOU EVERY
WAY A PLAYER CAN."

SPARKY ANDERSON

THE SPORTING NEWS, 1988

95 WADE BOGGS

His eyes lock into every pitch with a laser-like precision and his mind and body react instinctively. To swing or not to swing has never really been a question for Wade Boggs. The precise, instantaneous analysis, unwavering patience and perfect hand-eye coordination he brings to every at-bat is text-book and the .331 career average he brought into the 1998 season ranks among the best of all-time.

Boggs, a classic singles and doubles hitter who seldom strikes out, approaches his craft with machine-like consistency. He crouches slightly in his lefthanded stance, foot slightly closed, and wiggles the bat over the plate, ready to pounce. His hitting zone is sacred and nothing that penetrates it goes unchallenged. But anything out of the strike zone—no matter how slightly—will draw a swing. During his prime with the Boston Red Sox, Boggs had the frustrating ability to foul off ball after ball until he got what he wanted and his line drives shot to all fields—from any pitch location.

One of the best two-strike hitters ever, Boggs dominated the American League charts from his 1982 rookie season through 1989, an eight-year stretch in which he won five batting titles, topped 200 hits seven times, led the league in doubles twice, drew more than 100 walks four times and led the Red Sox to a 1986 World Series. Through 1989, Boggs carried a lofty .352 average.

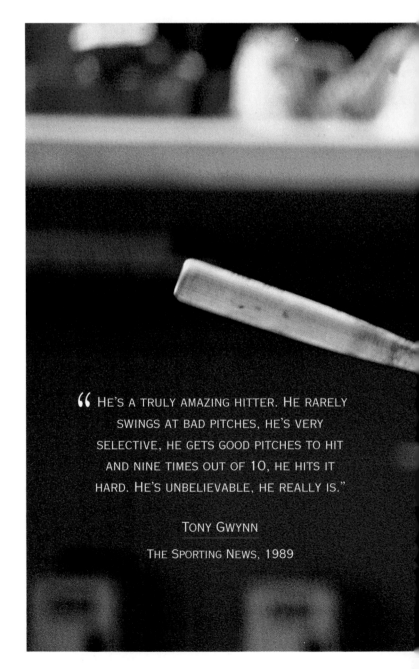

" HE'S A TRULY AMAZING HITTER. HE RARELY SWINGS AT BAD PITCHES, HE'S VERY SELECTIVE, HE GETS GOOD PITCHES TO HIT AND NINE TIMES OUT OF 10, HE HITS IT HARD. HE'S UNBELIEVABLE, HE REALLY IS."

TONY GWYNN
THE SPORTING NEWS, 1989

The sometimes-aloof, always-intense Boggs made a free-agent jump to the New York Yankees in 1993 and became a two-time Gold Glove winner, although his average fell into a slow decline. The 12-time All-Star performer helped the Yankees capture a World Series championship in 1996 and resumed his chase of career hit No. 3,000 in 1998 when he began his 17th big-league season—with the expansion Tampa Bay Devil Rays.

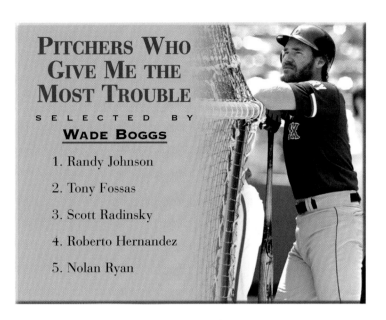

PITCHERS WHO GIVE ME THE MOST TROUBLE
SELECTED BY
WADE BOGGS

1. Randy Johnson
2. Tony Fossas
3. Scott Radinsky
4. Roberto Hernandez
5. Nolan Ryan

ROLLIE
FINGERS

The handlebar mustache made him look like the villain from a silent movie. His loose, carefree demeanor added a half inch to the smile hitters tried hard to suppress every time he strolled to the mound. But one fastball or slider from Rollie Fingers' strong right arm changed amusement to desperation and made it clear to everybody that a tense situation was under control.

The fun-loving, mustache-twirling, sometimes-flaky Fingers spent 17 major league seasons dousing late-inning fires as the premier reliever of his era. Not only did the lanky 6-4 righthander thrive from 1968 through 1985 with the Oakland A's, San Diego Padres and Milwaukee Brewers, he redefined the role that late-inning specialists would play in years to come. Fingers became the closer who could get the final few outs to protect a lead and he worked as often as needed.

Instead of banishing pitchers who couldn't make it as starters to the bullpen, teams began grooming late-inning specialists in the Fingers mold. They were influenced by the way the rubber-armed Ohioan anchored Oakland's three consecutive World Series championships from 1972-74 while saving games for starters Catfish Hunter, Kenny Holtzman and Vida Blue.

The amazing thing about Fingers was his durability and consistency over a long period. He used a lively fastball with a natural drop, the slider and a devastating forkball to carve out 341 career saves and a 2.90 ERA. The Oakland championships were nice, but Fingers enjoyed his greatest moment after the strike-shortened 1981 season when he became the first reliever to win both the Cy Young and MVP in the same season. That was the reward for a 28-save, 1.04 ERA performance at the tender age of 35.

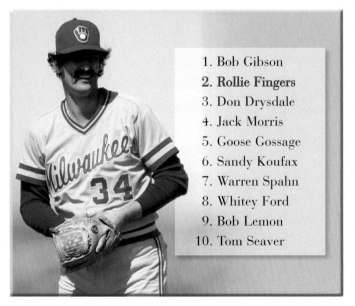

BEST BIG-GAME PITCHERS
SELECTED BY
SPARKY ANDERSON

1. Bob Gibson
2. Rollie Fingers
3. Don Drysdale
4. Jack Morris
5. Goose Gossage
6. Sandy Koufax
7. Warren Spahn
8. Whitey Ford
9. Bob Lemon
10. Tom Seaver

"ROLLIE IS THE BEST RELIEF PITCHER I'VE EVER
SEEN, AND HE'S BEEN CONSISTENTLY GREAT
THE LAST SIX OR SEVEN SEASONS."

ROGER CRAIG

THE SPORTING NEWS, 1977

"It has been my privilege to look at Koufax, Bunning, Newcombe, Erskine, Gibson and a lot of other good ones, but I've never found a pitcher mentally prepared to pitch with the consistency of Perry."

Roger Craig

The Sporting News, 1979

GAYLORD PERRY

97

He was a sleight-of-hand magician, an illusionist who misdirected the concentration of batters, managers and umpires. Gaylord Perry not only loaded up pitches with foreign substances banned by baseball rules, he loaded up the thoughts of opponents with distracting mind games. He was a 314-game winner who won as much with guile and intelligence as with a strong arm.

After Perry's 1983 retirement, he traced the origin of his notorious spitball to 1964, his third big-league season with the San Francisco Giants. Throughout the remainder of a 22-year career that featured stops in eight cities, he was cursed by hitters, screamed at by managers and undressed by umpires futilely searching for evidence. The laconic, broad-shouldered Perry simply displayed his good-old-boy smile and endured the flareups, knowing the distractions were only giving him a huge psychological edge.

Before every pitch, Perry would touch various parts of his anatomy—behind the ear, his forehead, his hair, the bill of his cap, his pants leg, his wrist—as hitters waited for the inevitable spitter, a pitch that would approach the plate like a fastball and drop abruptly. Their fear of the spitter only made Perry's above-average fastball and slider more effective and helped him top 20 wins five times and record six 300-inning seasons in an amazingly durable career that ended in Kansas City.

Perry won the first of two Cy Young Awards in 1972 when he recorded a 24-16 record with 29 complete games and a 1.92 ERA for the Cleveland Indians. The second came after a 21-6 record in 1978 for San Diego. But the five-time All-Star's only post-season fling came in 1971 when he was 1-1 in the Giants' National League Championship Series loss to Pittsburgh.

SMARTEST PITCHERS
SELECTED BY
JIM FREGOSI

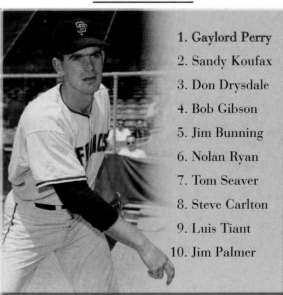

1. Gaylord Perry
2. Sandy Koufax
3. Don Drysdale
4. Bob Gibson
5. Jim Bunning
6. Nolan Ryan
7. Tom Seaver
8. Steve Carlton
9. Luis Tiant
10. Jim Palmer

"ECK ALWAYS THROWS STRIKES AND HE HAS THE HEART OF A GIANT. HIS NATURAL RESPONSE IS TO CHALLENGE A CRISIS HEAD-ON. THAT'S WHAT MAKES HIM SUCH A GREAT RELIEVER."

DAVE DUNCAN, 1988
ECKERSLEY'S LONGTIME PITCHING COACH

DENNIS ECKERSLEY 98

The wild-haired flamboyance has given way to controlled intensity and the cocky, hit-me-if-you-can attitude has become a quiet self-confidence. But make no mistake: Dennis Eckersley still pitches with the style, flamboyance and charisma he first exhibited in 1975 as a rookie righthander with the Cleveland Indians.

The Eckersley story is a two-parter. The first describes a care-free showman who compiled his own distinctive baseball vocabulary and more than 150 victories as a starter for the Indians, Boston Red Sox and Chicago Cubs. The second profiles one of the most successful closers in baseball history, a man who was able to make a mid-career conversion from the rotation to the bullpen and become the game's No. 2 all-time saves leader.

Eckersley's colorful early years included a no-hitter (1977 for Cleveland), a 20-win season (1978 for Boston) and a postseason appearance (1984) with the Cubs. It also included a winning bout with alcoholism and frequent tiffs with opponents who resented his in-your-face mound antics. Eck,

who delivered his pitches with a rhythmic, almost sidearm motion that ended with a dance-like follow-through, pumped his fist, taunted with his glares and generally invited negative reactions from frustrated opponents.

The dramatic transformation to reliever occurred in 1987 when he was traded to the Oakland Athletics and became the bullpen anchor for a team that won three American League pennants and a World Series from 1988 to 1990. The pinpoint control, emotional intensity and ability to set up hitters with his above-average fastball and sneaky slider remained a constant for the six-time All-Star and 1992 Cy Young winner through nine Oakland seasons, two more in St. Louis and another run in Boston.

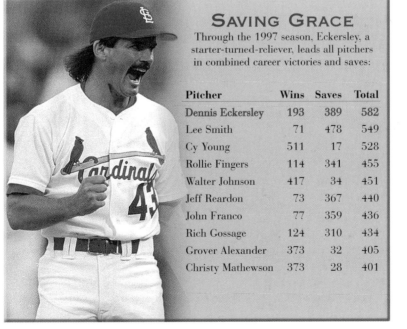

SAVING GRACE
Through the 1997 season, Eckersley, a starter-turned-reliever, leads all pitchers in combined career victories and saves:

Pitcher	Wins	Saves	Total
Dennis Eckersley	193	389	582
Lee Smith	71	478	549
Cy Young	511	17	528
Rollie Fingers	114	341	455
Walter Johnson	417	34	451
Jeff Reardon	73	367	440
John Franco	77	359	436
Rich Gossage	124	310	434
Grover Alexander	373	32	405
Christy Mathewson	373	28	401

99 PAUL MOLITOR

He chooses his words the same way he plays baseball—with sincerity, careful thought and fundamental precision. Everything about Paul Molitor, from his picture-perfect swing to the mistake-free daring with which he runs the bases, is part of a well-conceived master plan. Just wind him up and watch him execute.

Molitor's textbook approach and versatile talents have served him well over two unusual decades with the Milwaukee Brewers, Toronto Blue Jays and his hometown Minnesota Twins. He has played shortstop, second base, third base, center field and designated hitter; he has served as leadoff man and run producer; he has played in six All-Star Games and two World Series, and he has made his mark on the all-time offensive charts with more than 3,200 hits, 600 doubles and a .300-plus average.

Molitor attacks the pitch from a standup righthanded stance and drives the ball with power to all fields. His outstanding speed and aggressive baserunning skills cast him in the role of leadoff man for most of his 15 Milwaukee seasons—a role he filled with Rickey Henderson-like results. The only negative was Molitor's inability to stay off the disabled list, an injury jinx that cost him a lot of early-career games.

But that has not been a problem since 1990 and the now fortysomething Molitor continues to post eye-popping numbers. The Blue Jays, on their way to a second straight championship, saw his run-producing potential after signing him as a free agent in 1993 and Molitor responded by batting .332 with 22 homers and 111 RBIs. He has posted three 200-hit, two 100-run and two 100-RBI seasons since 1991, despite two strike-interrupted campaigns. And the 1,811 hits he posted in the 10-year stretch from 1988 to 1997 lead all major leaguers.

STREAKING

In 1987, Milwaukee's Molitor compiled the fifth-longest hitting streak since 1900:

No.	Player	Yr.
56	Joe DiMaggio	1941
44	Pete Rose	1978
41	George Sisler	1922
40	Ty Cobb	1911
39	**Paul Molitor**	**1987**
37	Tommy Holmes	1945
35	Ty Cobb	1917

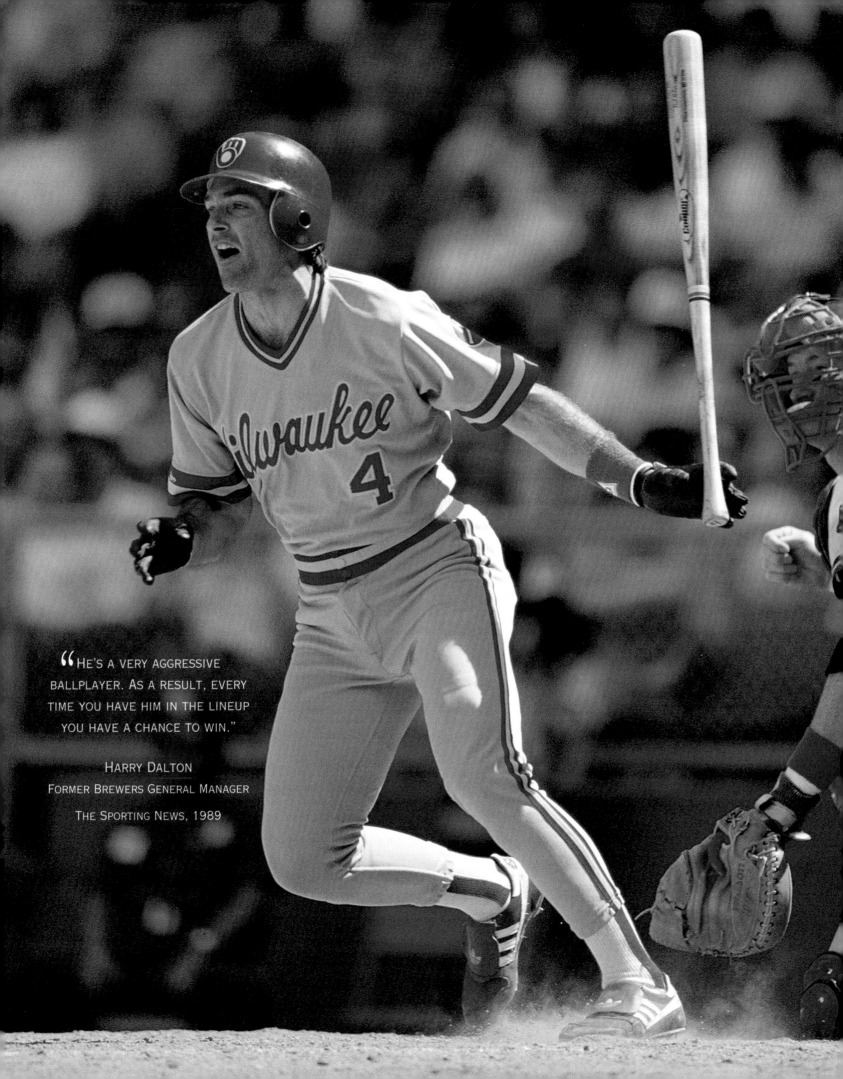

"He's a very aggressive ballplayer. As a result, every time you have him in the lineup you have a chance to win."

Harry Dalton
Former Brewers General Manager
The Sporting News, 1989

"That Wynn is a pretty tough pitcher. He's got everybody in the league scared. If I had to win one game, I'd have to say I'd want him to go. He knows just about all there is to know about pitching."

Casey Stengel

The Sporting News, 1959

100 EARLY WYNN

he raging eyes, masked by a sneering glare, was enough to unnerve any hitter. So was his reputation as one of the fiercest and meanest competitors ever to set foot on a pitching rubber. Every time Early Wynn stepped onto a major league mound, his one simple goal was to win—no matter what it took.

Wynn, a powerfully-built righthander, was a Depression-era throwback who thrived with a take-no-prisoners style over a 23-year career that touched parts of four decades and lasted until age 43. There was nothing fancy about the durable 6-foot, 210-pound wide body who approached every hitter as if he were the enemy and constantly looked for the intimidation edge with a rib-threatening fastball that was enough to test anybody's intestinal fortitude. "That son of a bitch is so mean he'd knock you down in the dugout," former Yankees great Mickey Mantle once complained.

That mean streak, combined with a driving intensity, a good fastball, a curve he learned in mid-career and a knuckleball, helped "Gus" forge

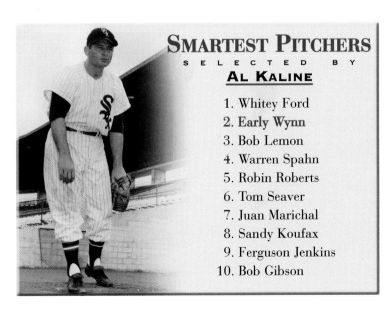

SMARTEST PITCHERS
SELECTED BY
AL KALINE

1. Whitey Ford
2. Early Wynn
3. Bob Lemon
4. Warren Spahn
5. Robin Roberts
6. Tom Seaver
7. Juan Marichal
8. Sandy Koufax
9. Ferguson Jenkins
10. Bob Gibson

out 300 career victories—72 for weak Washington teams in the 1940s, 164 in Cleveland, where he recorded four of his five 20-win records, and 64 for the Chicago White Sox. As affable off the field as he was tough on it, Wynn once took a line drive to the chin that knocked out seven teeth and required 16 stitches—and he wanted to stay in the game.

One of Wynn's more memorable seasons was 1954, when he won 23 times for an Indians team that recorded an American League-record 111 victories—only to lose in the World Series to the New York Giants. Another was 1959, when he recorded a 22-10 mark for the pennant-bound White Sox and was rewarded with the A.L. Cy Young.

By Position

The following list shows the position breakdowns for the Top 100 players based on a minimum of 500 games. Games are shown in parentheses and Negro League players are designated with NL. Nine players qualify at two positions and another, Pete Rose, qualifies at four.

FIRST BASE (16): Ernie Banks (1,259), Rod Carew (1,184), Jimmie Foxx (1,919) Lou Gehrig (2,136), Hank Greenberg (1,138), Harmon Killebrew (969), Buck Leonard (NL), Willie McCovey (2,045), Mark McGwire (1,301), Eddie Murray (2,214), Stan Musial (1,016), Pete Rose (939), George Sisler (1,970), Willie Stargell (848), Bill Terry (1,586), Carl Yastrzemski (765).

SECOND BASE (9): Rod Carew (1,130), Eddie Collins (2,650), Frank Frisch (1,775) Charley Gehringer (2,206), Rogers Hornsby (1,561), Nap Lajoie (2,036), Joe Morgan (2,527), Jackie Robinson (751), Pete Rose (628).

THIRD BASE (9): Wade Boggs (2,063), George Brett (1,692), Harmon Killebrew (792), Eddie Mathews (2,181), Paul Molitor (791), Brooks Robinson (2,870), Pete Rose (634), Mike Schmidt (2,212), Pie Traynor (1,864).

SHORTSTOP (4): Ernie Banks (1,125), Cal Ripken (2,302), Ozzie Smith (2,188), Honus Wagner (1,888).

OUTFIELD (37): Hank Aaron (2,760), Cool Papa Bell (NL), Barry Bonds (1,709), Lou Brock (2,507), Oscar Charleston (NL), Roberto Clemente (2,370), Ty Cobb (2,933), Sam Crawford (2,297), Joe DiMaggio (1,721), Goose Goslin (2,188), Ken Griffey Jr. (1,169), Tony Gwynn (2,063), Harry Heilmann (1,587), Rickey Henderson (2,266), Joe Jackson (1,289), Reggie Jackson (2,102), Al Kaline (2,488), Willie Keeler (2,040), Ralph Kiner (1,382), Chuck Klein (1,620), Mickey Mantle (2,019), Willie Mays (2,843), Joe Medwick (1,853), Stan Musial (1,896), Mel Ott (2,313), Kirby Puckett (1,696), Frank Robinson (2,132), Pete Rose (1,327), Babe Ruth (2,238), Al Simmons (2,142), Duke Snider (1,918), Tris Speaker (2,700), Willie Stargell (1,293), Paul Waner (2,288), Ted Williams (2,151), Dave Winfield (2,437), Carl Yastrzemski (2,076).

CATCHER (6): Johnny Bench (1,742), Yogi Berra (1,696), Roy Campanella (1,183), Mickey Cochrane (1,451), Bill Dickey (1,712), Josh Gibson (NL).

DESIGNATED HITTER (2): Reggie Jackson (638), Paul Molitor (1,060).

PITCHER (29): Grover Alexander (R), Steve Carlton (L), Roger Clemens (R), Dizzy Dean (R), Dennis Eckersley (R), Bob Feller (R), Rollie Fingers (R), Whitey Ford (L), Bob Gibson (R), Lefty Gomez (L), Lefty Grove (L), Carl Hubbell (L), Walter Johnson (R), Sandy Koufax (L), Greg Maddux (R), Juan Marichal (R), Christy Mathewson (R), Satchel Paige (R), Jim Palmer (R), Gaylord Perry (R), Eddie Plank (L), Robin Roberts (R), *Babe Ruth (L), Nolan Ryan (R), Tom Seaver (R), Warren Spahn (L), Ed Walsh (R), Early Wynn (R), Cy Young (R).

* Ruth pitched 158 games for the Boston Red Sox before earning lasting distinction as an outfielder for the New York Yankees.

TOP 100 BR

By Birthplaces

The following list breaks down the states and cities in which Top 100 players were born.

ALABAMA (6): Hank Aaron (Mobile); Willie Mays (Westfield); Willie McCovey (Mobile); Satchel Paige (Mobile); Ozzie Smith (Mobile); Early Wynn (Hartford).

ARKANSAS (3): Lou Brock (El Dorado); Dizzy Dean (Lucas); Brooks Robinson (Little Rock).

CALIFORNIA (11): Barry Bonds (Riverside); Joe DiMaggio (Martinez); Dennis Eckersley (Oakland); Lefty Gomez (Rodeo); Tony Gwynn (Los Angeles); Harry Heilmann (San Francisco); Mark McGwire (Pomona); Eddie Murray (Los Angeles); Tom Seaver (Fresno); Duke Snider (Los Angeles); Ted Williams (San Diego).

FLORIDA (1): Steve Carlton (Miami).

GEORGIA (4): Ty Cobb (Narrows); Josh Gibson (Buena Vista); Jackie Robinson (Cairo); Bill Terry (Atlanta).

IDAHO (1): Harmon Killebrew (Payette).

ILLINOIS (3): Rickey Henderson (Chicago); Kirby Puckett (Chicago); Robin Roberts (Springfield).

INDIANA (2): Oscar Charleston (Indianapolis); Chuck Klein (Indianapolis).

IOWA (1): Bob Feller (Van Meter).

KANSAS (1): Walter Johnson (Humboldt).

LOUISIANA (2): Bill Dickey (Bastrop); Mel Ott (Gretna).

MARYLAND (5): Jimmie Foxx (Sudlersville); Lefty Grove (Lonaconing); Al Kaline (Baltimore); Cal Ripken (Havre de Grace); Babe Ruth (Baltimore).

MASSACHUSETTS (2): Mickey Cochrane (Bridgewater); Pie Traynor (Framingham).

MICHIGAN (1): Charley Gehringer (Fowlerville).

MINNESOTA (2): Paul Molitor (St. Paul); Dave Winfield (St. Paul).

MISSISSIPPI (1): Cool Papa Bell (Starkville).

MISSOURI (2): Yogi Berra (St. Louis); Carl Hubbell (Carthage).

NEBRASKA (4): Grover Alexander (Elba); Wade Boggs (Omaha); Sam Crawford (Wahoo); Bob Gibson (Omaha).

NEW JERSEY (2): Goose Goslin (Salem); Joe Medwick (Carteret).

NEW MEXICO (1): Ralph Kiner (Santa Rita).

NEW YORK (10): Eddie Collins (Millerton); Whitey Ford (New York City); Frank Frisch (Bronx); Lou Gehrig (New York City); Hank Greenberg (New York City); Willie Keeler (Brooklyn); Sandy Koufax (Brooklyn); Jim Palmer (New York City); Warren Spahn (Buffalo); Carl Yastrzemski (Southhampton).

NORTH CAROLINA (2): Buck Leonard (Rocky Mount), Gaylord Perry (Williamston).

OHIO (6): Roger Clemens (Dayton); Rollie Fingers (Steubenville); Pete Rose (Cincinnati); Mike Schmidt (Dayton); George Sisler (Manchester); Cy Young (Gilmore).

OKLAHOMA (4): Johnny Bench (Oklahoma City); Mickey Mantle (Spavinaw); Willie Stargell (Earlsboro); Paul Waner (Harrah).

PENNSYLVANIA (8): Roy Campanella (Philadelphia); Ken Griffey Jr. (Donora); Reggie Jackson (Wyncote); Christy Mathewson (Factoryville); Stan Musial (Donora); Eddie Plank (Gettysburg); Honus Wagner (Mansfield); Ed Walsh (Plains).

RHODE ISLAND (1): Nap Lajoie (Woonsocket).

SOUTH CAROLINA (1): Joe Jackson (Pickens County).

TEXAS (8): Ernie Banks (Dallas); Rogers Hornsby (Winters); Greg Maddux (San Angelo); Eddie Mathews (Texarkana); Joe Morgan (Bonham); Frank Robinson (Beaumont); Nolan Ryan (Refugio); Tris Speaker (Hubbard).

WEST VIRGINIA (1): George Brett (Glen Dale).

WISCONSIN (1): Al Simmons (Milwaukee).

OTHER COUNTRIES (3): Rod Carew (Gatun, Canal Zone); Roberto Clemente (Carolina, Puerto Rico); Juan Marichal (Laguna Verde, Dominican Republic).

BY PRIMARY TEAMS

The following list breaks down the primary teams of Top 100 players, excluding the four who played only in the Negro Leagues. Players need 500 or more games to qualify for a team's roster. Pitchers qualify with 100 games. Game totals are shown in parentheses next to player names. The list does not include the pre-1900 teams of Cy Young, Honus Wagner and Willie Keeler.

NEW YORK YANKEES (13): Yogi Berra (2,116), Wade Boggs (602), Bill Dickey (1,789), Joe DiMaggio (1,736), Whitey Ford (498), Lou Gehrig (2,164), Lefty Gomez (367), Rickey Henderson (596), Reggie Jackson (653), Willie Keeler (873), Mickey Mantle (2,401), Babe Ruth (2,084), Dave Winfield (1,772).

PHILADELPHIA/KANSAS CITY/ OAKLAND A'S (11): Mickey Cochrane (1,167), Eddie Collins (1,156), Dennis Eckersley (525), Rollie Fingers (502), Jimmie Foxx (1,256), Lefty Grove (402), Rickey Henderson (1,552), Reggie Jackson (1,346), Mark McGwire (1,329), Eddie Plank (566), Al Simmons (1,290).

ST. LOUIS CARDINALS (11): Grover Alexander (116), Lou Brock (2,889), Steve Carlton (190), Dizzy Dean (273), Dennis Eckersley (120), Frank Frisch (1,311), Bob Gibson (528), Rogers Hornsby (1,580), Joe Medwick (1,216), Stan Musial (3,026), Ozzie Smith (1,990).

BOSTON RED SOX (10): Wade Boggs (1,625), Roger Clemens (383), Dennis Eckersley (191), Jimmie Foxx (887), Lefty Grove (214), Babe Ruth (391), Tris Speaker (1,065), Ted Williams (2,292), Carl Yastrzemski (3,308), Cy Young (327).

Frank Robinson (left), Brooks Robinson

EAKDOWNS

NEW YORK/SAN FRANCISCO GIANTS (10): Barry Bonds (732), Frank Frisch (1,000), Carl Hubbell (535), Juan Marichal (458), Christy Mathewson (634), Willie Mays (2,857), Willie McCovey (2,556), Mel Ott (2,730), Gaylord Perry (367), Bill Terry (1,721).

ST. LOUIS BROWNS/BALTIMORE ORIOLES (8): Eddie Murray (1,884), Satchel Paige (126), Jim Palmer (558), Cal Ripken (2,543), Robin Roberts (113), Brooks Robinson (2,896), Frank Robinson (827), George Sisler (1,647).

CLEVELAND INDIANS (7): Dennis Eckersley (103), Bob Feller (570), Joe Jackson (674), Napoleon Lajoie (1,614), Gaylord Perry (134), Tris Speaker (1,519), Early Wynn (343).

DETROIT TIGERS (7): Ty Cobb (2,806), Sam Crawford (2,114), Charley Gehringer (2,323), Goose Goslin (524), Hank Greenberg (1,269), Harry Heilmann (1,991), Al Kaline (2,834).

PHILADELPHIA PHILLIES (7): Grover Alexander (338), Steve Carlton (499), Chuck Klein (1,405), Napoleon Lajoie (624), Robin Roberts (529), Pete Rose (745), Mike Schmidt (2,404).

PITTSBURGH PIRATES (7): Barry Bonds (1,010), Roberto Clemente (2,433), Ralph Kiner (1,095), Willie Stargell (2,360), Pie Traynor (1,941), Honus Wagner (2,433), Paul Waner (2,244).

WASHINGTON SENATORS/MINNESOTA TWINS (6): Rod Carew (1,635), Goose Goslin (1,361), Walter Johnson (802), Harmon Killebrew (2,329), Kirby Puckett (1,783), Early Wynn (191).

BROOKLYN/LOS ANGELES DODGERS (5): Roy Campanella (1,215), Willie Keeler (565), Sandy Koufax (397), Jackie Robinson (1,382), Duke Snider (1,923).

CINCINNATI REDS (5): Johnny Bench (2,158), Joe Morgan (1,154), Frank Robinson (1,502), Pete Rose (2,722), Tom Seaver (158).

BOSTON/MILWAUKEE/ATLANTA BRAVES (4): Hank Aaron (3,076), Greg Maddux (157), Eddie Mathews (2,223), Warren Spahn (714).

CHICAGO WHITE SOX (4): Eddie Collins (1,670), Joe Jackson (648), Ed Walsh (426), Early Wynn (157).

SAN DIEGO PADRES (4): Rollie Fingers (265), Tony Gwynn (2,095), Ozzie Smith (583), Dave Winfield (1,117).

ANAHEIM/CALIFORNIA ANGELS (3): Rod Carew (834), Reggie Jackson (687), Nolan Ryan (291).

CHICAGO CUBS (3): Grover Alexander (242), Ernie Banks (2,528), Greg Maddux (212).

HOUSTON ASTROS (2): Joe Morgan (1,032), Nolan Ryan (282).

MILWAUKEE BREWERS (2): Rollie Fingers (177), Paul Molitor (1,856).

NEW YORK METS (2): Nolan Ryan (105), Tom Seaver (367).

TEXAS RANGERS (2): Gaylord Perry (112), Nolan Ryan (129).

KANSAS CITY ROYALS (1): George Brett (2,707).

SEATTLE MARINERS (1): Ken Griffey Jr. (1,214).

Hank Greenberg (left), Charley Gehringer

TOP 100 QUIZ

Each of the Top 100 players is the answer to a question in the following quiz.

Answers on page 224.

1. He's the only player to collect four hits in both an All-Star Game and a World Series game.

2. He was the last player to hit a home run at Brooklyn's Ebbets Field.

3. This Philadelphia Athletics player was walked intentionally with the bases loaded in 1901—the first known instance of a team intentionally walking home a run.

4. After playing his only minor league season in the Brooklyn Dodgers' organization, this player was drafted by the team for which he would spend his entire Hall of Fame career.

5. His 41-game hitting streak stood as an American League record until Joe DiMaggio hit in 56 straight games in 1941.

6. In 1984, this player hit his 500th career home run on the 17th anniversary of his first big-league homer.

7. Victimized by a fatal stroke at age 35, he was the youngest of the Top 100 players to die.

8. This player, who first achieved national attention by leading Texas to the College World Series championship, narrowly missed winning a major league World Series three years later in a memorable seven-game classic.

9. This player, who homered in his only two All-Star Game appearances, holds the distinction of playing in the most World Series games (50) without hitting a home run.

10. He is one of two pitchers (Ted Lyons is the other) to surrender a home run to Babe Ruth during his 60-homer 1927 season and a hit to Joe DiMaggio during his record 56-game hitting streak in 1941.

11. This Hall of Famer won consecutive batting titles with averages that were lower than his eventual lifetime average.

12. He won American League batting titles in every odd-numbered year from 1921 through 1927.

13. He played on the same Los Angeles-area Little League team as another Top 100 player who went on to fame as a career 500-home run hitter.

14. In 1971, he became the first player voted into the Hall of Fame by the special Committee on Negro Leagues.

15. He's the only man to play for the Boston Braves, Milwaukee Braves and Atlanta Braves.

16. He's the only man to win a Cy Young Award while pitching for a last-place team.

17. This righthander made his last major league appearance memorable by beating Mordecai "Three Finger" Brown, another future Hall of Famer who was pitching in his last major league game.

18. This pitcher made a near-perfect major league debut, allowing only a two-out, eighth-inning single to Phillies pinch-hitter Clay Dalrymple.

19. The first rookie to play in an All-Star Game went on to be named to his league's All-Star squad in each of his 13 big-league seasons. He played every inning of every All-Star Game for seven consecutive years.

20. During his four-game 1942 debut, this lefthander was 0-0 despite a complete-game effort in a contest that ended in forfeit. He didn't earn his first major league decision until four years later and still went on to win more than 300 games.

21. He was the first of two players who won two triple crowns.

22. He was the first player to hit 300 home runs and steal 300 bases.

23. He was the last player-manager in baseball.

24. This 500-home run man hit his last homer in a season-opening game.

25. This player was drafted by teams in three professional sports: baseball, basketball and football.

26. He hit more career home runs than any player who never led or tied for a league homer title.

27. He was his younger brother's teammate on three different major league clubs.

28. Although he won "only" 15 games for the Texas Rangers in 1977, this pitcher defeated each of the other 13 teams in his league at least once.

29. He is the last player to equal or exceed a league team's entire home run total for a season. He did it in 1949, when his American League-leading 43 home runs matched the Chicago White Sox's team total.

30. He is the oldest pitcher to throw a no-hitter.

31. This pitcher started five of the first six All-Star Games.

32. This Hall of Famer collected four hits, including two triples, in his major league debut.

33. This player's career ended prematurely when he was hit on the head by a pitched ball.

34. His .356 career batting average is the highest among players (minimum 1,500 hits) not in the Hall of Fame.

35. He is the only player to hit home runs in three consecutive All-Star Games.

36. He is the only player to hit 200 or more home runs in both the American and National leagues.

37. This Hall of Fame charter member holds distinction as the only starting pitcher in World Series history to bat anywhere but ninth in the order.

38. He is the only American League player other than Ty Cobb to win a batting title from 1907 through 1919.

39. This Hall of Famer's son halted Joe DiMaggio's 61-game hitting streak—the longest in minor league history.

40. He lost the first World Series game in 1903.

41. He hit the first pinch-hit home run in World Series history.

42. In 1934, after pitching a three-hitter in the first game of a doubleheader, he watched his brother throw a no-hitter in the nightcap.

43. This player holds the record for most home runs in a season by a batting champion.

44. He's the only pitcher in history to defeat the Boston Braves, Milwaukee Braves and Atlanta Braves.

45. He gave up Babe Ruth's first National League home run.

46. He was the first player to bat in a major league game in Canada.

47. His .690 winning percentage is tops among pitchers with 200 or more victories.

48. He won his only batting title and enjoyed his only 200-hit season when he was 20 years old.

49. He is half of the only father-son combination in the 300-homer fraternity.

50. Name the only player to hit three World Series home runs in consecutive years.

51. This player shares the same birthday (November 21) and city of birth (Donora, Pa.) with Stan Musial.

52. He is the only player to collect five hits in one World Series game.

53. He is the only pitcher to record 300 career saves and throw a no-hitter.

54. This longtime Pittsburgh infielder was Pirates manager the day Chicago's Gabby Hartnett beat them with his pennant-winning "Homer in the Gloaming" in 1938.

55. This player spiced his four-homer game by hitting two of them off brothers.

56. This player was an accomplished college basketball player and a 1981 NBA draft pick.

57. He homered in a record five different Championship Series.

58. He is the only major leaguer to win MVP honors in three consecutive odd-numbered years.

59. This Phillies slugger set a National League record when he hit 43 home runs, but it lasted for only one season.

60. He struck out 10 or more batters in a World Series game a record five times.

61. This Hall of Famer, known for his legendary speed and baserunning exploits, played until age 43 and reportedly hit over .400 in his final season.

62. When the Hall of Fame's first class was elected in 1936, this player was its oldest member and among its most accomplished—a perennial batting champ in the century's first decade.

63. This pitcher compiled the lowest ERA (2.14) over a six-year span in the post-World War II era.

64. He is the New York Yankees' all-time leader in stolen bases with 326.

65. He hit 17 lifetime home runs off Hall of Famer Don Drysdale.

66. In 1940 he became the only pitcher to hurl a no-hitter on opening day.

67. This Hall of Famer is the only player other than Rickey Henderson to collect at least 600 stolen bases and 250 home runs.

68. This player, known more for his glove than his bat, was on the losing team in a record 15 of the 18 All-Star Games in which he played.

69. He received the most votes from fans in the nationwide newspaper poll that was used to select the teams for the first All-Star Game in 1933.

70. He holds the major league record for fewest singles (53) in a season among players competing in at least 150 games.

71. In 1934, he managed in his first of three All-Star Games. He also was a National League starter and the league's leading batsman (.367) at the All-Star break.

72. In 1936, this Hall of Famer led American League regular second basemen in fielding percentage while tying for the league lead in second base errors.

73. This righthander, who holds the American League record for seasons pitched with 23, ended his big-league career with exactly 300 victories.

74. He's the only player to hit 500 home runs and steal fewer than 20 bases.

75. He once was managed by his father at the major league level.

76. Although he led the major leagues with 103 RBIs at the All-Star break in1935, this slugger was not selected to his league's All-Star Game squad.

77. This Top 100 player starred for a team that recovered from three-games-to-one deficits to win both the Championship Series and World Series in the same year.

78. This pitcher was credited with the first World Series victories for both the Philadelphia Phillies and St. Louis Cardinals.

79. He earned entry into the Hall of Fame with 425 votes out of 430 ballots cast for a record 98.84 percent.

80. He is the only man to play major league baseball in the same year he was elected to the Hall of Fame.

81. In each of his first two major league seasons, this Hall of Famer's club made it to the World Series. Although eligible for both, he did not play in either.

82. In 1970, he became only the second player to win All-Star Game MVP honors despite playing for the losing team.

83. He's the only player to hit 500 career home runs without hitting more than 33 in any single season.

84. Despite batting more than 500 times in his rookie season, he failed to hit a home run. Two seasons later, he hit 31.

85. He was the first player to win Most Valuable Player awards in consecutive seasons.

86. Nicknamed the "Hoosier Comet" by his fans, this Indianapolis-born Top 100 player began his illustrious professional career at age 18 with his hometown team.

87. Just short of his 21st birthday, he became the youngest pitcher to throw a complete-game World Series shutout.

88. He collected his 3,000th major league hit on the same day Tom Seaver collected his 300th big-league victory.

89. This Hall of Famer, born in the Civil War battlesite city of Gettysburg, Pa., twice lost World Series games by 1-0 scores.

90. This player's single broke Carl Hubbell's string of five straight strikeouts in the 1934 All-Star Game.

91. This Hall of Famer, who was nicknamed after his birthplace, led the National League in home runs one year and the American League seven years later.

92. He achieved fame as a member of Connie Mack's pennant-winning Athletics teams and was later an innocent member of the infamous 1919 Chicago White Sox.

93. This slugger made history when he shared a league MVP award—a major league first.

94. This player spent his entire career with one major league team. When he was traded to the Giants, he decided to retire a month later, nullifying the deal.

95. This one-club pitcher hurled seven opening-day shutouts.

96. He owned baseball's longest consecutive-game hitting streak until Joe DiMaggio put together his 56-game run in 1941.

97. He became the first relief pitcher to win a Cy Young and MVP in the same season.

98. Name the only player since 1900 to collect 200 or more hits in seven consecutive seasons.

99. He won consecutive MVP awards despite playing for losing teams both years.

100. At a time when Lou Gehrig, Hank Greenberg and Jimmie Foxx were the dominant major league first basemen, some considered this player the best at the position in the professional ranks.

TOP 100 ROLL CALL

(Statistics are through the 1997 season. Years for Cool Papa Bell, Oscar Charleston, Josh Gibson and Buck Leonard reflect time spent in the Negro Leagues. Eddie Plank's statistics include one season in the Federal League.)

BATTERS

Pg.	Player (years)	Born	Died	Hall of Fame Election	MVP	G	AB	H	R	HR	RBI	Avg.	SB
18	Hank Aaron (1954-76)	2-5-34	—	1982	1957	3,298	12,364	3,771	2,174	755	2,297	.305	240
86	Ernie Banks (1953-71)	1-31-31	—	1977	1958, 59	2,528	9,421	2,583	1,305	512	1,636	.274	50
144	Cool Papa Bell (1922-46)	5-17-03	3-7-91	1974	—	—	—	—	—	—	—	—	—
40	Johnny Bench (1967-83)	12-7-47	—	1989	1970, 72,	2,158	7,658	2,048	1,091	389	1,376	.267	68
90	Yogi Berra (1946-65)	5-12-25	—	1972	1951, 54, 55	2,120	7,555	2,150	1,175	358	1,430	.285	30
204	Wade Boggs (1982-present)	6-15-58	—	—	—	2,227	8,453	2,800	1,422	109	933	.331	20
78	Barry Bonds (1986-present)	7-24-64	—	—	1990, 92, 93	1,742	6,069	1,750	1,244	374	1,094	.288	417
122	George Brett (1973-93)	5-15-53	—	—	1980	2,707	10,349	3,154	1,583	317	1,595	.305	201
128	Lou Brock (1961-79)	6-18-39	—	1985	—	2,616	10,332	3,023	1,610	149	900	.293	938
110	Roy Campanella (1948-57)	11-19-21	6-26-93	1969	1951, 53, 55	1,215	4,205	1,161	627	242	856	.276	25
134	Rod Carew (1967-85)	10-1-45	—	1991	1977	2,469	9,315	3,053	1,424	92	1,015	.328	353
146	Oscar Charleston (1915-50)	10-14-1896	10-5-54	1976	—	—	—	—	—	—	—	—	—
48	Roberto Clemente (1955-72)	8-18-34	12-31-72	1973	1966	2,433	9,454	3,000	1,416	240	1,305	.317	83
14	Ty Cobb (1905-28)	12-18-1886	7-17-61	1936	1911*	3,035	11,434	4,189	2,246	117	1,937	.366	892
142	Mickey Cochrane (1925-37)	4-6-03	6-28-62	1947	1928†, 34	1,482	5,169	1,652	1,041	119	832	.320	64
56	Eddie Collins (1906-30)	5-2-1887	3-25-51	1939	1914*	2,826	9,949	3,315	1,821	47	1,300	.333	744
182	Sam Crawford (1899-1917)	4-18-1880	6-15-68	1957	—	2,517	9,570	2,961	1,391	97	1,525	.309	366
126	Bill Dickey (1928-46)	6-6-07	11-12-93	1954	—	1,789	6,300	1,969	930	202	1,209	.313	36
30	Joe DiMaggio (1936-51)	11-25-14	—	1955	1939, 41, 47	1,736	6,821	2,214	1,390	361	1,537	.325	30
38	Jimmie Foxx (1925-45)	10-22-07	7-21-67	1951	1932, 33, 38	2,317	8,134	2,646	1,751	534	1,922	.325	87
190	Frank Frisch (1919-37)	9-9-1898	3-12-73	1947	1931	2,311	9,112	2,880	1,532	105	1,244	.316	419
20	Lou Gehrig (1923-39)	6-19-03	6-2-41	1939	1927†, 36	2,164	8,001	2,721	1,888	493	1,995	.340	102
102	Charley Gehringer (1924-42)	5-11-03	1-21-93	1949	1937	2,323	8,860	2,839	1,774	184	1,427	.320	181
44	Josh Gibson (1930-1946)	12-21-11	1-20-47	1972	—	—	—	—	—	—	—	—	—
192	Goose Goslin (1921-38)	10-16-1900	5-15-71	1968	—	2,287	8,656	2,735	1,483	248	1,609	.316	175
84	Hank Greenberg (1930-47)	1-1-11	9-4-86	1956	1935, 40	1,394	5,193	1,628	1,051	331	1,276	.313	58
200	Ken Griffey Jr. (1989-present)	11-21-69	—	—	1997	1,214	4,593	1,389	820	294	872	.302	123
108	Tony Gwynn (1982-present)	5-9-60	—	—	—	2,095	8,187	2,780	1,237	107	973	.340	308
120	Harry Heilmann (1914-32)	8-3-1894	7-9-51	1952	—	2,148	7,787	2,660	1,291	183	1,539	.342	113
114	Rickey Henderson (1979-present)	12-25-58	—	—	1990	2,460	8,931	2,550	1,913	252	921	.286	1,231
26	Rogers Hornsby (1915-37)	4-27-1896	1-5-63	1942	1925†, 29†	2,259	8,173	2,930	1,579	301	1,584	.358	135
80	Joe Jackson (1908-20)	7-16-1889	12-5-51	—	—	1,332	4,981	1,772	873	54	785	.356	202
106	Reggie Jackson (1967-87)	5-18-46	—	1993	1973	2,820	9,864	2,584	1,551	563	1,702	.262	228
166	Al Kaline (1953-74)	12-19-34	—	1980	—	2,834	10,116	3,007	1,622	399	1,583	.297	137
162	Willie Keeler (1892-1910)	3-3-1872	1-1-23	1939	—	2,123	8,591	2,932	1,719	33	810	.341	495
150	Harmon Killebrew (1954-75)	6-29-36	—	1984	1969	2,435	8,147	2,086	1,283	573	1,584	.256	19
194	Ralph Kiner (1946-55)	10-27-22	—	1975	—	1,472	5,205	1,451	971	369	1,015	.279	22
198	Chuck Klein (1928-44)	10-7-04	3-28-58	1980	1932	1,753	6,486	2,076	1,168	300	1,201	.320	79
68	Napoleon Lajoie (1896-1916)	9-5-1874	2-7-59	1937	—	2,480	9,589	3,242	1,504	83	1,599	.338	380
104	Buck Leonard (1933-50)	9-8-07	11-27-97	1972	—	—	—	—	—	—	—	—	—
42	Mickey Mantle (1951-68)	10-20-31	8-13-95	1974	1956, 57, 62	2,401	8,102	2,415	1,677	536	1,509	.298	153
138	Eddie Mathews (1952-68)	10-13-31	—	1978	—	2,391	8,537	2,315	1,509	512	1,453	.271	68
12	Willie Mays (1951-73)	5-6-31	—	1979	1954, 65	2,992	10,881	3,283	2,062	660	1,903	.302	338
124	Willie McCovey (1959-80)	1-10-38	—	1986	1969	2,588	8,197	2,211	1,229	521	1,555	.270	26
196	Mark McGwire (1986-present)	10-1-63	—	—	—	1,380	4,622	1,201	811	387	983	.260	10
172	Joe Medwick (1932-48)	11-24-11	3-21-75	1968	1937	1,984	7,635	2,471	1,198	205	1,383	.324	42
212	Paul Molitor (1978-present)	8-22-56	—	—	—	2,557	10,333	3,178	1,707	230	1,238	.308	495
132	Joe Morgan (1963-84)	9-19-43	—	1990	1975, 76	2,649	9,277	2,517	1,650	268	1,133	.271	689
168	Eddie Murray (1977-97)	2-24-56	—	—	—	3,026	11,336	3,255	1,627	504	1,917	.287	110
28	Stan Musial (1941-63)	11-21-20	—	1969	1943, 46, 48	3,026	10,972	3,630	1,949	475	1,951	.331	78

| | | | | Hall of Fame | | | | | | | | | |
Pg.	Player (years)	Born	Died	Election	MVP	G	AB	H	R	HR	RBI	Avg.	SB
94	Mel Ott (1926-47)	3-2-09	11-21-58	1951	—	2,730	9,456	2,876	1,859	511	1,860	.304	89
186	Kirby Puckett (1984-95)	3-14-61	—	—	—	1,783	7,244	2,304	1,071	207	1,085	.318	134
170	Cal Ripken (1981-present)	8-24-60	—	—	1983, 91	2,543	9,832	2,715	1,445	370	1,453	.276	36
174	Brooks Robinson (1955-77)	5-18-37	—	1983	1964	2,896	10,654	2,848	1,232	268	1,357	.267	28
52	Frank Robinson (1956-76)	8-31-35	—	1982	1961, 66	2,808	10,006	2,943	1,829	586	1,812	.294	204
98	Jackie Robinson (1947-56)	1-31-19	10-24-72	1962	1949	1,382	4,877	1,518	947	137	734	.311	197
58	Pete Rose (1963-86)	4-14-41	—	—	1973	3,562	14,053	4,256	2,165	160	1,314	.303	198
10	Babe Ruth (1914-35)	2-6-1895	8-16-48	1936	1923†	2,503	8,399	2,873	2,174	714	2,213	.342	123
66	Mike Schmidt (1972-89)	9-27-49	—	1995	1980, 81, 86	2,404	8,352	2,234	1,506	548	1,595	.267	174
96	Al Simmons (1924-44)	5-22-02	5-26-56	1953	—	2,215	8,759	2,927	1,507	307	1,827	.334	88
76	George Sisler (1915-30)	3-24-1893	3-26-73	1939	1922†	2,055	8,267	2,812	1,284	102	1,175	.340	375
188	Ozzie Smith (1978-96)	12-26-54	—	—	—	2,573	9,396	2,460	1,257	28	793	.262	580
180	Duke Snider (1947-64)	9-19-26	—	1980	—	2,143	7,161	2,116	1,259	407	1,333	.295	99
64	Tris Speaker (1907-28)	4-4-1888	12-8-58	1937	1912*	2,789	10,195	3,514	1,882	117	1,529	.345	432
176	Willie Stargell (1962-82)	3-6-40	—	1988	1979	2,360	7,927	2,232	1,195	475	1,540	.282	17
130	Bill Terry (1923-36)	10-30-1898	1-9-89	1954	—	1,721	6,428	2,193	1,120	154	1,078	.341	56
152	Pie Traynor (1920-37)	11-11-1899	3-16-72	1948	—	1,941	7,559	2,416	1,183	58	1,273	.320	158
34	Honus Wagner (1897-1917)	2-24-1874	12-6-55	1936	—	2,792	10,430	3,415	1,736	101	1,732	.327	722
136	Paul Waner (1926-45)	4-16-03	8-29-65	1952	1927†	2,549	9,459	3,152	1,627	113	1,309	.333	104
24	Ted Williams (1939-60)	8-30-18	—	1966	1946, 49	2,292	7,706	2,654	1,798	521	1,839	.344	24
202	Dave Winfield (1973-95)	10-3-51	—	—	—	2,973	11,003	3,110	1,669	465	1,833	.283	223
156	Carl Yastrzemski (1961-83)	8-22-39	—	1989	1967	3,308	11,988	3,419	1,816	452	1,844	.285	168

PITCHERS

| | | | | Hall of Fame | | | | | | | | | |
Pg.	Pitcher (years)	Born	Died	Election	MVP	Cy Young	W	L	ERA	IP	ShO	SO	Sv.
32	Grover Alexander (1911-30)	2-26-1887	11-4-50	1938	—	—	373	208	2.56	5,190.0	90	2,198	32
70	Steve Carlton (1965-88)	12-22-44	—	1994	—	1972, 77, 80, 82	329	244	3.22	5,217.1	55	4,136	2
118	Roger Clemens (1984-present)	8-4-62	—	—	1986	1986, 87, 91, 97	213	118	2.97	3,040.0	41	2,882	0
184	Dizzy Dean (1930-41)	1-16-10	7-17-74	1953	1934	—	150	83	3.02	1,967.1	26	1,163	30
210	Dennis Eckersley (1975-present)	10-3-54	—	—	1992	1992	193	170	3.49	3,246.0	20	2,379	389
82	Bob Feller (1936-56)	11-3-18	—	1962	—	—	266	162	3.25	3,827.0	44	2,581	21
206	Rollie Fingers (1968-85)	8-25-46	—	1992	1981	1981	114	118	2.90	1,701.1	2	1,299	341
116	Whitey Ford (1950-67)	10-21-28	—	1974	—	1961	236	106	2.75	3,170.1	45	1,956	10
72	Bob Gibson (1959-75)	11-9-35	—	1981	1968	1968, 70	251	174	2.91	3,884.1	56	3,117	6
158	Lefty Gomez (1930-43)	11-26-08	2-17-89	1972	—	—	189	102	3.34	2,503.0	28	1,468	9
54	Lefty Grove (1925-41)	3-6-1900	5-22-75	1947	1931	—	300	141	3.06	3,940.2	35	2,266	55
100	Carl Hubbell (1928-43)	6-22-03	11-21-88	1947	1933, 36	—	253	154	2.98	3,590.1	36	1,677	33
16	Walter Johnson (1907-27)	11-6-1887	12-10-46	1936	1913*, 24†	—	417	279	2.17	5,914.1	110	3,509	34
62	Sandy Koufax (1955-66)	12-30-35	—	1972	1963	1963, 65, 66	165	87	2.76	2,324.1	40	2,396	9
88	Greg Maddux (1986-present)	4-14-66	—	—	—	1992, 93, 94, 95	184	108	2.81	2,598.1	23	1,820	0
154	Juan Marichal (1960-75)	10-20-37	—	1983	—	—	243	142	2.89	3,507.1	52	2,303	2
22	Christy Mathewson (1900-16)	8-12-1880	10-7-25	1936	—	—	373	188	2.13	4,780.2	79	2,502	28
46	Satchel Paige (1948-53)	7-7-06	6-8-82	1971	—	—	28	31	3.29	476.0	4	288	32
140	Jim Palmer (1965-84)	10-15-45	—	1990	—	1973, 75, 76	268	152	2.86	3,948.0	53	2,212	4
208	Gaylord Perry (1962-83)	9-15-38	—	1991	—	1972, 78	314	265	3.11	5,350.1	53	3,534	11
148	Eddie Plank (1901-17)	8-31-1875	2-24-26	1946	—	—	326	194	2.35	4,495.2	69	2,246	23
160	Robin Roberts (1948-66)	9-30-26	—	1976	—	—	286	245	3.41	4,688.2	45	2,357	25
92	Nolan Ryan (1966-93)	1-31-47	—	—	—	—	324	292	3.19	5,386.0	61	5,714	3
74	Tom Seaver (1967-86)	11-17-44	—	1992	—	1969, 73, 75	311	205	2.86	4,782.2	61	3,640	1
50	Warren Spahn (1942-65)	4-23-21	—	1973	—	1957	363	245	3.09	5,243.2	63	2,583	29
178	Ed Walsh (1904-17)	5-14-1881	5-26-59	1946	—	—	195	126	1.82	2,964.1	57	1,736	34
214	Early Wynn (1939-63)	1-6-20	—	1972	—	1959	300	244	3.54	4,564.0	49	2,334	15
36	Cy Young (1890-1911)	3-29-1867	11-4-55	1937	—	—	511	316	2.63	7,356.0	76	2,803	17

* The Chalmers Award honored MVPs from 1911-14.
† The League Award honored MVPs from 1922-29.

1. Joe Medwick
2. Duke Snider
3. Napoleon Lajoie
4. Roberto Clemente
5. George Sisler
6. Reggie Jackson
7. Josh Gibson
8. Roger Clemens
9. Frank Frisch
10. Lefty Grove
11. Ty Cobb
12. Harry Heilmann
13. Ozzie Smith
14. Satchel Paige
15. Eddie Mathews
16. Steve Carlton
17. Christy Mathewson
18. Juan Marichal
19. Joe DiMaggio
20. Warren Spahn
21. Rogers Hornsby
22. Willie Mays
23. Pete Rose
24. Mel Ott
25. Dave Winfield
26. Stan Musial
27. Paul Waner
28. Gaylord Perry
29. Ted Williams
30. Nolan Ryan
31. Lefty Gomez
32. Willie McCovey
33. Mickey Cochrane
34. Joe Jackson

35. Ralph Kiner
36. Frank Robinson
37. Babe Ruth
38. Tris Speaker
39. Ed Walsh
40. Cy Young
41. Yogi Berra
42. Dizzy Dean
43. Mickey Mantle
44. Robin Roberts
45. Carl Hubbell
46. Lou Brock
47. Whitey Ford
48. Al Kaline
49. Barry Bonds
50. Goose Goslin
51. Ken Griffey Jr.
52. Paul Molitor
53. Dennis Eckersley
54. Pie Traynor
55. Mike Schmidt
56. Tony Gwynn
57. Johnny Bench
58. Roy Campanella
59. Chuck Klein
60. Bob Gibson
61. Cool Papa Bell
62. Honus Wagner
63. Greg Maddux
64. Rickey Henderson
65. Hank Aaron
66. Bob Feller
67. Joe Morgan
68. Brooks Robinson

69. Al Simmons
70. Mark McGwire
71. Bill Terry
72. Charley Gehringer
73. Early Wynn
74. Harmon Killebrew
75. Cal Ripken
76. Hank Greenberg
77. George Brett
78. Grover Alexander
79. Tom Seaver
80. Lou Gehrig
81. Sandy Koufax
82. Carl Yastrzemski
83. Eddie Murray
84. Kirby Puckett
85. Jimmie Foxx
86. Oscar Charleston
87. Jim Palmer
88. Rod Carew
89. Eddie Plank
90. Bill Dickey
91. Sam Crawford
92. Eddie Collins
93. Willie Stargell
94. Jackie Robinson
95. Walter Johnson
96. Willie Keeler
97. Rollie Fingers
98. Wade Boggs
99. Ernie Banks
100. Buck Leonard